WATERGATE AND "THE GRAVE NATIONAL SECURITY MATTER"

The World Turn'd Upside Down

JERRY ROGERS

Dedication — In Memoriam

Patricia Elizabeth Parsons Rogers
ca 1968, RAF Upper Heyford, England Officers Club
Air Force Officer's Wife, Mother, Grandmother
Career Elementary School Teacher, with honors
b: 27 November 1939, Ft. William, Ontario, Canada
d: 22 April 1998, Riverside, California
Interred: Columbarium, Riverside National Cemetery, California

Acknowledgments

This is a book many years in research and writing. Research began in earnest in April 1994 following the death of President Richard Nixon that month. It involved reading volumes of books on Watergate, including by Watergate principals, reading volumes of US Congressional testimony, and newspaper research. Also involved were numerous hours listening to Watergate tapes at the National Archives in College Park, Maryland, and paid audio enhancement of tapes.

Chapter 20 cites the names of persons and agencies that were contacted to provide information. This includes many Watergate principals with indications of their response and extent of cooperation.

The research has been very extensive and intensive. I began to record and write up my own experiences, which has led to the creation of this book. Nearly all aspects of my work have been shared with members of my immediate family and their spouses: my son Ryan T. Rogers, my daughter, Brooke M. Rogers Dodson, and my son Erik O. Rogers. Also, my beloved wife, Judy Casanova, my confidante and companion, has rendered invaluable advice and encouragement to this project. I also wish to thank her daughter, Anabella Casanova.

My writings have been shared with persons, including spouse or partner, who have known me though various stages of my life, both military and civilian, and going back to my growing-up years in Colton, California. These persons will forever remain anonymous, as per my promise and their wishes.

I wish to thank the following staff members of the Presidents Collection, Nixon Watergate Tapes Section, at the Miller Center at the University of Virginia in Charlottesville, Virginia: Kenneth Hughes and Barbara Perry.

Lastly, I wish to thank following archivist staff at the Nixon Presidential Materials Project at Archives II at College Park, Maryland: Karl Weissenbach, Cary McStay (Watergate tapes supervisor), Steve Greene, David Paynter, and Sahr Conway Lanz. I also thank archivist Ryan Pettigrew at the Nixon Museum and Library in Yorba Linda, California.

Judy Casanova and Jerry Rogers
US Marine Corps Birthday Ball November 10, 2003
Officers Club Camp Pendleton, CA

Contents

Preface and Prologue

—

"…this was a very serious tragic time in America. We almost lost our democracy and our constitutional government."

Samuel Dash, Minority Counsel,
Watergate Senate Select Committee

—

THREATENED BY IMPEACHMENT, PRESIDENT NIXON resigned from office in disgrace on August 9, 1974, because of discoveries of criminal and questionable activity, constituting abuse of power, all associated with Watergate.

It was disclosed that President Nixon had authorized money payment of a blackmail demand by E. Howard Hunt, a member of the White House Special Investigations Unit (a.k.a. Plumbers). The blackmail threat was directly tied to what was described by President Nixon as a "grave national security matter" that should never be disclosed. That matter involved various crimes, all done under color of national security in Plumbers operations led by Hunt, against an active-duty military intelligence agent, American counterspy, who was a suspected leaker of classified information and believed Soviet agent. It was feared at that time that public disclosure of that matter would threaten the military's command and control system as well as the end of the Republic. This military aspect of the Watergate tragedy has remained unresolved and undisclosed as public disclosure risked dire consequences.

Now after forty years, the unfinished business of the military aspect, "the grave national security matter," should be disclosed as the American people have a right and need to know what happened, with the matter to be dealt with now by the US Justice Department and US Congress.

"For God's sake, don't get caught!" This was the hurried warning given to E. Howard Hunt and G. Gordon Liddy, both White House Plumbers, by their supervisor Egil Krogh on September 1, 1971, shortly before their departure to Chicago and then to Los Angeles to perpetrate a break-in of a psychiatrist's office in Beverly Hills. The break-in was successful in that they did not get caught, at least immediately. This was one of the first such criminal acts done under color of **national security** at the orders of the Nixon White House. Other nefarious acts were committed up until the time they were caught breaking into the offices of the Headquarters of the Democratic National Committee at the Watergate Hotel and Offices in Washington, D.C., in June 1972. So Watergate in essence began before Watergate. President Nixon referred to these events as "matters totally unrelated to Watergate." They were matters that authorities were to avoid and leave alone, in part because they involved very sensitive **grave national security** matters. Getting caught was inevitable. With guile, hubris, bravado, and self-delusion, the culprits overestimated their abilities in "successful" criminal operations and underestimated the possibilities of discovery by chance or accident, ignoring those old wisdoms, "What can go wrong, will go wrong," and "If you do it enough times, you will get caught." Getting caught is even more likely if persons are not professional in their trade and become blinded by their own prowess. Once they were caught, it was inevitable that prior offenses would surface. The Plumbers were caught later rather than sooner. Dr. Lewis Fielding was the Beverly Hills psychiatrist who had been treating Daniel Ellsberg, a RAND Corporation think-tank analyst, who publically leaked the *Pentagon Papers*. The goal of the office break-in was to locate adverse medical information in files which could be used to discredit Ellsberg.

The *Pentagon Papers*

Watergate arose out of the Vietnam War and with what came to be known as the *Pentagon Papers*, officially titled *United States – Vietnam Relations, 1945–1967: A Study Prepared by the Department of Defense.* A United States Department of Defense history of the United States' political-military involvement in Vietnam from 1945 to 1967, the papers were first brought to the attention of the public on the front page of *The New York Times* in 1971. A 1996 article in *The New York Times* said that the *Pentagon Papers* "demonstrated, among other things, that the Lyndon Baines Johnson administration had systematically lied, not only to the public but also to Congress about a subject of transcendent national interest and significance." The DOD task force report was declassified and publicly released in June 2011.

Ellsberg, the RAND Corporation researcher, knew the leaders of the task force well. An aide to Assistant Secretary of Defense John T. McNaughton from 1964 to 1965, he worked on the study for several months in 1967; and in 1969, Leslie Gelb and Morton Halperin, DOD staffers, approved his access to the work at RAND. Opposing the war, Ellsberg and his friend Anthony Russo photocopied the forty-seven-volume study in October 1969, intending to disclose it. Ellsberg approached Nixon's National Security Advisor Henry Kissinger, Senators William Fulbright and George McGovern, and others, but none were interested, so Ellsberg approached a *New York Times* reporter who accepted the papers. Publication began in 1971.

To put the *Pentagon Papers* in context of the times, the Vietnam War created tremendous turmoil in the country with massive anti-Vietnam War protests occurring in large cities such as Washington, D.C., Los Angeles, Chicago, and New York City as well as on many college campuses. The late 1960s and early 1970s have been described as a "season of treason" and are referred to as such in Watergate tapes. On May 22, 1973, President Nixon released a public statement characterizing the country's turmoil and giving a justification for the 1970 "Huston Intelligence Plan" (described below):

"In the spring and summer of 1970, another security problem reached critical proportions. In March, a wave of bombings and explosions struck college campuses and cities. There were four hundred bomb threats in one twenty-four-hour period in New York City. Rioting and violence on college campuses reached a new peak after the Cambodian operation and the tragedies at Kent State and Jackson State. The 1969-70 school year brought nearly 1,800 campus demonstrations and nearly 250 cases of arson on campus. Many colleges closed. Gun battles between guerrilla-style groups and police were taking place. Some of the disruptive activities were receiving foreign support."

Agencies of the US government took strong actions to understand and counter the turmoil. The FBI in the 1960s ran Counterintel Pro, which was an extensive domestic intelligence surveillance program that violated many citizens' civil liberties in the name of **national security**. Separately and with no other agency coordination, the CIA operated Operation Chaos which included both domestic and international surveillance for the purpose of determining if there was any foreign penetration of US antiwar groups. Aspects of these programs were only discovered in the Senator Frank Church hearings of the late 1970s. In those prior times, military intelligence agencies were also involved in domestic intelligence, and large police departments, such as Los Angeles, New York City, Chicago and Washington, D.C., operated extensive domestic intelligence/surveillance programs. All these programs also targeted college campuses with recruitment of student informants, a feature especially desired by President Nixon. There was no Congressional oversight of the federal programs and none by local jurisdiction city councils and/or civilian police review boards of police domestic intelligence/surveillance. A comprehensive description and analysis of all these domestic intelligence programs has never been published. In essence, in the late 1960s and early 1970s, a state of repression bordering on a police state existed in the US.

The 1970 Huston Intelligence Plan proposed extensive domestic intelligence surveillance programs to be led by the FBI, CIA, DIA, and NSA. The plan was ostensibly in operation for four days, at which time FBI Director J. Edgar Hoover withdrew his agency, fearing repression of citizen civil liberties. Actually, the FBI's Counterintel Pro and CIA's Operation Chaos continued all during the Nixon/Watergate era and without the knowledge of President Nixon or his administration. Furthermore, the CIA and FBI continued their programs without much coordination; the programs were security-compartmentalized. It is in dispute that that the Huston Plan was ever rescinded. The goal of all these intelligence efforts was to determine if there existed foreign intelligence penetration of and influence upon domestic peace/protest groups. This was never proven; however, over the years US domestic intelligence and investigative agencies thoroughly penetrated domestic peace/protest groups.

In his May 22, 1973, statement, President Nixon then proclaimed:

"On Sunday, June 13, 1971, the *New York Times* published the first installment of what came to be known as "the *Pentagon Papers*." Not until a few hours before publication did any responsible government official know that they had been stolen. Most officials did not know they existed. No senior official of the government had read them or knew with certainty what they contained.

All the government knew, at first, was that the papers comprised forty-seven volumes and some seven thousand pages, which had been taken from the most sensitive files of the Departments of State and Defense and the CIA, covering military and diplomatic moves in a war that was still going on.

Moreover, a majority of the documents published with the first three installments in the *Times* had not been included in the forty-seven-volume study—raising serious questions about what and how much else might have been taken.

There was every reason to believe this was a security leak of unprecedented proportions.

It created a situation in which the ability of the government to carry on foreign relations even in the best of circumstances could have been severely compromised. Other governments no longer knew whether they could deal with the United States in confidence. Against the background of the delicate negotiations the United States was then involved in on a number of fronts—with regard to Vietnam, China, the Middle East, nuclear arms limitations, US-Soviet relations, and others—in which the utmost degree of confidentiality was vital, it posed a threat so grave as to require extraordinary actions.

Therefore, during the week following the *Pentagon Papers* publication, I approved the creation of a Special Investigations Unit within the White House, which later came to be known as the "Plumbers." This was a small group at the White House whose principal purpose was to stop security leaks and to investigate other sensitive security matters. I looked to John Ehrlichman for the supervision of this group.

Egil Krogh, Mr. Ehrlichman's assistant, was put in charge. David Young was added to this unit, as were E. Howard Hunt (a retired career CIA clandestine services operator) and G. Gordon Liddy (a former FBI agent).

The unit operated under extremely tight security rules. Its existence and functions were known only to a very few persons at the White House. These included Messrs. Haldeman, Ehrlichman, and Dean.

At about the time the unit was created, Daniel Ellsberg was identified as the person who had given the *Pentagon Papers* to the *New York Times*. I told Mr. Krogh that as a matter of first priority, the unit should find out all it could about Mr. Ellsberg's associates and his motives. Because of the extreme gravity of the situation, and not then knowing what additional national secrets Mr. Ellsberg might disclose, I did impress upon Mr. [Egil] Krogh the vital importance to the **national security** of his assignment. I did not authorize and had no knowledge of any illegal means to be used to achieve this goal."

The White House Special Investigations Unit: The Plumbers

The above governmental domestic intelligence programs contributed to the climate that made formation of the White House Special Investigations Unit (the Plumbers) possible in early July 1971. Hunt came highly recommended to the Plumbers by CIA Director Richard Helms (Hunt is "ruthless," he said) and White House Aide Charles Colson, who strongly advocated Hunt's hiring based on his extensive CIA operational experience and via Colson-Hunt mutual affiliation with a university alumni association.

This White House tape reflects President Nixon's priorities and requirements for the position Hunt soon filled:

Conversation 534-3 between the President, H. R. Haldeman, and Henry Kissinger
July 1, 1971, 8:45-9:52 a.m.
Abuse of Power, **Stanley Kutler, pages 7-8**
Excerpts:

HALDEMAN:	Yeah. Absolutely.
PRESIDENT NIXON:	Now, do you see what we need? ... I need a son of a bitch like Huston who will work his butt off and do it dishonorably. You know what I mean? Who will know what he's doing, and I want to know, too. And I'll direct him myself. I know how to play this game, and we're going to start playing it.

***

PRESIDENT NIXON:	When you get to Ehrlichman, now, will you please get—I want you to find me a man by noon...a recommendation of a man who will work directly with me... I want somebody just as tough as I am for a change. We are up against an enemy, a conspiracy. They're using any means. *We are going to use any means.* Is that clear?

None of these Plumbers operations, Houston Intelligence Plan, or other White House secret operations from 1970 to 1972 came to light until the unraveling of events following the discovered break-in of the Democratic National Committee (DNC) Headquarters at the Watergate Hotel and Office complex in Washington, D.C. A goal of the June 17, 1972, operation was to plant electronic surveillance devices at DNC Headquarters. Seven individuals were apprehended by police, and two of them, G. Gordon Liddy and E Howard Hunt, were identified as White House-connected. Three of the individuals were contracted Cubans (formerly CIA contract employees) hired by Hunt. The Nixon Administration immediately discounted the break-in as a "third-rate burglary."

President Nixon's first known opportunity to discuss the Watergate break-in with anyone of his key staff was on Tuesday, June 22, 1972, when he had a seventy-nine-minute conversation with H. R. Haldeman, his chief of staff. An unsolved mystery is an eighteen-and-a-half-minute tape gap in that conversation. Haldeman's notes indicate this part of the conversation did not deal with the break-in, so one can only speculate on its content. General Alexander Haig, President Nixon's **national security** advisor and later chief of staff, referred to this gap as being caused by "a sinister force." There were efforts then and in later years to technically raise the conversation but with no success: The missing part had been manually erased many times, and the original recording had been permanently obliterated. Access to this recording was limited to President Nixon, Presidential Secretary Rosemary Woods, General Haig, and H. R. Haldeman, who had more than a week of unfettered access to the tape at the White House following his being fired by President Nixon on April 30, 1973. Haldeman's access to the tape containing the mysterious tape gap was never investigated at the time or subsequently.

The Plumbers and the Grave National Security Matter: News Articles

During the period from November 21, 1973, through January 18, 1974, a number of articles appeared in the following newspapers dealing with Watergate, **national security**, and Plumbers operations:

1. **November 20, 1973:** *Washington Star News*, "Security Could Imperil 'Plumbers' Prosecution," by Barry Kalb **Appendix 1**

2. **November 21, 1973:** "Jaworski to Push on 'Plumbers'" by Mary Russell and Susanna McBee, *Washington Post* staff writers **Appendix 2**

3. **November 29, 1973:** *Washington Star News*, page A-3: "Plumbers' Goal: Hide Spying on Soviets," by Dan Thomasson, Scripps Howard News Service **Appendix 3**

4. **December 7. 1973:** *The Pittsburgh Press*, "Nixon Cites National Security: 'Plumbers' Trials Pose Threat," by Dan Thomasson, Scripps-Howard Staff Writer **Appendix 4**

5. **December 8, 1973:** *New York Times*, Part 1 of 2 parts, pages 75-76: "The President and the Plumbers: A Look at Two Security Questions," by Seymour M. Hersh **Appendix 5**

6. **December 10, 1973:** *The New York Times,* page 1: "Nixon's Active Role on Plumbers: His Talks with Leaders Recalled," by Seymour Hersh **Appendix 6**

7. **December 30, 1973:** *Watergate: Chronology of a Crisis*, page 472: Baker on 'Grave Matter' **Appendix 7**

8. **Jan 15, 1974:** *Washington Post,* "Security Secret is a Puzzle," by Laurence Stern **Appendix 8**

9. **January 18, 1974:** *Washington Post*, "Chasing a Spy Ring: Its Secret is Safely Locked Away in Confusion," by Laurence Stern, *Washington Post* staff writer **Appendix 9**

This is a consolidated summary of the contents of the above articles; for sourcing of paragraphs, reference above numbered newspaper articles. As clarification, although the Plumbers' operations against the US intelligence officer are known by various names: "The Grave **National**

Security Matter," "The California Caper," "The Missing Link" (Senator Baker), and various references here to **national security**.they deal with one event (3)

The existence of a serious **national security** operation conducted by the White House Plumbers first came to public attention when Presidential Aide John Ehrlichman broached the matter while discussing known activities of the Plumbers with the special Senate Watergate Committee's Republican investigators during the summer of 1973. Ehrlichman related that the matter was too sensitive to discuss and invoked executive privilege during his June 1973 testimony. When Senator Baker, the committee co-chair, pressed to know more, White House attorneys J. Fred Buzhardt and Leonard Garment briefed committee Democratic co-chair Senator Sam Ervin (NC), Republican co-chair Senator Howard Baker (TN), and their chief counsels Samuel Dash (D) and Fred E. Thompson (R). (3)

"Certain information was brought to our attention," Senator Baker said. "The matter, of course, has not been fully resolved by the committee, but I really think at this time I have absolutely nothing further to say about it." There were some reports that the **national security** matter involved Pentagon snitching of National Security Council documents. Senator Baker, in 1973, confirmed that the White House regarded the matter of a "very urgent importance" and acknowledged that he did not know the specific basis of White House concern or the nature of the documents which passed from NSC to the Pentagon. Per Senator Baker, the NSC matter is different from the "sensitive **national security** matter" also referenced here. (3)

Senator Ervin did not think the committee had authority to pursue this matter, but he said that the panel (the committee) would discuss it further. "A participant in the July 1973 secret Watergate Committee meeting said Ervin's reaction was that 'it was more like the Keystone

Cops—comical rather than sinister—everyone in the room played it down and thought it was embarrassing." (8)

Ervin refused to permit the Watergate Committee to probe more deeply into the operation despite contentions by Senator Baker that it was a vital "missing link" to the overall Watergate investigation. According to Baker, "The tip of the iceberg may be the only thing showing; I'm not sure we can put it together because of this major 'missing piece.'" In a 1973 appearance on ABC's television program *Issues and Answers*, Senator Baker, citing a "matter of **grave national security** importance," said, "There are animals crashing around in the forest. I can hear them, but I can't see them." (7) To this date, Senator Baker has never disclosed the true nature of the "missing link." The matter was also known as "The California Caper," a term used by Hunt in Senate Committee executive testimony and by a committee staff member. [Caper defined: an activity or escapade, particularly one that is illegal or ridiculous. Synonyms: frolic, stunt, prank, trick, foolery, antics, lark.]

Former Attorney General Elliot L. Richardson gave a hint of this matter in his confirmation hearings in May 1973 before the Senate Judiciary Committee affirming that he had omitted certain passages from notes he had taken on a meeting with Egil Krogh, former White House aide and Plumbers chief. He asserted that the omission referred to a genuine **national security** item and that the CIA had informed him the words left out were subject to classification because their disclosure would prejudice an intelligence source. Richardson stated he was told by White House Special Counsel J. Fred Buzhardt during summer 1973 about "a very significant **national security** problem" associated with Plumbers' super-secret operations. (2)

President Nixon told Assistant Attorney General Henry E. Petersen, who handled the Watergate probe for the US Justice Department until May 1973, "that **national security** matters were not matters that should be investigated because there were some very highly sensitive, not only in Ellsberg, but another matter so sensitive that even Senators Ervin and Baker decided they should not be delved into further." President Nixon told him in April 1973, "That is a **national security** matter. You stay out of that. Your mandate is to investigate Watergate." (2)

Baker and others, including Leonard Garment, Presidential Counsel, urged President Nixon to disclose the matter. It was asserted that most of those informed of the matter contended disclosure of the matter would help President Nixon's case in Watergate and that he had steadfastly refused to do so. One source observed, "The only thing that makes me sympathize at all with the President's plight is the fact that, in this at least, he is sincerely motivated."

CIA Involvement in Watergate and with Plumbers

As of July 30, 1971, a highly secure facility was set up in Room 16 of the Old Executive Office Building, adjacent to White House, for use by Hunt and Liddy. The Plumbers were provided with a secure phone (encrypted technology) with direct connection between Room 16 to "mostly talk to the CIA at Langley."

The following CIA personnel were identified as having operational contacts with Hunt and/or Liddy and/or David Young even after General Cushman cut off aid in late August 1971: Richard Helms, CIA Director; Howard J. Osborn, CIA Director of Security; John Paisley, CIA Office of Security; Richard Ober, CIA officer; Dr. Bernard Malloy, CIA psychiatrist; John Hart, CIA European Division Chief; John Caswell, Executive Officer, CIA European Division; Thomas Karamessines, CIA Director of Plans (Clandestine Services); Peter Jessup, CIA officer with the National Security Council; Dr. Edmund Gunn, CIA doctor. For over twenty years, Ober served under James Angleton as CIA's deputy chief counterintelligence officer and operated CIA's CHAOS.

Hunt's liaison to the CIA was John Paisley, Office of Security (OS), of which Hunt was once a member. An August 9, 1971, David Young memo indicates he had a meeting with Paisley and OS Director Howard Osborn in which Paisley provided a list of objectives for the Special Investigations Unit 5—a clear indication the CIA had a heavy role in identifying objectives and providing assistance to the Plumbers.

On August 18, 1971, Hunt requested that a certain CIA secretary stationed at the CIA Paris field station, previously known to Hunt and acceptable because of her "loyalty factor," be assigned to the Plumbers. The CIA TSD technician recommended taking this request to General Cushman. According to Hunt, this secretary would be involved in a highly sensitive assignment and did not want her CIA division chief to know the White House was involved in the request for this thirty- to ninety-day assignment. The secretary request was denied. This matter was furnished to the Senate Watergate Committee but apparently was never pursued in following investigations.

Liddy had meetings with CIA officials to receive official briefings of sensitive CIA projects and/or information he needed in his capacity as a Plumber.

In 1973, Senator Majority Leader Mike Mansfield (D-MT) instructed certain Federal agencies to not destroy any Watergate files. One day later on June 18, 1973, CIA Director Helms destroyed CIA files.

In 1974, the Senate Armed Services Committee called upon the US Ambassador to Iran to testify on Watergate. When Helms stated he would disclose sensitive **national security** information if called to testify, the hearing was canceled.

FBI Involvement in Watergate and with Plumbers

In his book *Will* (1980), Liddy stated he had a meeting with William C. Sullivan, Assistant FBI Director, Domestic Intelligence, and Charles

Brennan, Assistant Director in charge of Domestic Intelligence on August 2, 1971. Mentioned were the SALT, U-2, and Jack Anderson leaks. The SALT and Jack Anderson leaks are known in Watergate literature as having been undertaken by the Plumbers.

In the FBI's Watergate Summary Report, dated July 5, 1974, no **national security** matters were considered as a part of the FBI's investigation.

However, in the same FBI report, it was stated that the FBI wanted to interview Kathleen Chenow, the Plumbers' secretary. Her interview was delayed by Acting FBI Director Grey based on "**national security** considerations." Dean had a pre-interview meeting with Chenow on her statements. There is no record of any statements or testimony of **national security** information provided by Chenow.

Per a 1974 FBI Watergate summary, it was related that John W. Dean, former White House Counsel, had admitted that he had destroyed two notebooks that had been taken from Hunt's White House safe two days after the Watergate break-in. Dean stated he found the notebooks in White House file materials in January of 1973. Dean claimed that the notebooks contained names and addresses of people connected with the Watergate break-in and related crimes. At the time, Hunt was greatly distressed that his operational materials had been taken from his White House safe. These were possibly the notebooks related to the Ellsberg-Fielding break-in and "The California Caper."

Plumbers' activities involved:

- Investigation of Ellsberg who had leaked the so-called *Pentagon Papers* to the *New York Times*_for publication. This leak was a causative force in formation of the Plumbers, in part because both the CIA and FBI had refused to become involved in domestic intelligence operations of this nature. Sources asserted that Ellsberg may have been a Soviet intelligence informer and that he was capable of turning over details of the most closely held nuclear-targeting secrets of the United States.

- Supervision of a 1971 massive leak investigation within the Department of Defense. That investigation focused on a mid-echelon military official with considerable foreign travel and intelligence agencies exposure. This military official was still on active duty, his identity not disclosed. (4) Related to this, The Plumbers supervised a 1971 massive leak investigation within the Department of Defense. This military official was operating as an American counterspy and would be compromised by continued inquiry by the Watergate Special Prosecutor and Senate Watergate Committee into the Ellsberg case. Furthermore, this military official was believed to be a highly placed Soviet agent of the K.G.B., the Soviet intelligence agency. (5) There was fear that disclosure of the details would endanger the life of a US intelligence source to the highest Russian officials. One source aware of the operation stated, "I have no doubt that it is highly likely a life would be snuffed out. It would, in the words of the CIA, put an individual in 'extreme prejudice.'" (5)

The Watergate Special Prosecutors and National Security

Professor Archibald Cox of Harvard Law School was the first Watergate Special Prosecutor, and Richardson stated that in September 1972 he had raised this **national security** matter with Cox as a serious problem. They agreed that it would have to be thought through and anticipated. Cox was fired by President Nixon, possibly because he had pressed too hard on the cited **national security** aspects of Plumbers operations, and he was succeeded by Texas attorney, Leon Jaworski, on November 1,

1972. Soon thereafter, Jaworski was briefed on this sensitive **national security** matter by Buzhardt and General Haig, White House Chief of Staff. According to Jaworski, Buzhardt and Haig "did call to my attention a matter related to **national security** and a problem which could arise from that." Buzhardt and Haig promised to let Jaworski or a member of his staff listen to tapes and to any **national security** problem. (2)

Jaworski believed he would not have to invade that **national security** area when pursuing prosecutions and indictments on other matters. In Senate questioning, Senator Edward Kennedy requested that the veil of secrecy not be drawn over the matter, and Jaworski replied: "One, much as I respect the issue of **national security**, I'm not going to be blinded by it; and, two, there was no resistance by Buzhardt or Haig when I thought some indictments could be brought, and I was going to pursue them." (2)

In mid-November 1973, President Nixon, at an Associated Press (AP) editors conference at Disney World in Orlando, Florida, stated that **national security** matters were not matters that should be investigated because leaders of the Senate Watergate Committee had decided that there were some very highly sensitive matters into which they should not delve further.

At the AP conference in November 1973, President Nixon stated: "I don't mean we're going to throw the cloak of **national security** over something because we are guilty of something. I'm simply saying that where **national security** would be disserved by having an investigation, the President has responsibility to protect it, and I'm going to do so." (2)

Other reasons and concerns for not disclosing the sensitive **national security** matter involved:

- Discouragement of criminal indictments of Plumbers activities involving John D. Ehrlichman, Charles Colson and Egil Krogh.

President Nixon was strongly committed to avoiding criminal liability for key White House staff members. He used the concept of "Presidential Executive Privilege" to avoid incriminating disclosures.

- Fear by President Nixon and his national security advisor, Henry A. Kissinger, that a full inquiry into the Ellsberg case would eventually result in disclosure of United States nuclear secrets and compromise of a Soviet KGB (intelligence) official operating as an American counterspy (above). (6)

- A desire by President Nixon to keep the matter secret to protect the "whole military command structure." (9)

In his televised speech to the nation on April 29, 1974, President Nixon again expounded his version of the conversation at that meeting on March 21, 1973, one of those for which the tape was sought by both the special prosecutor and the House Judiciary Committee. He prefaced his account with the statement that "in many places on the tapes there were ambiguities—statements and comments that different people with different perspectives might interpret in drastically different ways."

As to Hunt's blackmail threat, President Nixon also stated:

- "I returned several times to the immediate problem posed by Mr. Hunt's blackmail threat, which to me was not a Watergate problem, but one which I regarded, rightly or wrongly, as a potential **national security** problem of very serious proportions. I considered long and hard whether it might in fact be better to let the payment go forward, at least temporarily, in the hope that the **national security** matter would not be exposed in the course of uncovering the Watergate cover-up.

- "I believed then, and I believe today, that I had a responsibility as President to consider every option—including this one—where production of sensitive **national security** matters was at issue, protection of such matters. In the course of considering it and of 'just thinking out loud,' as I put it at one point, I several times suggested that meeting Hunt's demands might be necessary.

- "But then I also traced through where that would lead. The money could be raised. But money demands would lead inescapably to clemency demands, and clemency could not be granted. I said, and I quote directly from the tape: 'It is wrong, that's for sure.'"

White House Watergate Tapes and Transcripts National Security and the Plumbers' Other Operation: "The California Caper"

There are volumes of transcripts made from conversations involving President Nixon based on 3,342 hours of secret recordings from three physical sites in the White House: Oval Office, Old Executive Office Building (President's office), and the Cabinet Room. Recordings were also made from the White House telephone system and at Camp David. Of the tapes, thirty-seven hours continue to be withheld due to **national security**. Perhaps it would be well for the US government, under independent safeguards, to force immediate disclosures of these **national security** withholds.

Many of the tapes, often of conversations between the President and H. R. Haldeman, showed President Nixon concerned about Howard Hunt: "Hunt's going to blow!" "Hunt knows too much," "The guy you have to control is Hunt." Hunt's demands resulted in blackmail against the President. The demands were directly related to "The California Caper." In the White House tapes, President Nixon refers to Hunt and Liddy as "crazy bastards" and "those jackasses."

The following conversation references concerns about "The California Caper" and its relationship to fears of **national security** disclosures:

Conversation 898-12, Meeting between President Nixon, H.R. Haldeman, John Ehrlichman and Ronald Ziegler, Oval Office, April 17, 1973. 12:35-2:20 p.m.

Excerpts:

EHRLICHMAN: Well, I think you have to charge Henry Petersen or whoever you get, gets as a man in charge here with protecting your privilege, and then that's got to go down to Silbert, and Silbert has to be cautioned that he is not to go into matters of executive privilege, and he is not to go into matters of **national security** importance.

PRESIDENT NIXON: Any matters involving a conversation with the President involve **national security**. If they want to know anything, they can ask me.

EHRLICHMAN: Now, ah, the question comes up, I don't know how far this will run, but this **caper in California,** for instance. Ah, Colson asked me.

PRESIDENT NIXON: **Which caper?**

EHRLICHMAN: This, this thing of Hunt's out there, the **national security** thing they connected Ellsberg.

PRESIDENT NIXON: That's right. They haven't found it yet.

EHRLICHMAN: Well, Petersen knows about it. I think. It's laying around somewhere, but ah, if the question comes up, Colson says, "How do I handle that?" I said, "Chuck, well, if I were asked that, I would say that that is a **national**, that was a **national security** project, and I'm not in the position to answer a question on that, ah, because I think it falls within the ambit of executive privilege."

PRESIDENT NIXON: That's right.

EHRLICHMAN: "Now, I would have to refer it to the President for a waiver of executive privilege on that if he desired to do so." And he said, "Well, can I say the same thing?" And I said, "Well, I don't know whether you can or not." He said, "Well, what would the President say if it's referred to him?" And I said, "I don't know, I haven't asked him."

PRESIDENT NIXON:	That's what we'd say.
EHRLICHMAN:	Okay? Can I tell him that...?
PRESIDENT NIXON:	Yeah.
EHRLICHMAN:	For you?
PRESIDENT NIXON:	All right.
EHRLICHMAN:	All right.
PRESIDENT NIXON:	...anything (unintelligible) anything, anything in leak thing, the plumbing thing was **national security**.
EHRLICHMAN:	That's what it was.
PRESIDENT NIXON:	Anything in the plumbing thing and, and, and that the, the ITT thing, no I can't plead it was that, you know. Uh, Hunt did there. It's quite apparent...
HALDEMAN:	**RESTRICTED-"B"**
PRESIDENT NIXON:	**RESTRICTED-"B"**
HALDEMAN:	**RESTRICTED-"B"**
UNIDENTIFIED:	**RESTRICTED-"B"**

EHRLICHMAN: **RESTRICTED-"B"**

RESTRICTED-"B" is a **national security** matter withheld by the National Archives.

HALDEMAN: I doubt if Dean knew about that. I don't— See, Dean and Colson never tracked particularly well together, I don't think. Well, I don't know if they did or not.

EHRLICHMAN: Ah, whoever, whoever operates this at the Justice Department has to be told that the inquiry must not jeopardize your privilege. Someday, they're going to try and put you in a crunch spot.

PRESIDENT NIXON: Sure.

EHRLICHMAN: And they'll put a question to me, and I'll say I can't take that question.

PRESIDENT NIXON: (Unintelligible).

EHRLICHMAN: And then I'll be back to you.

PRESIDENT NIXON: No problem…wa

EHRLICHMAN: And ah, it's going to be hard.

PRESIDENT NIXON: No, for me at all, it's **national security**. It's in a **national security** area, and that is a **national security** problem.

In an **April 25, 1973, Conversation 430-22, Haldeman with President Nixon** addressed the **national security** aspect of Hunt's blackmail demand:

Excerpts:

HALDEMAN: You're being blackmailed, here on this specific question of, of the **national security** point. Because what Hunt was holding ya up on, was not on the Watergate.

PRESIDENT NIXON: Still, still…

HALDEMAN: But on the other seamy work for Ehrlichman. All the other defendants were involved in this.

Ellsberg and the Target in the other operations were considered by the President, his closest aides, and the Plumbers as "national traitors" and "enemies of the state." Both were to be discredited and dishonored with operations against them with the goal to destroy them professionally and personally. The operant term was "neutralization." Neither could be trusted. Ellsberg and Target were believed to be involved in a conspiracy. In the Watergate White House tapes, this second Plumbers' operation is often referred to as "the other matter."

The Watergate tapes make references to "the SC thing," "the pre-Watergate thing," "the matter totally unrelated to Watergate," "highly sensitive thing," "military area," and similar cryptic, coded phrasing. In 1971, there is reference to the other operation on Target, also known as "the California Caper." John Ehrlichman and/or Charles Colson, directed and/or sanctioned the following criminal activities (seamy work for Ehrlichman) by the Plumbers, all conducted under color of **national security.**

Clandestine Interview and Photographing of a Questionable Person using CIA Equipment

In July 1971, Hunt met at the CIA Headquarters offices of General Robert Cushman, USMC, and Deputy CIA Director with request for CIA support. The purpose was to assess in a clandestine manner a person (Target) whose ideology was in question. Requested were fictitious identification documents for Hunt and Liddy, physical disguise for Hunt, and notional pocket litter. Also requested and received was a Tessina spy camera secreted in a cigarette pouch. The Tessina, a subminiature camera manufactured in Switzerland, takes 14/21mm pictures on standard 35mm film roll with thirty-six exposures loaded into a special cassette. It required a CIA technician to load and unload the film roll into the cassette. This particular camera was used because the photography was to be taken in a darkened corridor. (Such suggests that a casing operation was conducted beforehand to come up with the photographic venue lighting characteristics, likely around August twenty-fifth, the same day the Ellsberg/Fielding casing operation occurred.) The low-light operational challenges meant that the camera was loaded with high-speed film. According to Liddy, the camera's aperture and shutter speed were preset. The camera was secreted in a tobacco pouch. Hunt and Liddy were CIA-trained on use of the camera, and upon completion of the

July 1971 mission, the camera was returned for processing as it required technical expertise to unload the film. During the Watergate hearings, seven prints from the Tessina showed Hunt and Liddy outside the Beverly Hills office of Ellsberg psychiatrist, Dr. Fielding. The negatives were retained by the CIA, and the Watergate hearings never mentioned what other photographs existed of the Target. Presumably, the CIA still retains in file all photographs from the film, including the twenty-nine unaccounted negatives and print. According to Liddy, the CIA provided the Plumbers with prints from the roll of film after it was developed.

There is no mention in any of the Watergate literature that the Tessina camera was used in any other Plumbers operation. It was returned to the CIA because it did not work out operationally. A different camera, a Polaroid, was used to photograph the results of the psychiatrist's office after the break-in. According to Liddy in his book *Will*, a Retina IIIC 35mm camera with 80mm lens was used in the Ellsberg/Fielding break-in. The Retina IIIC was Liddy's personal camera, and there is no reporting of photographs taken with this camera or any other details. Neither Hunt nor Liddy participated in the actual entry of Dr. Fielding's psychiatric office as they were prohibited by Ehrlichman from doing so. The actual break-in was done by three contracted Cubans (the same ones who participated in the break-in at the Watergate DNC Headquarters.)

Hunt's meeting with General Cushman's CIA office was surreptitiously recorded. The transcript of that conversation was furnished to the Senate Watergate Committee and placed in the Congressional record. There was no apparent follow-up as to the identity of the Target.

Probable Telephone Tap of This Person's (Target's) Telephone

Telephone taps are a standard counterintelligence and special operations technique, and the Plumbers had access to the means for doing so. The Plumbers telephone-tapped Ellsberg, and this was done by the FBI.

Also, Hunt and the Plumbers installed electronic surveillance equipment at the Democratic National Headquarters offices at the Watergate Hotel and Office Complex.

It is probable that a telephone tap was used in the other operation involving Target. US government records would reflect the details and possible actual transcripts of conversations.

Probable Covert Search and Clandestine Photography

In Liddy's book *Will*, there is a photograph shown of an automatic Minolta C subminiature/spy camera with accessories, including those for copying documents (a camera stand) and film-developing equipment and chemicals. In the book, it is stated that this equipment was used in the Ellsberg/Fielding break-in. Watergate hearings indicated neither Hunt nor Liddy participated in the physical break-in as this was done by the Cubans, and a Polaroid camera was used there. The Minolta spy camera was not used in the Ellsberg/Fielding break-in except where Liddy used it to photograph an external door lock at Dr. Fielding's office. The Minolta spy camera was not furnished by the CIA. This camera along with camera stand and film-developing chemicals were purchased by Hunt and Liddy at a Beverly Hills, California, camera shop. It is likely that a covert search was conducted by the Plumbers of Target's venue over Labor Day weekend 1971, using the Minolta spy camera to photograph documents (the same Labor Day weekend of the Ellsberg/Fielding break-in), and at the location of the darkened corridor photographic venue. A possible date is Saturday, September 4, 1971, in part because there is no accounting for activity on that day by either Hunt or Liddy. The Ellsberg/Fielding break-in occurred on Friday, September third, and the Plumbers returned to Washington, D.C., on Sunday, September fifth. What documents were photographed, and what were the results? It is possible that the three Cubans participated in the covert search. Hunt and Liddy asserted that they had prior experience with surreptitious entry (also known as "black bag jobs"), Hunt with CIA and Liddy with FBI.

This April 26, 1973, Conversation 905-8 between President Nixon and Haldeman is relevant:

Excerpts:

PRESIDENT NIXON: Did you hear about it?

HALDEMAN: No, not until I heard that tape yesterday… I, I still don't know what that means—you mean they took a picture, when they broke in, and that picture was in Hunt's file in the stuff they turned over to the FBI?

PRESIDENT NIXON: That's why Dean's saying that, the uh, Ehrlichman is uh, uh, that, that Hunt's going to blow the whistle on him, is blackmailing.

HALDEMAN: Does Ehrlichman know that, that photo was in the file?

PRESIDENT NIXON: Yes, he does. But Ehrlichman, Ehrlichman says he, he knows about the break-in.

Probable Extortion Attempt of Target

In the book *Will* (page 262), Liddy cites the value of exploitation of sexual weaknesses. "During one of our trips to California, Hunt attempted to recruit one woman suggested by Jackson (a California friend) and a woman suggested by Hunt's friend. The woman I was working with was ideal as a plant. She was flashy, good-looking, young, had secretarial skills and experience, and appeared able to attract men sexually if she wished, probably even the candidate." Liddy would need her services through August (1971); however, over dinner Liddy purposely burned his hand severely at a dinner table, and the woman refused Liddy's lucrative offer. When Liddy returned to the hotel, he learned that Hunt had obtained a preliminary commitment from another woman. The purpose of the probably sexual exploitation—an extortion attempt of Target. The prior discussion of Hunt's CIA secretary use applies here.

Was the purpose of the extortion attempt to create a spy out of the Target in order to blackmail and control him? The following is a conversation between President Nixon and Haldeman:

Conversation 422-20 the President and H. R. Haldeman, March 22, 1973, 9:11-10:35 a.m., Executive Office Building.
Excerpts:
<u>Begins 25 min/01 sec</u>

PRESIDENT NIXON:	How does John answer the Ellsberg thing? That's the other point I wanted to raise, that, uh, John [Ehrlichman] seems to say, well…
HALDEMAN:	He says, "I didn't know anything about it." He, he says, "I didn't think they, I—"
PRESIDENT NIXON:	Talked about the oversight.
HALDEMAN:	No, he didn't. He says he didn't find out about that.

PRESIDENT NIXON: Krogh, Krogh did. But what, what was, what were we doing at that meeting? *What was he talking about then?* [Is the whole point (unintelligible)?] I'm rather curious to know myself.

HALDEMAN: Well, you better ask John, 'cause I don't really know. All I know is...

PRESIDENT NIXON: All I know is that I think it was part of that whole operation of John and [David] Young, where we were just looking into the whole business of leaks. Henry [Kissinger] was in on that. Henry must be aware of some of that. I've got to—

HALDEMAN: What they—the enterprise out of there, which is the key thing—that, that Hunt, you see, Hunt—what **Hunt says is that he'll uncover some of the sleazy work he did for Ehrlichman.** He said particularly remind him of the...

PRESIDENT NIXON: Yeah.

HALDEMAN: ...of the...

PRESIDENT NIXON: That's Ellsberg's affair. That's what Dean told me.

HALDEMAN: Alright, and the Ellsberg affair…

PRESIDENT NIXON: Yeah, what happened?

HALDEMAN: I'm not sure what happened, but it has something to do with they sent Hunt out, and I guess the Cubans…

PRESIDENT NIXON: Yeah.

HALDEMAN: …to break in…

PRESIDENT NIXON: To a doctor's office.

HALDEMAN: …to a psychiatrist's office to get a report…

PRESIDENT NIXON: Yeah.

HALDEMAN: …on Ellsberg's mental analysis or something like that, and they bungled, bungled the break-in. They didn't get what they were supposed to get or something, and then they came back and said could they go back again, and that request got to Ehrlichman, and he said, "Absolutely not," he says. And they didn't, apparently. That's—

PRESIDENT NIXON: Why did they want a report on (unintelligible)?

HALDEMAN: I don't know, but they had—there was a lot of stuff. They had a lot of interesting stuff on Ellsberg that showed he was, that was—we got some of it.

PRESIDENT NIXON: What was the purpose of it though? I mean, to discredit—

HALDEMAN: I forgot—yes. (Unintelligible)

26 min/18 sec

PRESIDENT NIXON: (Unintelligible)

HALDEMAN: *But they'd make a spy out of him*, and, uh...

PRESIDENT NIXON: Oh, I see.

HALDEMAN: Uh, uh.

PRESIDENT NIXON: Did, did, uh, it make him look as bad after all that **national security** was involved and so forth?

HALDEMAN: Well...

PRESIDENT NIXON: I'm not sure *it would..*

HALDEMAN: And why were we using private people? Because the question, there was a valid, or, a real question here as to where the CIA and the FBI fit into it.

PRESIDENT NIXON:	Also, whether *they* were leaking—
HALDEMAN:	(Unintelligible) because things were leaking from all over.
PRESIDENT NIXON:	*They* were leaking from all over, and somebody had to find a way—
HALDEMAN:	And it had to be done independently.
PRESIDENT NIXON:	It had to be done independently because of possibility of, uh, leakage.

There were no known efforts to make Ellsberg into a spy, and he was already considered a spy, a Soviet agent. This making of someone into a spy is related to someone else, but this is not directly apparent from this tape. President Nixon's statement "make a spy out of him" reflects direct "guilty knowledge."

Spying is espionage. Espionage committed against the US is treason. The act of making a spy of someone is <u>subornation of treason,</u> which IS treason.

Possible Electronic Surveillance "Bugging" of Target

The following conversation between President Nixon and Henry Pedersen, Assistant Attorney General, is relevant. It shows guilty knowledge on the part of President Nixon that a crime was committed and that he wanted it masked under "executive privilege."

Conversation 902-3, of a meeting between President Nixon and Henry Pedersen, Oval Office, April 19, 1973 10:12-11:07 a.m.
This is portion of a Watergate tape as part of the Watergate Special Prosecution Task Force held by the National Archives.

In-Camera submission, April 30, 1974, U.S. v. Ehrlichman

Excerpts:

PRESIDENT NIXON: My purpose in the Hunt thing in calling you is simply to say it is, it was a **national security** investigation. It is not related in any way to the Watergate thing.

PEDERSEN: Correct.

PRESIDENT NIXON: And that the purpose of it was…

PEDERSEN: Well, is there any other—you know I can't stay away from that which I don't know.

PRESIDENT NIXON: Certainly. Did Hunt do anything else?

PEDERSEN: Is there any other **national security** stuff that we could—

PRESIDENT NIXON: Yes.

PEDERSEN: …inadvertently get into through Hunt.

PRESIDENT NIXON: Yes, you could get into other things. For example, Hunt, Hunt involved in <u>bugging</u>, apparently. He tried, for example, on one occasion, he was—it was basically (unintelligible) Ellsberg period, you know, this place was leaking like a sieve, and you remember Kissinger's National Security people.

PEDERSEN: Yes, sir. I do.

PRESIDENT NIXON: We had a horrible time, and frankly the country was in jeopardy because I—it was imperative that our situation with foreign governments and a lot of others that I'd get Hoover in and say, "Damn it, we've got to (unintelligible)." (Unintelligible) for myself. You know how [J. Edgar] Hoover was. You know, but he hated to get into anything involving press. So when you—I think, though, quite candidly, Hoover for years—you should know this—bugged the—**RESTRICTED-"B"**

PEDERSEN: I remember the situation, but I don't (unintelligible)

PRESIDENT NIXON: I can't tell you—

PEDERSEN: I remember the entire thing, I remember. I

know who you mean, but I can't recall his name, either.

PRESIDENT: **RESTRICTED-"B"** And I know that when I first came intooffice, he used to send that stuff over here by the carload. He used to love that sort of thing. That we discontinued also. We discontinued that.

****

PRESIDENT NIXON: I want you to understand that I have never used the word **national security** unless it is. As far as Watergate is concerned, or any of that crap, you just—but when I called you the other day, I said I am not going to let any stone unturned, and that is what you and I have got to understand. But I am anxious to get one or two things, Henry, very important. In terms of privilege, that you, that, one: any conversations with the President are obviously privileged.

PEDERSEN: Yes, sir. I understand that.

RESTRICTED-"B" is a **national security** matter withheld by the National Archives.

There is no evidence that Hunt/the Plumbers ever employed electronic surveillance/ eavesdropping (bugging) on Ellsberg.

It appears that none of the above operations were conducted without a court order. All were done "clandestinely," and in violation of the Fourth Amendment of the US Constitution. Crimes of an egregious nature were perpetrated and civil liberties callously violated of both the Target and his family. Were the venues for each of the five Plumbers operations at Target's California home?

Both Hunt and Liddy possessed handguns. A handgun was found in Hunt's White House Plumbers' safe, and Liddy describes owning a "sterile (non-traceable) CIA handgun" as well as Browning fold-down knife, which Liddy carried on the Ellsberg/Fielding break-in, per his book *Will*. Were these lethal weapons carried on them during any of the above operations? Were there any plans or intent to use them during any operation?

More on Plumbers Activity and Colson's Involvement

Conversation 423-3 of a meeting among President Nixon, Haldeman, Ehrlichman and Ronald Ziegler on March 27, 1973, 11:30 a.m.-1:30 p.m. Executive Office Building:

Excerpts:

PRESIDENT NIXON: In that case—

EHRLICHMAN: That's correct. And I had no occasion to tell you anything about Colson's involvement...

PRESIDENT NIXON: That's my point.

EHRLICHMAN: Ah, Young and Krogh operated that, the whole Operation from the beginning, as a matter of fact, with the other leaks, the Tad Szulc leaks and so on, and they carried on through and, and Krogh is very frank in saying, "I authorized this, ah, this operation in Los Angeles, no two ways about it." He says, uh, "If I am asked," uh, he says, "that's what I'll say, and I'll resign and leave the Department of Transportation and get out of town." He said, "I, uh, thought at the time we were doing the right thing and…"

PRESIDENT NIXON: Should he?

EHRLICHMAN: ..and so forth. I don't think he'll have to. Number one, I don't think Hunt, uh, I don't think Hunt will strike him [Krogh]. If he did, I would, I would put the **national security** tent over this whole operation.

PRESIDENT NIXON: I sure would.

EHRLICHMAN: And say, "Look, there are a lot of things that went on in the national interest there that involved taps. They involved entry. They involved interrogation. They involved a lot of things, and I don't, I don't propose to open that up to scrutiny."

PRESIDENT NIXON: Right.

The above conversation partially corroborates aspects of the above Plumbers' activity. However, there is no evidence that the Plumbers interviewed or interrogated Ellsberg. A clandestine interview is a form of interrogation. Telephone taps and entry were employed.

Given Target's presumed intelligence agent skills, is it possible that Plumbers operations at the time were detected and compromised by Target, and the Plumbers were unaware?

The exact reasons for Plumbers operations against the Target, or his identity, have never been disclosed in US Congressional record, Watergate books, and related materials such as Watergate tapes. The exact nature of Target's leak(s) has never been revealed. Apparently, the Plumbers' leak investigations gained no result. Again, who was Target? By whom and on what were grounds for identifying Target as a Soviet agent? An "**Enemy of the State**"? A "**National Traitor**"? What was betrayed or leaked?

In an April 28, 1973 Conversation 038-154, President Nixon addressed that issue:

"…that, my God, this is a **national security** investigation—was—but it didn't produce anything."

Possibly Target's identity can be learned from a 1974 FBI Watergate report. Of relevance here is a partially redacted (hidden content) document based on **national security** grounds concerning contact and directives from the CIA Director Helms to the FBI not to interview a person associated with Howard Hunt.

From FBI Watergate Summary, pages 58, 59

"On June 28, 1972, Mr. Gray was confidentially informed by CIA Director Helms that (**redacted**) therefore, should not be interviewed.

The Field was so instructed; however, prior to the receipt of that information, (**redacted**) been interviewed, resulting in no information of value. (**Redacted**) never interviewed, and no reasons to interview him are now known.

"At the time that WFO discovered the (**redacted**). On July 7, 1972, WFO advised that the (**redacted**)

"Alexandria was instructed to conduct appropriate investigation regarding (**redacted**) to develop his identity and association with Hunt and other subject. On July 11, 1972, our Alexandria office advised that CIA could furnish information concerning (**redacted**) only to Acting Director Gray. On July 28, 1972, a handwritten note was personally delivered by General Walters to Mr. Gray. (**Redacted**) who was in contact with Hunt during August 1971. General Walters also (**redacted**) supplied a Uher recorder pursuant to Hunt's request; helped him get it in shape for overt, not covert, use; and there was no attempt to make the recorder useful for clandestine purposes."

Alexandria, above, refers to Alexandria, Virginia, FBI Field Office. General Walters is Lieutenant General Vernon Walters, US Army, Deputy Director CIA, who succeeded General Cushman.

In 2010 and 2011, the FBI was requested to declassify and release the unredacted version of this document under the provisions of the Freedom of Information Act. The request was refused on both occasions citing **national security.**

Pages 58 and 59 of the above FBI Summary Report contain other **national security** redactions on the same subject matter needing release.

Charles Colson

Colson, who supervised Hunt, was a very close confidant of President Nixon both during the time Colson served as a White House counsel and after leaving to go into private legal practice. Sometimes there were two or three conversations in one day, in White House offices and by telephone. The following is a telephone conversation between President Nixon and Colson about the **grave national security** matter:

Conversation 45-65 between President Nixon and Charles Colson, April 30, 1973, 11:24-11:28 p.m., White House Telephone

Abuse of Power, Stanley Kutler, page 386

PRESIDENT NIXON: Incidentally, on this—you know, all this business about you know, the Plumbers operation, good God, that's totally justified, isn't it?

COLSON: Yes sir.

PRESIDENT NIXON: Or is it?

COLSON: Well, I don't think there's any doubt about it. I don't intend to talk about it. They—I don't think they can make me because that's, at least what I know about it, it's a **national security operation**, and Ehrlichman talked to me about that some time ago, and that was something that I wouldn't discuss. I wouldn't have any reason to discuss it.

PRESIDENT NIXON: Right. You just say—but you say, "Look, we were protecting the security of this country.

White House tapes show that President Nixon in a May 1973 conversation with General Alexander Haig voiced identical concerns to that of the Watergate Special Prosecution Task Force about the end of the Republic and that he wanted all Presidential records suppressed based on **national security**.

Conversation 913-8 between the President and General Alexander M. Haig, May 9, 1973, 9:40-10:02 a.m. Oval Office
Excerpts:
Abuse of Power, Stanley Kutler p 423

PRESIDENT NIXON: You and I both know that the main thing we've got to do is keep our iron hand on the presidential papers for the other reason. **National security. National security**.

HAIG: That's essential.

PRESIDENT NIXON: **National security**—that's what the *Times* and others are nibbling about Ellsberg—Goddamned people stole those Pentagon papers, and now they want to get out there and the whole goddamned files, and we're trying to stop them. We're not going to allow that. You know that—that's, that's too hot. That's too hot, Al… It would really destroy N government, wouldn't it? I mean, goddamn it, we've got leaks all the time. What the hell do we do, for example we—

Kutler text has "unintelligible" in lieu of N, which appears in actual tape. Likely N refers to national, meaning national government.

HAIG: We know that (unintelligible).

PRESIDENT NIXON;   Huh?

HAIG: It just would be inconceivable if that ever got out, and it's always been true. You know this isn't any different than with any other presidency or any other—you just do not do it. You cannot!

PRESIDENT NIXON: Just say this is a **national security** matter. It involves **illegal activities.** It involves **national security**. I have no comment and will not go beyond that. Mitchell…

The last portion of the conversation is not in the Kutler book but is on the actual tape. There is other discussion on Ellsberg but not on this matter. This above omission adds meaning to the sentence. In other conversations, President Nixon coached others to use term illegal activities rather than criminal activities in an effort to soften the characterization.

Question: Based on all the above, was President Nixon, in his capacity as Commander in Chief, justified in going along with Hunt's blackmail threat in order to avoid public disclosure of the Plumbers' "**national security**" operations?

August 9, 1974

President Nixon resigned from office in disgrace. In his brief remarks given at the White House in the morning with many present and the nation watching on television, he stated, "Greatness comes not when things go always good for you, but the greatness comes, and you are really tested when you take some knocks, some disappointments, when sadness comes, because only if you have been in the deepest valley can you ever know how magnificent it is to be on the highest mountain.

> "We want you to be proud of what you have done. We want you to continue to serve in government, if that is your wish. Always give your best, never get discouraged, never be petty; always remember, others may hate you, but those who hate you don't win unless you hate them, and then you destroy yourself."

After taking the oath of office at mid-day August 9. 1974, President Gerald Ford, speaking to the nation on television, declared, **"My fellow Americans, our long national nightmare is over.** Our Constitution works; our great Republic is a government of laws and not of men. Here the people rule. But there is a higher Power, by whatever name we honor Him, who ordains not only righteousness but love, not only justice but mercy. In all my public and private acts as your President, I expect to follow my instincts of openness and candor with full confidence that honesty is always the best policy in the end."

In that speech President Ford declared, "I believe that **truth** is the glue that holds government together, not only our Government but civilization itself. That bond, though strained, is unbroken at home and abroad."

For those Americans who witnessed all of this, President Ford's words were so very soothing after the tumultuous and terrible events of Watergate: the Congressional hearings, President Nixon's public statements and speeches, trials and testimony, and news accounts of questionable and criminal activity. Indeed, the nation did live through a nightmare, and all welcomed a fresh start to heal the nation under

President Ford's competence. People wanted Watergate forever banished and to move on to a saner existence and civil society.

What Do We Do Now?

The American people have an absolute right and need to know what happened during these times. As is evident from the above, the full story has not been told. For the reasons cited by Judge Breyer and President Nixon, the whole truth of Watergate could not be told at that time for fear of dire consequences. Telling the truth at this time will accomplish what President Nixon could not or would not do then. As President Ford stated, truth is the glue that holds a nation as well as civilization together.

The final chapters of Watergate need to be revealed and written, without fear or favor. The Department of Justice and the US Congress are key actors in discovery of the truth. The Republic and the US military will survive, will endure, and will be affirmed with truth-telling now forty five years later.

This is consistent with the notion of **national security**.

Truth IS **national security**.

National Security is Personal Privacy.

Truth may not forever be hidden from history.

For many years, radio-listening audiences were treated to daily news presented by broadcaster Paul Harvey Senior and his headliner part of the show called "The Rest of the Story." He would tell little-known facts about a person, providing interesting characterizations about that person's journey and key events through life, all without identifying that person by name. Then came "the rest of the story" where folks were surprised learning that person's identity and explanation of prologue and prologue.

Similarly, here the reader is presented with the "rest of the story" of that person considered by President Nixon as a **National Traitor** and **Enemy of the State**, subjected to egregious criminal acts by the White House Special Investigations Unit, also known as the Plumbers. That person is me.

In the chapters that follow cover my personal Watergate story, including over twenty-one years on active duty in the Air Force as a Special Agent and Intelligence Officer. The "rest of the story" recounts the various stages and progression of my military career as a person as well as professional intelligence officer and how I dealt with Watergate at the time. It includes my awareness of Plumber operations against me.

The reader is requested to take the chapters in progression as there are building blocks in telling "the rest of the story."

Chapter 1:
So Help Me, God!

19 APRIL 1962: NELLIS AFB, NEVADA

Dick and I were in our Special Agent civilian clothes and standing in his office. "Okay, Jerry, are we ready?" Dick asked.

"I'm ready!"

"Raise your right hand," he said, and we both did. "Now, repeat after me... I, Percy Gerald Rogers, 69251A, having been appointed a Second Lieutenant, United States Air Force, do solemnly swear that I will support and defend the Constitution of the United States against all enemies foreign and domestic; that I will bear true faith and allegiance to the same; that I take this obligation freely, without any mental reservation or purpose of evasion; that I will well and faithfully discharge the duties of the office upon which I am about to enter. So help me, God."

I repeated him, line for line, and when we were done, he exclaimed, "Great, Jerry! Congratulations!" We shook hands and then went on to sign the paperwork. I signed, and then Dick signed. The papers were sworn to and subscribed before me at Nellis AFB, Nevada, this nineteenth day of April 1962.

Now, some fifty-five years later, I clearly recall that reading from a darkened Thermo-Fax copy of an AF Form 133 "Oath of Office (Military Personnel)." Captain Richard A. "Dick" Noble was my immediate supervisor and Commander of Detachment 1909 of the Air Force Office of Special investigations, the Air Force's version of the Federal Bureau of Investigation.

This time, the oath was for a commission in the Regular Air Force; I was then serving in the temporary grade of First Lieutenant. So this wasn't the first time I had taken such an oath. There were two previous times, and both are vivid in my memory. The first time was on 5 February 1960 (military date) at the Armed Forces Recruiting Center in downtown Los Angeles. It seems to me that the Center was located in a seedy part of downtown LA, and the large common room was full of recruiters and recruits from all branches of service processing paperwork. It was my first experience of "hurry up and wait." It took all morning for all of us to get the paperwork done, forms signed. Then the announcement came to assemble in another larger room. It was an interesting room with overhead glass panels for available sunlight and a well-worn wooden floor, but it was still poorly lit. We were going to be sworn in. There were probably one hundred people in the room, all men, I think, and mostly younger than me at barely age twenty-two. A short, burly Army sergeant entered the room and stood before us, all of us spread out in ranks. This guy was pretty impressive with many rows of military ribbons on his uniform shirt. We all stood at attention while he said, "You are now about to take the oath of enlistment. If there is any reason you feel you cannot take the oath, leave the room now!" No one did. "Raise your right hand, and repeat after me... Say your own name."

"I, Percy Gerald Rogers, do solemnly swear... So help me, God!" At the instant we finished, I thought to myself, "I may have just signed my own death warrant here." It was indeed a solemn and sobering moment. Anyone who has ever taken an oath in the armed forces will definitely recall that event—the time they took the "blood oath." As a member of the armed forces, there is no guarantee that one will survive the enlistment. Too, while I understood the oath, the phrase "domestic enemies" seemed strange. What seemed even stranger was that in years later, that phrase would come back to haunt me while I was at the same time under the oath's warrant.

So, I was now officially an Airman Basic in the United States Air Force and headed for Lackland Air Force Base in San Antonio, Texas, for Air Force Officer Training School (OTS), Class 60C.

As an Officer Candidate, I could drive my own car to Lackland and didn't have to take the train or bus as the enlistees for military basic training did. Soon afterwards, I was joined by newlyweds Tim and Betsy S. for the drive to Texas. As we drove off that February day I looked back and Mom was crying as she walked back into the house. THAT was hard to take! Tim and I were fraternity brothers at UC Berkeley and had both investigated the Air Force commissioning program. Sometime in May 1959, shortly before graduation on June 11, we both took the mental and physical tests at Travis AFB and met a board of officers for an oral interview. The OTS program was perfect since one was guaranteed an Air Force specialty upon graduation. My first choice was the Air Force Office of Special Investigations, the career specialty being called "Special Investigations and Counterintelligence Officer." My second choice was Tim's "Air Police Officer." Tim's college major was psychology while mine was criminology, with a law enforcement emphasis.

OTS was a three-month-long program, hence the name "Ninety-Day Wonder School." Quite frankly, I had never had any previous interest in being in the military or serving as an officer. My interest was getting into a law enforcement career right after graduation from college; this OTS program seemed like an excellent avenue for doing so. The military draft was still about though it didn't seem likely that I would be called up in those times. OTS was a "Gentleman's Course" compared to the other two programs going on at the same time at Lackland: Aviation Cadets and Office Candidate School (OCS). These were six-month-long programs with plenty of harassment, like "chicken walks" of 140 count cadence (very fast walking pace) whether alone or in formation, and mandatory washouts (kicked out) throughout the programs (fear factor). The "Washout Parties" at the service club were beer-guzzling spectacles. Washouts stood on tables, slamming down pitchers of beer with no gulping, straight down the hatch. It was humorous and pathetic at the same time. It all seemed like an effort to anesthetize manufactured failure. After witnessing a couple of the parties, I didn't go again. I was very happy we in OTS were not treated that way; we were indeed treated as gentlemen. We did have one OTS candidate washout for academics. He was a popular fellow, and so whenever our squadron was marching in formation, for instance to chow hall, we would march in a "missing man" formation, meaning we kept his marching slot vacant. This was our silent form of protest. I think we got away with that for a couple days until the training staff told us to knock it off. We made our point even though the candidate was on his way home.

I fully enjoyed OTS. The thirty-eight of us who graduated in our squadron (there were four squadrons total) were from all over the United States, so you could hear English spoken in a variety of dialects from Maine to Mississippi. In one humorous situation, we had to get a translator for a conversation between Davy, graduate of U Maine, from Bangor (say "Bangah") and Fred C "Horsefly" from Ole Miss, (draw that out) with his deep-voiced Southern-gentleman speak. "Now, Fred, this is what Davy said."

"Now, Davy, this is what Fred said." It was a riot.

I was in One Squadron, "The Hawks," under the absolutely motivating supervision of tactical-training officer, fighter pilot Captain

Fred Haeffner (later Major General+). He gave us the name of "Hawks" and developed a mystique/élan for us. Once he flew really low over the squadron area in his fighter aircraft, and we all cheered on when he did it. (I don't think that could be done these days.) After five weeks of schooling, Class 60B graduated, leaving those of us in 60C to help train the new guys in Class 60D. For the final five weeks in the program, I was the "B Flight Commander," meaning it was my job to drill and march the new class while the "A Flight Commander" was in charge of Class 60C "veterans." I don't know how it was that I acquired this position, but I liked doing it. Only five weeks earlier, I was one of the clueless new guys. My roommate was the One Squadron Commander, Officer Candidate Major Louis Giacobbe, later C5A pilot, a Korean War Marine Corps veteran, who at eighteen years of age had participated in the Inchon Bay invasion. Lou, originally from Philly but then from Florida, was an "old man at age twenty-six or twenty-seven." Lou recounted some of his Korean War experiences, half-kidding to me that he missed out getting the Purple Heart, which is every Marine's dream. He was blown about a bit but never combat wounded.

Saturday morning personnel and barracks inspections were some of my more memorable times (with GI parties going on until the late Friday night hours): making sure the heads were microscopically clean, the hardwood floors buffed out to perfection and clear of "woolybuggers" (large lint balls), and personnel lockers totally "squared away" with clothing hanging neatly in a prescribed manner in the closets and personnel items securely affixed with tape to towels lining the pull out drawers. The real toothpaste and shaving cream was ingeniously secreted in hiding places, far away from the searching eyes of nit-picky inspecting officers. It was kind of funny in those few minutes before the inspecting officer would walk into the barracks because we would be getting ready and standing around in our uniform shirts, polished shoes, and underwear briefs. At the last minute, we'd put on our trousers. This was done to make sure there were absolutely no creases in the pants that would get us a demerit, what we called a "gig." Gigs could get you restricted to base or area and "ramp time," silent drill on the march pad and doing "square corners." Pat once questioned, "Why is it that you always put your pants on last?"

"Well, so I don't get creases. OTS training, my dear!"

One last story: Our four OTS Squadrons marched in the annual Fiesta Day parade in downtown San Antonio in late April 1960. Our entire unit was positioned at the end of the parade and right behind a loud cha-cha band. We were badly out of step, and the crowd was yelling at us, "GET IN STEP!" So we invented a way to get in step. We called out cadence through the center ranks, marching ten abreast, and from front to back and back to front. That really helped; however, it was dicey marching over, around, through and in the horse manure on the street. What an experience and one never to forget! Olé!

Graduation from OTS on 10 May 1960 was a "sweet day," even though the US was in a major crisis with the shoot down of US U-2 pilot Francis Gary Powers over the Soviet Union on May 1, 1960. For graduation, we assembled in the OTS area auditorium, heard a short commissioning speech, and then took the commissioning oath: "I, Percy Gerald Rogers, do solemnly swear… So help me, God!" After that we walked across the front stage to receive our commissions and later lined up, single-file, outside to receive our first salute as newly minted Second Lieutenants from the Non-Commissioned Officer in Charge, each providing him with a dollar bill to commemorate the event. The movie *Officer and a Gentleman* has a scene which depicts this "ceremony."

Several weeks after having received the third oath of office in 1962, I received the official commission. The script if hard to read and understand, so here is the plain text version:

Seal
The President of
The United States of America
Presidential Seal
to all who shall see these presents greeting:

Know ye, that reposing special trust and confidence in the patriotism, valor, fidelity and abilities of Percy Gerald Rogers I do appoint him a Second Lieutenant in the Regular Air Force United States Air Force to rank as such from the tenth day of May, nineteen hundred and sixty. This officer will therefore carefully and diligently discharge the duties of the office to which appointed by doing and performing all manner of things thereunto belonging.

And, I do strictly charge and require those Officers and other personnel of lesser rank to render such obedience as is due an officer of this grade and position. And this Officer is to observe and follow such orders and directions, from time to time, as may be given by me, or the future, President of the United States of America, or other Superior Officers acting in accordance with the Laws of the United States of America.

This commission is to continue in force during the pleasure of the President of the United States of America, for the time being, under the provisions of those Public Laws relating to Officers of the ARMED FORCES OF THE UNITED STATES OF AMERICA and the component thereof in which this appointment is made.

Done at the City of Washington, this nineteenthday of April in the year of our Lord one thousand nine hundred and sixty-two, and the Independence of the United States of America the one hundred and eighty-sixth.

Signed By the President
Signed By Lieutenant General, USAF Air Force Seal Secretary of the Air
Force Deputy Chief of Staff Personnel

Chapter 2:
First Assignment – LA Roadrunner
Los Angeles, California: 1960-1962

I HAD JOINED THE AIR Force to see the world, so when assignment day came out at Lackland, I was disappointed. I was being assigned to Los Angeles, California, to a duty station called Cheli Air Force Station (AFS) at Maywood, California, wherever that was. I was essentially being shipped back home.

Commissioned as a Second Lieutenant on 10 May 1960, I left the next day, driving back in my 1956 Chevy convertible with Tim and Betsy. As Tim recently recalled, it was a trip from hell; on one occasion as we drove across a bridge, it was sunny, and by the time we got to the other side, the car, with top down, was filled with rainwater. It was proof of what they say about Texas: "If you don't like the weather now, just wait five minutes." It was sooner for us. We drove straight back to California, and after checking in with Mom in Colton, I went on to Belmont Shores, California, a southern suburb of Long Beach. Shortly thereafter, I moved into an apartment with Byron B., another UC Berkeley fraternity brother, and two other guys. Belmont Shores was about thirty miles from Cheli AFS by Pacific Coast Highway and the Long Beach Freeway.

I soon found out what Cheli AFS was all about. It was a military depot with all sorts of WWII warehouses and some single-story office buildings with entrance at Atlantic and Bandini, just off the Long Beach Freeway. Then, I checked into my duty assignment at District Office 18, Office of Special Investigations whichwas the headquarters for all of the OSI offices in Southern California—from Vandenberg AFB, near Lompoc, to George AFB, near Victorville to San Diego. The dilapidated condition of the Headquarters buildings contributed in some measure to psychological demotivation; the place was disgusting, and this was my first Air Force assignment. Welcome to the "real world." The Headquarters also served as the investigative center for the greater Los Angeles area. I couldn't go to work as an investigator right away because I had to complete Basic Investigator's Course to open up in September 1960 in Washington, D.C.

To help out, for three months from July through September 1960, I was assigned to a desk job in the Personnel Security Investigations Division. This office had overall responsibility for conducting and doing the paperwork reports of personnel security investigations for Air Force military and civilian personnel as well as Air Force contractor employees (i.e., Boeing, North American, Lockheed). The work was to do background investigations for top-secret clearances on these people, using their completed DD Form 398 Statement of Personal History (SPH) as a basis for checks on their education, work experience, and personal references. It also involved doing local agency checks such as at police departments where the person resided or had resided. We also checked all periods of listed employment which meant going to the company or institution to check employment records as well as conducting job-site coworker interviews. In some cases, we would do neighborhood investigations, especially when unfavorable information was listed or detected. It was actually a pretty thorough process, considering the number of investigators involved and their varied investigative styles.

So in that three-month period, without being OSI-schooled and -credentialed, my job was to take Thermo-Faxed copies of pages of the DD Form 398 and grid them. This meant looking up the specific address where the investigation was to be conducted and locating the grid coordinates from Thomas Brothers map books. The grids would then be written down on the Thermo-Faxed paper to send to the field investigator. There developed a lot of repetition, so over time I knew by heart the grid coordinates for any police department, university, or major contractor. I began to know Los Angeles and Orange County fairly well. My immediate supervisor, Major John Pizzo (now deceased), was very nice and very apologetic about the menial work to which I had been assigned. But at that point in time, there was no one else to do the work, and it had to be done. The completed work was then funneled out to the field agents for investigations. When I departed for OSI Basic School in September 1960, I was replaced by an E2, Airman Third Class. As a junior officer, I was replaced by a junior enlisted person. Oh well, humble pie time.

I completed Basic School in December 1960, and when I got back, I was assigned to the field investigation unit to become a "Roadrunner," or a "doorbell ringer." There were about twenty of us total doing this sort of work, all of us in civilian clothes. There were about three to four of us second lieutenants (butter bars; we were new to the service and very green) assigned with the rest, experienced enlisted men (yes, all men at that time), most of whom were senior sergeants with extensive military and investigative experience going back to Army Criminal Investigations Division (CID) and Army Counterintelligence Corps (CIC) before the Air Force was founded in 1947.

We were assigned to LA regions, and mine was the San Fernando Valley, from North Hollywood to Chatsworth and Pacoima. It included Burbank, Glendale, and Sun Valley, to mention a few. A major Air Force contractor in the area was Lockheed Aircraft Corporation. At that time, there seemed to be a number of Lockheed employees needing top-secret clearances, and I would go to the company security office there to set up employment checks as well as reference interviews. This meant interviewing work colleagues as listed references on the SPH or what we called "throw-offs," meaning developed references. At other times, I ran PSI investigations in Beverly Hills, Hollywood, Santa Monica, and West LA.

For all reference interviews, we had a standard spiel, which went like this:

"Hello, I am Air Force Special Agent Rogers. We're doing a background check on So-and-So, and he has listed you as reference for an Air Force position of trust. In what way do you know him? How long have you worked together? In what capacity? Do you believe he is of good character and reputation? Is he stable? Free from any mental or nervous illness? Do you believe that he is, honest…trustworthy… loyal? Do you know of any foreign travel or connections? (If so, please describe in detail.) Do you know of anything or have any information about this person that would affect his suitability for a position of trust with the United States Air Force or US government? Would you recommend this person for a position of trust?"

The questioning each time would need to appear fresh, and that was sometimes difficult to do because of constant repetition. So much in interviewing is dependent upon sincerity and a need to gain trust and rapport in a very short period of time in the encounter. I specifically noticed when interviewing at Lockheed that the security director, a former FBI agent, would be very into my business and wanting to know what had happened in the interview. In essence, he was debriefing me at the end of the reference interviews. It was a little off-putting. I didn't realize it then, but I was probably running background investigations on employees of Lockheed's "Skunk Works," the on-site top-secret design and development center for the U-2, A-11, A-12 and follow on aircraft. In retrospect, he probably wanted to know if any of the projects there were being compromised through my questioning. I don't think that ever happened. I only realized all this many years later.

The work could be quite varied. I recall one day interviewing the President of Lockheed Aircraft Corporation in his prestigious office and then right afterwards interviewing a housewife in her robe with her hair up in curlers at the kitchen table of a simple house somewhere in the Valley. I got pretty good at navigating the streets in the region and laying out an itinerary for maximum efficiency. All of us in the business became efficient in street navigations, lead generations, and completion. In those two years from 1960 through early 1962 I got to see a lot of varied lifestyles and people. I interviewed many, many different people under a variety of circumstances. At residences, offices, and shops I interviewed store owners, corporate executives, psychiatrists, movie industry people, housewives, educators, scientists, technicians, and people of all races, ages, and orientations. When I first started PSI investigations upon completion of OSI Basic School, I was very nervous and unsure of myself. By the time I left there two years later, I had developed a lot of confidence in interviewing anybody under any circumstances. As we investigators shared our mutual experiences, we felt that we could size a person up and assess right at the start if we were going to get any unfavorable information. At some level, we got good at assessing people. I don't think it was an instinctive thing; it was just based on a whole lot of experience.

Some interesting experiences at DO 18:

- The field operations area was located at a small single-story complex adjacent to the main building. There, field agents at desks would scurry around getting leads paperwork lined up for the day's work. It was a hubbub of activity with agents making pre-visit phone calls, coordinating with various other entities, and getting guidance from our civilian special agent supervisor. The rule was that we needed to be in the office by seven thirty in the morning and had to depart the building by eight fifteen. Anyone who didn't leave would get yelled at, as I was once. We each had a daily production quota of fifteen lead accomplishments per day. It wasn't unreasonable, but it did require good planning to make it happen.

However, in the LA area, it was impossible to get to our field destinations in a timely manner leaving the office at eight fifteen. The freeways were always clogged with morning rush-hour traffic. So we all dutifully complied and got out of there by eight fifteen sharp. Then we would all rendezvous at Michael's Coffee Shop nearby at the corner Atlantic and Commerce. It was a rather large coffee shop, and we gathered to have coffee, doughnuts, and rolls in a big room way in the back. There the sergeants would hold court. Butter bars (Second Lieutenants) were invited. A whole lot of informal learning happened there. We newbies learned the lore and legends of OSI, names of key functionaries, and how duty was at various air bases in the US and overseas. We would also learn about cases the experienced ones had worked on in their careers, which were quite extensive, varied, and interesting. For example, we heard of the airman caught having sex with a young woman in a

Dempsey Dumpster of all places. (Probably not an OSI case). There would be discussions of how various field interviews had gone down. There would be enactments of the interviews as had gone on between the agent and the interviewee. For example, in a rundown neighborhood, the purpose of the investigation was to interview a reference listed on the subject's SPH. The door bell was rung, and there was no answer right away. Someone inside said, "Hello."

"Hello, I'm Special Agent Packey from the Air Force."

"Yes?"

"We're doing a background investigation on Airman Johnny Jones. Do you know Airman Jones?"

The voice just inside said, "No, don't think I know him! Nooooo, don't think I do."

"Well, he's being considered for a position of trust with the Air Force, like a new and better job."

"Oh, yeahhhh, I know that boy! Oh, yeahhhh, he's my cousin. Are you with the p-o-l-i-c-e? Is he in any trouble? Come on in."

Then there was the sound of deadbolts being opened and chains being released. The door opened, but Packey couldn't see inside because it was dark, and the screen door was dirty and obscuring.

Special Agent Packey then entered into an unknown world.

There would be other interview enactments and discussions at the coffee shop. Some of these enactments or tales were very serious, others lighthearted. With a group of twenty or so, you needed to choose which discussion group to join or be able to listen in on. It was a pretty fast-paced thirty to forty-five minutes.

I had an unexpectedly bad experience with a civilian woman I interviewed at the security office of a defense contractor. She was up for a top-secret clearance to maintain her job; however, she had a lengthy record of psychiatric treatment as self-disclosed on her SPH. My job that day was to interview her about that to find out about where her treatment had occurred and by whom. I also needed from her a signed release statement for examination of her psychiatric records and interview of the psychiatrist. During the interview, she totally broke down right in front of me. It was horrifying. As per procedure, I immediately terminated the interview and went for help. I was very saddened and shaken up by this experience and felt so very sorry for her. As evidenced, she was in fragile health, and my procedural questioning had incited a psychological reaction. I don't know what happened to her after that, but that job was necessary for her livelihood.

The senior agents had great camaraderie. Even though in civilian clothes, those lieutenants of us were always treated with respect and addressed by our rank, at least in a group situation. Those morning coffee klatches were a great real start of the day and often gut-busting hilarious.

However, leaving Michael's at nine o'clock, we could still reach our outbound destination on time. Because of traffic, we couldn't have made any better time leaving headquarters at eight fifteen. At Michael's we were really just in hiding.

Our military supervisor of the PSI Division was a Lieutenant Colonel Uptight, who was not "one of the guys." One morning, someone came running in at Michael's shouting "Uptight's on his way!" It was an "oh s---!" moment. Everyone evacuated in a heartbeat. We all burst through the rear double doors, hitting the emergency panic bars to access the rear parking lot. It was like a Strategic Air Command (SAC) scramble alert, guys running for their cars. All our OSI cars were lined up as if on flight line. Most of us were driving new, gutless 1959 four-door Plymouth sedans, all painted Air Force blue with no markings. These were covert, clandestine plainclothes cars? Cars were speeding out, up alleys, down narrow streets, and onto main streets, all away from the scene of the crime and to the sanctuary of the freeways. What a getaway! Just visualize it!

We didn't know how all this happened. Had there been a leaker? Did some sorry son of a bitch leak on us? This was my first experience with leaks and leakers. Or, was that thing a fake warning, just a joke or prank? Was it disinformation? Anyway, we had to change our rendezvous coffee shop to the City of Bell under conditions of greatest secrecy. That coffee shop fiasco was my first experience in being involved in a clandestine, secret operation.

• After about a year on the road, I was transferred inside to the PSI Division as a PSI case reviewer. There I would assemble all finished investigative work and, according to detailed manuals, get the report ready for Major Pizzo to review before he sent it to the typing pool for a final rendition. Sometimes there was another lieutenant there as a case reviewer, but the regulars, about six in all, were experienced, seasoned special agent sergeants. One of them had been on the Bataan Death March. The sergeants had great spirit and were always helpful in teaching me the ropes. This leads to the next story.

- The District Commander was not well respected and not a people person or leader. Two things he did really upset the troops. Here we were in an urban situation, and he had the troops with families sign out on a day's leave if they were taking any family member to a hospital or dispensary for care. This was not done elsewhere in the Air Force, and this practice was greatly resented. Then the Colonel had a new restroom created in the headquarters building in what had formerly been a small photo lab. I think the straw that broke the camel's back was the commander's decision that this new head was only to be used by officers. The enlisted were to continue using the old, terribly smelly head. Dick, one of the PSI case writers, had previously worked at OSI Directorate (Headquarters) in Washington, D.C., in the main file room. In that capacity, he knew many senior OSI officers. One of them had told him that if he ever came across anything that needed attention out there, Dick should call him. The "head situation" caused a caucus amongst the sergeants (I heard it going on, and those guys were really angry). A phone call was made to D.C. Within a few days, DO 18 Headquarters was surprise-visited by two senior OSI Headquarters colonels en route home from the Pacific. I had heard of these colonels: Colonel Kenneth Atchley, with a reputation as a "hatchet man" (I really didn't know what a hatchet man was or did, only that it was something bad) and Colonel Kirby Gillette, considered a very fair man. Then, the

Inquisition began. The colonels set up a hearing room in the commander's office. One by one, we were called in; that would include about seventy to eighty District personnel total.

There was a solo chair right in front of the colonels' table. I was scared because I didn't know what to expect or if I was in trouble in any way. I made sure that I was looking sharp in my uniform that day and reported in to them in military fashion with salute. I told them what I knew, which wasn't much. The colonels asked what kind of Officer Effectiveness Report (OER) I had received from my civilian supervisor when last rated. I told them it was "typically effective," meaning straight down the middle. As a junior officer, I think my military bearing impressed them. They both expressed heated displeasure at the non-competitive OER, and both instructed me to get it removed from my military records at once. I found that strange because I didn't know that could be done, and I didn't know how to get the OER removed. Being so new to the service, I didn't know that this OER might be a killer for my Air Force career. Later on, I realized my transfer from Roadrunners to inside PSI case reviewer was a plan to get me away from the civilian boss to a military supervisor, Major Pizzo, who would then write me a fairer, more competitive OER. My career was being saved, and I didn't even know it. Major Pizzo was my mentor, protector, and overseer. What Major Pizzo ever saw in me I never knew.

For some unrecalled reason, I did not take action to get that OER removed; however, in about October 1961, I received an invitation from the Air Force to become a regular officer. The invitation included a green sheet which was a promise to send me to graduate school whenever possible. Major Pizzo gave me strong counseling to accept the commission. (He had been a RIF'd [Reduction in Force: downsized force] bomber pilot from WWII, so he had been passed over for Lt Colonel though he was later promoted.) Anyway, the Inquisition resulted in the District Commander Colonel being fired and reassigned. We got a new commander, Lt Col Paul Nold, who was very approachable. I did approach him in late 1961 and asked to be reassigned to an airbase, so I could get involved in doing criminal investigations, which is why I had joined the Air Force and OSI in the first place. I think I made my case with him as soon thereafter, I received orders for assignment to OSI Detachment 1909 at Nellis Air Force Base in Las Vegas, Nevada.

DO 18 Lessons Learned:

- Get a mentor; be a mentor.

- Learning occurs all the time, under the most unusual circumstances, and in the most unexpected places.

- I learned a lot about people in many situations and locales. I eventually became very proficient in interviewing all sorts of people. The PSI experience in the field and in the office really developed me professionally. Actually, it was an experience of a lifetime because I saw so much humanity in many varied conditions and forms. It helped my powers of observation as well as my interpersonal and intrapersonal perception immensely. Those experiences helped me to place people in settings and locales.

- Be aware of the power of lower-level participants in the organization. Over time, they develop their own communication channels and power base. So...

- "Don't mess with the troops, or the troops will mess with you!" Or, "Take care of the troops, and they will take care of you!" (It cuts both ways.)

- Sometimes it's easy to assess a person; at other times, it can be very difficult or impossible. Everybody does it differently. People do the darnedest things and can surprise you in ways you've never thought of. Sometimes the circumstances can be controlled; other times not so.

- Don't be quick to judge.

- If you're ever in a jam with a military superior, be sure to show up next day (a) in a fresh, clean uniform, (b) with shiny shoes, (c) and a freshly cut regulation haircut and (d) say sir a lot. Example: Sir! Yes, sir! Sir! (Repeat as often as needed).

Chapter 3:
Nellis Air Force Base Assignment,
Las Vegas, Nevada; 1962-1964

My wife Pat and I arrived in Las Vegas in early 1962. It was exciting to be starting out our new marriage there, where we had gotten married the previous December second, always the day after payday... Good planning.

Because of unavailability, we weren't able to move into base housing at Nellis AFB, which is located to the east of North Las Vegas, Nevada. We found a relatively new apartment on Sherwood Lane, about two blocks to the south of the Sahara Hotel on the Las Vegas strip at Las Vegas and Sahara Boulevards. We were definitely on our own now and moving on with our lives. Pat had graduated in 1960 with a bachelor's degree in education from Long Beach State and had student-taught a year at an elementary school in Bixby Knolls, a wealthy neighborhood in north Long Beach. She located a teaching opportunity at an elementary school in North Las Vegas. She was usually a fourth or fifth grade teacher.

We enjoyed living behind the Sahara Hotel in part because after dinner at the apartment, we could go over to the hotel's Casbah Lounge for an after dinner cocktail and take in the Louis Prima show. It was gorgeous music which we'd never heard before, really uptempo and brash.

It was a small ensemble with a drummer, piano, string base, trombone player, and then Louis on trumpet and Sam Butera on saxophone. The group was called Louis Prima, Sam Butera, and Witnesses. Their singer was his much younger wife, Gina Miaone, whom he and had married after divorcing from Keely Smith. Gina had a wonderful voice, as did Keely whom I heard later in Palm Springs. We loved all their songs, which often had vocals by Louis and/or Gina. Those were unforgettable songs: "Oh, Marie," "Just a Gigolo," "Bona Sera," and "Five Months, Two Weeks, Two Days." Two of my all-time favorites were "Greenback Dollar Bill" and "Next Time" by Sam and Louis. I play them today fifty years later. Suggestion: play these songs on YouTube.

I reported in to the office: Detachment 1909, Air Force Office of Special Investigations. The Detachment Commander was USAF Captain (Special Agent) Richard A. "Dick" Noble, mentioned in Chapter 1. He had been with the organization since the 1950s. It was a small office complex located within a larger, single-story WWII office building. I was there to replace Chief Warrant Officer (CWO-4) (Special Agent) Ray I. Turner. I think the "I" was for Ivan. We called and referred to him as "Ray I." He had served in the Army in WWII and then at some point transferred over to the Air Force after its founding in 1947. I believe most of Ray I.'s duty assignments in the Army and Air Force were criminal investigations. In the Army, it was CID, in the Air Force, OSI. Ray I. didn't retire until two months after I arrived, so we had face-to-face training and turnover time. That was really to my advantage because I knew nothing of running any sort of criminal investigation. Ray I. was a total master of the art form. He took me under his wing and started showing me the ropes.

He took the lead in some of the cases that came up shortly after my arrival:

- <u>Toolbox theft</u> from the flight line by a punk-type airman. He thoroughly established elements of the crime, but he was not successful in getting a full confession from the airman. The airman received a general court martial and a punishment I don't recall.

- <u>Rape allegation</u>: An entire Air Force squadron, aircraft and personnel, came in from the east coast for bombing and gunnery training. Shortly after the squadron arrived, we had two women show up, and one alleged rape by one of our airmen, possibly from this transient unit.

From their appearances, these were two honky tonk floozies, barroom angels, and I'll give them names: Suzy Q, the complainant, and Lulu Mae, her friend. I don't know where these women came from. I think because of their hillbilly accents and twangs, they were from Texas or elsewhere. Suzy Q was very distraught and alleging rape. Suzy Q had a front tooth busted out and stringy, unkempt hair; maybe at one time she had looks but was now pretty beat up and haggard, especially in her simple, rumpled party dress. We got her age, and I think it was late twenties. She was accompanied by Lulu Mae, a much larger woman, in similar dress and appearance. Lulu was the dutiful and caring friend, often having her arm wrapped over Suzy Q's shoulder. These were definitely barroom floozies, but each rape allegation has to be taken seriously, regardless of appearances or position. This was my first encounter with authentic bar room angels.

Well, Suzy Q gave a description of the culprit and stated that his unit had just come in. The alleged rape incident had happened in the early morning hours that day. She and the culprit had met in this low-down, trashy North Las Vegas honky tonk. Ray I. and I went down there to look it over. Yep, sure enough, it was a low-down honky tonk dive. It was everything you ever wanted in a place like that.

Immediately Ray I. had Suzy Q medically examined at the Base Hospital for evidence of sexual assault. (No physical evidence of rape was found later.) From what Suzy Q said, Ray I. believed it could only be this certain Temporary Duty (TDY) squadron that had arrived the day before. So Ray I. contacted the unit commander to arrange for a special lineup to identify the culprit. He had all the unit's some one hundred personnel lined up in ranks and formation on the flight line's aircraft parking area. Then, he had the men slowly file to the inside of the nearby hangar via a small room inside the building. It was a strange way to run a lineup, but it really made sense. This kind of lineup was not in the book; there were so many suspects for Suzy Q to view in an expeditious matter.

At the small hangar room, Suzy Q was whimpering, and Lulu Mae was soothing her. So the squadron's troops slowly filed by the two women for identification. The troops would furtively glance over at the two women, and then quickly glance away, straining hard to turn their face profiles so as not to be identified. There must have been a lot of guilty minds left over from the night before. There was disappointment on the part of Suzy Q as there was no positive identification, but there was exuberance on the part of the airmen for that same reason.

Earlier, Ray I. interviewed Suzy Q in the soundproofed interview/ interrogation room at the OSI Detachment Office. In rape, an element of the crime is penis penetration of the vagina. So Ray I. was attempting to determine this and asked her to describe what went on. Suzy Q replied, "Well, he put his dick right up here next to my pussy." Then with her hands, she animated it over the top of her dress. I got up immediately and left the room. I rolled around the outer offices in gut-busting laughter. It struck me so funny as I was so new to investigations, and her statement was so unexpected. After composing myself, I went back into the interview. Ray I. established via interview that there had been no penetration or rape. Still, we needed to interview the culprit. Later Ray I. asked me: "Jerry! What the hell happened to you? Where did you go?" I told him.

It turned out that the rape suspect was a young sergeant. He was not present at the hangar lineup for some reason, but when he found out about the situation, he turned himself into his commander, and Ray I. interviewed him. He was a married man.

Ray I. interviewed Sergeant Culprit, who admitted he had met Suzy Q at the North Las Vegas honky tonk and that he had accompanied Suzy Q back to her single-wide trailer in a drunken state. As he was about to mount her, he came out of his drunkenness and discovered just how ugly and disgusting he felt Suzy Q and the situation were. He never penetrated Suzy Q and left immediately. Suzy Q felt rejected and disappointed and then got angry. She then decided to declare rape.

Ray I. cleared Sergeant Culprit, and he was most grateful. Ray I. had run a very professional and thorough investigation. Some of those other squadron members must have felt relieved, not to sin again for a while. Through persistent effort, Ray I. closed the case in just two days.

So Ray I. retired and sometime later got a job at the FBI Las Vegas Field Office as an administrative type. Ray I., now dead, was a terrific, one-of-a-kind guy in my book.

I then began doing my share of the criminal investigation work along with Dick Noble. We were busy. Here are some of the cases we worked on:

- Rape in a Catholic Church: We received a notification from the local police that an airman assigned to the base had raped a teenage Catholic schoolgirl of diminished mental capacity in the pews of a Catholic church. The girl was walking home from school, and he forced her into the church to rape her. The local police and authorities took the lead, and we monitored the case. I don't know what the culprit's punishment was.

- General's Horse Case: We got a call from the Las Vegas Police Department about a con man they ran across at a downtown Las Vegas "Glitter Gulch" hotel. This con man had persuadedan Army First Lieutenant to get some crime tools for him. The lieutenant was totally gullible and "nervous in the service." The lieutenant had received a direct commission into the Army Chemical Corps. He was en route to Dugway Army Proving Grounds in Utah for his first duty assignment. The con man said he was a veterinarian and needed certain equipment to perform surgery on the base general's horse because the horse had the gout or bloat. He wanted the lieutenant to get specific surgery equipment for him from the base: pliers, wrenches, hammers, vice grips, drills, etc. Just what was the lieutenant thinking? That the military still had a cavalry? Or that a vet needed drills and wrenches to perform an operation? On a horse? Odd! Very odd!

Anyway, the crime was quashed, but the lieutenant just couldn't believe he was being had. He exclaimed, "He seemed like such a nice man...such a nice man!"

- Stealthy Burglary: There was a theft of an entire box of Pall Mall cigarette cartons from the Base Commissary. That box contained ninety-six cartons of cigarettes, so the theft was sizeable even though the cigarettes were sold at discount military prices. It was the slickest theft I ever saw. There were no clues. How did they get into the building? There was no evidence of forced entry.

How could anyone leave the building with that box? How did anyone, if civilian, get on or off the base? It was all very stealthy. It was a very clean operation. It seemed like the perfect crime.

Several days later, we received a call from the Las Vegas Police Department that they had busted some Indians from Rosebud, South Dakota, who were found drunk in their vehicle. Inside the vehicle were the military-stamped cigarettes, the ones we were looking for. They had booked the Indians into the Clark County Jail. So this crime involved civilians, and it was classed as a "Crime on a Federal Reservation" under the jurisdiction of the FBI.

I accompanied the FBI agent in charge of the investigation to the jail. There he interviewed each one of the four Indians, and this is the story they gave: They were from the Indian Reservation at Rosebud, South Dakota, and had heard they were casting Indians for a Hollywood movie. They drove to LA but did not get casted, so they headed for Las Vegas and found a small Indian settlement just off Las Vegas Boulevard in North Las Vegas. They were hanging out there but needed money and smokes, so they knocked over the base commissary.

These were some kind of Indians. A couple had historic Indian names, like Black Cloud, Running Deer, and the like; a few had English sounding names; but they all had Indian aliases. This was a bit difficult to sort out. It was a challenge to get all this right in the subject/title header of the official tones. They would have been good in the movies. It was dicey calling them by name because you wouldn't want to call one by the wrong name.

It turned out that one or two of the Indians had visited a white woman who was conducting a vigil at Sunrise Mountain, near the city, and living in a cave in the side of the mountain. They had given her a carton or two of cigarettes, and these needed to be recovered. This woman's vigil had been written up in the *Las Vegas Sun*. So the FBI agent and I went out to Sunrise Mountain. There we hiked up a trail in the heat and met the vigil woman at her tent near the cave. She showed us her visitor's log (a visitor's log, even!), and sure enough, it showed that White Cloud had signed in and had given a carton of cigarettes to her. The carton was confiscated as evidence. This whole episode was bizarre and a real challenge to write up in the ROI.

I don't know what happened to the Indians, but in reflection, I hope the judge just shipped their butts back to Rosebud pronto. Just put them on a Greyhound bus with police escort all the way.

- Cookie Crumble: We received word that an airman in the barracks was eating someone else's cookies. Airman Culprit had found a way to reach into a small postal box to filch the delivery slip for a package. The airman presented the slip at the window of the Military Post Office and received the package. I got a search authorization (warrant) from the base commander and found the partially consumed box of cookies in the airman's barracks room. The cookies were seized and put in our office evidence room. The airman admitted to the theft. He was general court-martialed, where I testified, and the airman received a dishonorable discharge with a two-year sentence to Ft. Leavenworth Military Penitentiary in Kansas. I thought then as now that the sentence was over the top. He was basically a nice kid who got caught doing a stupid-ass crime. However, one does not steal from the mail system. I sincerely hope he got his life together after all that.

- Harassing Phone Caller: At the Detachment Office, we received a complaint from an airman's wife that someone, she thought from her husband's squadron, had called her on two occasions harassing her with suggestive, near-lewd phone calls. I took a statement from her, and she recounted that there was a hint as to the perpetrator's identity in three words he had used. I immediately went to the Central Base Personnel Office, where all military records were kept and had all personnel records pulled of the some one hundred persons in the squadron. The individual records ranged from thick to thin with documents. I went through each record one by one, page by page, line by line and eventually got a match on one with the three words. I called the alleged perpetrator in to the office, read him his rights, laid out all the evidence I had, and he immediately confessed. I testified at his court-martial. He was found guilty, and I don't recall what his sentence was. The complainant wife was grateful for the action.

- Attempted Suicide: We got a report of an attempted suicide at Indian Springs Auxiliary Airfield about fifty miles from Nellis. I responded, speeding up to that base, and got stopped by the Nevada Highway Patrol. I showed the officer my OSI credentials and explained the situation. He let me go, and I got up to Indian Springs at about two a.m. The airman had already been transported to Nellis AFB Hospital, and he was not in critical condition. It was blustery cold, and I needed to photograph the crime scene, where he had attempted to shoot himself. It was a small Renault Dauphine automobile. To photograph the scene, I was using an issued, old Speed Graphic photographer's camera with Polaroid Land Back. The flash bulbs had to be changed on every flash exposure (hot and ouch!), and the Polaroid film wrappings were blowing all over the inside of the car. The shoot was very cramped because it was small car, with me a big guy using a bulky camera. It was tough keeping the crime scene a crime scene as the sand was blowing in also. It was a wonder I got the job done, and I interviewed the airman next day. His sad love situation just didn't seem to me to be a justification for attempting to take his own life. I believe the airman was medically discharged from service.

- Toolbox thefts: We would have rashes of aircraft mechanic toolbox thefts at the flight line. This was a bad situation because the tools were needed to conduct maintenance repairs on the aircraft. Tool boxes were mission essentials. I devised a crime-prevention program for this. With prior consent from the maintenance supervisors, I would drive the OSI vehicle onto the flight line and roar up to a hangar, stopping abruptly. Flying out the door, I would enter the hangar and go straight to the toolbox stowage location, making sure troops would see me. I would gruffly shake the cable securing the toolboxes on stowage rack, grumble about security, glare at them all, and then storm off. Then, I would go to the next hangar and so forth. It seemed to work for a while.

- Crime Prevention: I had two other physiological crime prevention techniques that I used occasionally. With a known culprit airman, I would find out his walking path on base. He would not know me by name. I would plan to walk past him and then speak his name out of the blue: "Hello, Airman Jones, how are you today?" He would be left to figure out how OSI knew him. Better watch out! The other technique was to call up a culprit airman's duty section on a Friday afternoon and ask his immediate supervisor to have him report to the OSI Office first thing on Monday. The airman had the weekend to worry things over, and the approach on Monday in a non-threatening, friendly tone was: "Hello, Airman Jones, how are you? Just thought you'd like to tell me something today. I have some concerns here and was wondering if you would like to help me out? Would that be so?" There were several objectives in this: one, to attempt to get a voluntary admission (via a provocation interview); two, if unable to get a voluntary admission, to put him on notice that the interview was a form of "informal warning or caution about future activity"; and three, to possibly recruit him as an informant.

- We had barracks thefts and office thefts of varying severities. I had suspects but couldn't make the case on them. Eventually, I came to the realization that a person committing crimes would continue to repeat and get more brazen when not caught. When and if the pattern of misconduct persisted, eventually they would get caught. It was axiomatic! A confession without corroboration was difficult to take to court for a conviction. Having been caught prior crimes could then be back investigated and solved. I found that people get caught for the most unusual reasons.

- Counterespionage operation: I believe I can safely discuss this particular case because of time and changing circumstances. I will be circumspect to protect aspects of the matter. We inherited an ongoing counterespionage operation (keyword: counterespionage) involving a controlled asset, a double agent (keyword: double agent) operation. Dick became the onsite counterespionage case officer, and he was under the direct supervision of the Counterespionage Operations Branch of the OSI Headquarters Counterintelligence Division, where I was assigned later in my OSI career. The case involved an Air Force sergeant and his wife. We'll call her Erika. She was from Germany and had relatives living in East Germany. She was blackmailed by the East German Intelligence Service, the MFS (Ministry for State Security, also known as STATSI [keywords: MFS East German Intelligence or STATSI.]) Her relatives' safety was threatened, and she was extorted to commit espionage against the USAF via her husband's access to classified information. I was on the periphery of this case and helped Dick whenever he directed me. I was his apprentice helper.

The case came about after the MFS threat. The sergeant reported it to Air Force authorities. Erika, because of her feisty, head-strong attitude, represented control challenges. Dick and the headquarters' counterespionage case superior had lengthy dialogue on how best to handle her. In CE Ops, you can't have the asset controlling the operation. That's the case officer's (handler's) job. He would be told to be very firm with her, and there would be discussion on just exactly what the language interaction should be.

For the operation, Dick was issued a Uher reel-to-reel portable tape recorder (heavy and bulky) with a leather carry case (keyword: Uber tape recorder.) The recorder case was also a concealment device for surreptitious interviewing, as is done in espionage and counterespionage operations. The tape recorder was concealed in the trunk of the OSI vehicle, with a microphone concealed inside in the passenger area. This is where the "personal meets" were to happen. One time a meeting happened in the OSI interview/interrogation room, and that meeting was tape-recorded. The MFS issued the couple two pieces of spy equipment: a hollowed-out nail in order to secret microdots and a small microdot camera (keyword: microdot camera). The camera was sleek. It was small and about the size of a snail on a small metal post, measuring no more than an inch and a half.

As I recall, the sergeant had no natural job access to classified material, so the spy equipment was not used. However, it had to be controlled and was brought to the OSI on demand for accounting. Otherwise, the couple kept it at their home in Las Vegas, just in case anyone from MFS showed up unexpectedly and wanted to see the gear as evidence of their bona fides This was my first encounter with an actual counterespionage operation. Although it was not so very active, it consumed a tremendous amount of Dick's time. Great planning occurred for any personal meet. Then, there was considerable time spent in post-meet action and critique. Great care was taken concerning operational security to make sure this double-agent operation was not compromised in any way. This was especially necessary since lives were at stake in East Germany. Every small detail of the operation was thought through, thought through, and then thought through again.

AFOSI Detachment 1909 Lessons Learned:

- The Rape Allegation Case run by Ray I.: He treated everyone in the case in a most professional manner and gave each person respect regardless of what his own personal feelings might have been. He stayed focused on the elements of the crime, didn't get distracted by the absurdities (as I did), and used an innovative technique in doing the lineup. He had solved the case within two days and absolved a sergeant from a very serious crime. He moved quickly, objectively and effectively, yielding a great example to me as a fledging investigator.

  Looking back, I see I was rather gullible at the outset. Then, I believed Suzy Q's rape allegation was true. How could a woman make such a serious allegation unless it were true? Thinking back, I don't think Ray I. thought for a moment this woman's allegation was true. I don't recall we ever talked about that during or after the investigation. What an honor to see Ray I. work as he was a master craftsman in criminal investigations. I had an emerging realization that criminal investigation can be an art form when done by artists such as Ray I.

- <u>General's Horse Case</u> Some people are gullible and can be inadvertently participate in a crime. A con man used an Army lieutenant to attempt provision of military tools to treat the General's horse on base, the tools to be used in local criminal activity. This was an expert con man and a very stupid lieutenant.

- <u>Rosebud Indians:</u> Even stealthy burglaries can be solved when the culprits mess up and get sloppy. There is no such thing as a perfect crime. The truth will always will out! This was an early lesson in my OSI and Air Force career and one to which I wholeheartedly subscribed at all times thereafter.

- <u>Rape in a Catholic Church</u>: This was one of the most despicable acts and cases I ever encountered. Rape is a cowardly act of violence from which no one ever recovers—victim, family, perpetrator.

- <u>Cookie Case:</u> Amateur criminals almost always get caught. In this case, he was hammered with his punishment. Military criminal justice can be brutal and harsh.

- <u>Harassing Phone Caller:</u> It is possible to solve crimes with mere fragments or shards of information, given enough time and persistence. That was a most gratifying case for me to solve. Ray I. would have been proud of me!

- <u>Attempted Suicide</u>: I only investigated one attempted suicide in my OSI career, never a completed suicide, thank goodness. The prospect of attending an autopsy never appealed to me. I came to realize that suicides don't really solve the problem; the family is left with egregious psychic trauma which may go on for years and through successive generations. It is a cowardly way out.

- <u>Crime Prevention Measures</u> are a short-term solution. It's best to let the crimes go on as criminals will believe their actions will go on as undetected. Given enough time, they will get caught, and back crimes will be solved. Just be patient. The forces of criminality will coalesce, and something will surface that will cause the crime to be detected and then processed. See perfect crime discussion above.

- <u>MFS Case</u>: Even the most relatively inactive CE case is very time-consuming, requiring exacting planning and execution. Dick and the CE case supervisor would spend considerable time in listening to the tape-recorded personal meet sessions over and over. They would be listening for all sorts of aspects of the case such as truthfulness, honesty, motivation, and possibilities of deception. They would listen to every voice inflection and intonation. They would critique Dick's performance. They would compare notes on what they had heard and develop theories as well as strategies for dealing with the issues and for following on.

I gained an appreciation for focused listening and realized just how much can be missed in an ongoing conversation or face-to-face interaction. Communication occurs at many levels. Doing replays helps one to understand and discern what has gone on before. Realization and learning occurs after repeated experiences. Few people have the opportunity to experience this in life.

Good CE Ops have considerable control at both local and headquarters levels.

It takes years to become a master craftsman at counterespionage operations. Masters are those persons who have made all the mistakes. Counterespionage operations are an art form, and watching an experienced counterespionage case officer in action is like watching a high-level artist in any other profession, especially noted artists and athletes. I was later told that to become a good counterespionage officer, one had to develop a solid track record as a criminal investigator.

Counterespionage work is best left to very experienced professionals. It is not slapdash kid stuff that can be done on a whim. It requires a skill knowledge base, meticulous research, investigation, and execution as well as exceptional creativity and stick-to-itiveness. Not many people have the aptitude to do this kind of work. I met two such officers in my career that could be called true artisans of the craft. I will cover this later.

This case demonstrated in real life what the East Germany state was all about: a police state that was brutal, pervasive, and repressive. The recent movie *Lives of Others* seems to be an excellent depiction of what went on in East Germany and the STATSI during those terrible years. It shows where secret government can lead if left to its own devices.

Chapter 4:
OXCART at Nellis AFB:
My Experiences (1962-1964)

THIS INFORMATION WAS FURNISHED TO Roadrunners Internationale (RI) for regular membership. RI members, mainly former/retired CIA and Air Force, who were involved in the testing and development of the A-11/A-12 spy plane at Groom Lake, Nevada (also known as Area 51 or The Ranch), during the 1960s. The A-11 and A-12 OXCART program, which was a successor to the U-2 and followed by the SR-71, was totally declassified by the US government in 1991. It was a joint CIA and Air Force program. I was not aware that the program had been declassified until July 2007.

****

I was a First Lieutenant, Regular Air Force, assigned as a Special Agent to Detachment 1909 Nellis AFB in Nevada from January 1962 through June 1964. Sometime around late 1962, I was informed by my AFOSI Detachment Commander, Captain R. A. Noble, that I was going to be briefed into a special, very sensitive program.

In preparation for that, I was required to complete a detailed DD Form 398 Statement of Personal History, which included information about my wife Patricia, a naturalized American citizen of Canadian birth. A deep background investigation was conducted on us.

To the best of my recollection, I was briefed at the Detachment Office by Mr. Ed White, Area 51 CIA Security Officer on OXCART. He impressed upon me just how secretive the whole project was. I then signed the CIA OXCART secrecy statement. He told me at the time that the high-performance aircraft was named A-11 and that it could fly high and at Mach 3.

Shortly thereafter, I was accompanied by SA Noble to Area 51, whereupon we were taken to a hangar where there were a number (maybe five or six) of A-11 aircraft positioned inside all parked very close together. We walked around the aircraft, climbed a ramp, and looked into a cockpit of one.

This was a totally mind-torqueing experience for me (a pee-pee in your pants sort of thing). I was totally impressed and astonished. Just as we were about to enter the hangar, there was all this loud jet-engine noise adjacent. We looked, and there was an A-11 just landed and starting to shut down. The pilot was in a special flight suit, and he seemed to have a shock of blond hair. He looked so gallant climbing out of the aircraft. That scene is indelibly etched in my memory. It really motivated me! I was later told that the pilot I spotted was probably the legendary Lou Schalk, Lockheed test pilot and who piloted the A-11 on its maiden voyage in 1962. That whole visit lasted about two hours.

There was another Air Force officer special agent assigned to the project. He was physically sited at CIA Headquarters. I learned he was the AFOSI liaison officer between us, the AFOSI Commander (office) and CIA Headquarters.

At those times, Area 51 was probably the most secret place on Earth. At that time, OXCART was not public. On my supervisor's orders, I did the following to support my role in doing off-site security:

1. <u>Established an AFOSI Contact Program on base.</u> This sort of program was totally new to me as well as AFOSI, so we actually did the prototype/test version of the contact program. Within about three months, I had recruited about thirty persons to the program, mostly enlisted personnel and some Air Force civilians. These persons were strategically located where possible indiscreet conversation/loose talk could occur about the program. Briefing these people on what to listen for was a challenge since I couldn't tell them exactly what the main objective of their participation was. I gave a general security briefing and then engaged them in a lot of elicitation interviewing (where I was probing for purpose, but they would be unable to determine of the true nature of the interview regime).

In all this, I contacted each source once a month, encouraging active listening and motivating them all the while. It was a challenge, and I learned a lot. During those two years doing monthly debriefings of the thirty sources, I probably did seven hundred elicitation-type interviews. I think I got very good at it and could usually detect if anyone was elicitation interviewing me.

We had no office help. I hand-typed all debriefing reports. The Commander of the 1129th Special Activities Squadron was always cited as the primary distributee.

2. <u>Debriefed assigned base pilots</u>, mainly in the fighter-training squadrons (F-100s and F-105s) and Thunderbirds. The base was very busy training F-105 pilots as this was early days of Vietnam, and that is where they were headed upon completion of training. In training, they were flying in the bombing and gunnery ranges to the north like Indian Springs, Tonopah Test Range, and other thereabouts bombing and gunnery ranges.

The Nellis AFB Wing Commander, BG Hubbard, had ordered all flying personnel via squadron commanders (down the chain) to voluntarily report any suspect sightings when flying on the ranges. They responded dutifully, and we were very busy. I did almost all the pilot debriefings, finding out what they had seen and then cautioning them not to talk about it further. Just forget it! I always enjoyed talking with the pilots.

As I look back on all that, I recall that the pilots were the bravest of the brave. All were really nice guys. Again, I enjoyed talking with them. I remember the names and faces of some.

As an aside, here are some of the pilots I debriefed:

Colonel (then Major) Lawrence Guarino, USAF: It was previously erroneously reported that he was killed in Vietnam in an F-105.

See this link for description of his distinguished service record of 30 years on active duty in the USAF: http://www.pownetwork.org/bios/g/g063.htm

Major Guarino was shot down in his F-105 over Vietnam on June 14, 1965, and was released from captivity as a POW on February 12, 1972, after nearly eight years in prison.

Colonel Guarino retired from the Air Force in 1975. Colonel Guarino flew many aircraft in his military career from P-51 Mustangs with the Flying Tigers in China to the F-105 in Vietnam. He received many distinguished military decorations, including the Air Force Cross.

Colonel (then Major) Fred Cherry, USAF: Colonel Cherry flew fifty-one missions in an F-84G in Korea and fifty-two missions in an F-105 in Vietnam. He was shot down on October 22, 1965, and released from captivity as a POW on February 12, 1972, after nearly eight years in prison.

Colonel Cherry had horrific experiences in captivity at the "Zoo" and at Hanoi Hilton. He was America's first black POW of the Vietnam War, and he was subjected to days upon days of harsh physical and psychological torture associated with his race. Colonel Cherry received the Air Force Cross.

Major (then Captain) Frank Leithan, USAF: He was previously erroneously reported as killed in a take-off from Nellis AFB.

On October 12, 1966, Major Frank Leithan and Captain Robert Morgan, both members of the Air Force Thunderbirds, were killed during a flight at Indian Springs Auxiliary Field in Nevada. Leithan was to have taken command of the field.

All these write-ups of pilot debriefings were sent directly to the Commander 1129th SAS with copy to the Commander AFOSI, BG Cappucci, in Washington, D.C., or his deputy.

This whole support program kept me busy almost full-time. At the same time, I was carrying a full load of criminal and personnel security investigations.

I was debriefed out of OXCART in June 1964 when I departed for one year of graduate school at Michigan State University. If you can believe it, going to graduate school was sort of a vacation after the workload I had experienced at Nellis AFB.

After MSU, I was assigned to RAF Upper Heyford in England. At some point in time, Colonel Robert S. Holbury was assigned at Commander of the Sixty-Sixth Tactical Reconnaissance Wing (RF-101s). It was there that we both discovered we had known of each other (sort of) from the OXCART and Area 51 days. He had been Commander of the 1129th Special Activities Squadron, and I had never known by name who the commander of that unit was. It was blind reporting to me.

Colonel Holbury was another tremendous person, leader, and Air Force officer. I have always hoped that some of his style rubbed off on me.

I consider OXCART one of three highlights of my Air Force career. It was really a challenge to do the job, and I absolutely thrived doing it. In terms of my Air Force career, I'm not sure it helped me too much. OXCART was so secret and hush-hush that any reference to it in my Air Force Officer Effectiveness Reports (performance reports) was very brief and vague, if at all. How does one justify an exemplary write-up if you just can't talk or write about it? Also because of this, I didn't receive any other form of Air Force recognition for the effort. However, in my own mind I absolutely knew I had done something significant over the period, and this was extremely gratifying if only to me and no or few others. As I discovered in my military career, this same sort of thing happened to others, so I was not alone. It comes with the territory of being in the military.

Other Thoughts on OXCART

As an Air Force Special Agent, I had worn civilian clothes all the time since 1960 when I had finished AFOSI Basic School in Washington D.C., and started carrying credentials on me for identification. In early 1962, upon invitation from the Air Force, I received a commission as a Regular Officer. I always deported myself as such even though I was wearing civilian clothes. When reporting in to a senior officer, be it in AFOSI or to a Base or Wing Commander, I always reported in with a salute and reporting as "Sir! Lt (Captain) Rogers reporting, sir!" and to that effect. If I ever saw the Base of Wing Commander driving by on base while I was afoot, I always rendered a military salute while in civilian clothes. The salutes were always returned, and the commander would read my lips of greeting and greet back and salute back. Whenever I was on base, I would always go to official Air Force social events like

New Year's Day receptions or Air Force Dining-Ins in my Air Force Mess Dress uniform. I wanted to announce myself as an Air Force officer and not some smug super-spook puke.

The regular caseload at Nellis AFB involved criminal investigations, which usually involved what I call "crumb bums," who had committed dumb crimes to which I would have to testify at various court-martial or administrative hearings. The other work involved personnel security investigations on and off base for persons needing top-secret clearances. This was important but b-o-r-i-n-g work.

OXCART was something completely new and invigorating to me. In our business, we called it counterintelligence collections. In light of all of the above, whenever I would debrief a pilot on sightings, I would always make it a non-threatening experience, done in a friendly, professional tone. Plus, I valued the fact that they were making reports "voluntarily," so that must be respected. I did not want the pilots in the squadrons or the squadron commanders to in any way think of us as "those assholes up at OSI." After a debriefing, if I saw one of the pilots around the base, we would exchange greetings, but only if I or he determined it was comfortable to do so. It was refreshing and Air Force motivating to talk to these cream-of-the-crop people as opposed to the bottom-of-the-heap people.

We had a lot of business on the debriefings. I believe had the pilots believed their military careers were in jeopardy by reporting in, we would have had no program at all, and the mission of understanding what was going on in the air by our pilots up around the target area would not have been achieved. Yes, there was a concern about damage to military careers over this voluntary reporting. I recall Captain Frank Leithan, above, approaching me the in the base housing area where we lived with grave concerns about his reporting and the prospect of damage to his military career. I assured Frank that he had done what he had been ordered to do, and there was absolutely no problem to his military career. Frank was a Naval Academy graduate, and I believed he would likely be a four-star general eventually. His death was a great loss to the Air Force.

Even though everything was hush-hush, I'm sure word got around in the squadrons about what was going on. Know and recall that these were very experienced pilots and officers, naturally observant and curious about anything flying around in "their space," especially sleek, strange stuff.

I believe that the cumulative reporting by the pilots helped create a greater understanding of what was going on in the target area, such that it was useful to the Area 51 Commander and other decision-makers on exposure of the A-11/A-12 aircraft while operational. In 1964, President Johnson publicly disclosed the OXCART program, and part of the rationale had to do with the increased number of sightings by aircraft in the area, including commercial airliners.

I recall on one occasion one of my sources reported overhearing a pilot engaging in loose talk about what he had observed in the air in the target area. The source immediately contacted me, and I wrote up a full report and hand-carried it to the Wing Commander's office. Shortly, I received a telephone call from BG Hubbard. He asked me to repeat exactly what had been reported, which I did. He then put me on the speaker phone to repeat the report. I could hear what I believed to be the alleged offender pilot in the background denying the report. I don't know what happened with the pilot, but I later thought that word might have gotten around the squadrons to "just watch it!" It also showed that GB Hubbard was right on top of the situation. No messing around! Period!

One last OXCART vignette on the deep investigation done on Pat and me: We heard from Uncle Roy, a Canadian GE executive, that one day the Royal Canadian Mounted Police (civilian-clothes types) appeared at his office and asked questions about his nephew in the American Air Force. Roy couldn't offer much as we had not met. This Mounties/Uncle Roy story circulated in the family for years. "Remember the time the Mounties questioned Uncle Roy about Jerry?" I knew then why Uncle Roy had been contacted but never told my wife about it and never disclosed my participation in OXCART, including up through the time of her passing in 1998. Pat never knew

A totally un-OXCART-related occurrence at Nellis AFB: Normally, aircraft departing the base flew eastbound over the desert and then straight up to the gunnery and bombing ranges, about fifty to seventy-five miles northbound. Because of winds on this one day, a solo, single-engine fighter aircraft took off in the other direction over populated North Las Vegas. As he got airborne, the pilot experienced engine problems (I think a flameout). Pat was an elementary school teacher at a school in North Las Vegas and within the flight path of departing aircraft. The pilot crashed the aircraft in an open field and thus avoided the school, which was in session with a lot of school children, as well as the densely populated surrounding housing area. People on the ground reported seeing the pilot move his head around just before crashing. He did not eject but instead dead-sticked the aircraft into the ground at a vacant piece of land, killing only himself and hazarding no one else.

Though I never talked to pilots about it, I believe they must go over in their minds worst-case scenarios and how they would respond. He would have pre-thought the what-ifs and then, in the immediacy of the situation, run though all those what-ifs again. The worst case in this case was a flameout over a populated area. I believe that this pilot in the diminishing seconds had already pre-decided what he would do: no ejection, fly the aircraft into the ground, dead-sticking it. In the final seconds, this pilot must have been struggling hard with the controls to crash land the aircraft with no loss of life on the ground other than his own. He had run though all the what-ifs, and it was over! There was a report of the accident in the local newspaper. Likely the pilot's identity is only known to the Air Force and members of his family. The accident is probably long forgotten in the neighborhood, but I never forgot about it and still do remember it from time to time, as here, even forty-plus years afterwards. Lesson: In the military, there is no guarantee you're going to get out alive or even in one piece. Where appropriate, go through your what-ifs. Through all his what-ifs, this pilot was getting it just right, and he got it just right!

As an unsolicited footnote, I received lifetime membership status in Roadrunners Internationale.

Chapter 5:
Michigan State University Assignment:
June 1964-June 1965

RECEIVING THE NOTIFICATION OF ASSIGNMENT to the School of Police Administration at Michigan State University for a one-year Master of Science degree program was a real surprise and joyous occasion. Recall that I had signed up for a regular commission in the Air Force with a promise of a graduate degree at some future time. I had then completed all the required paperwork, which included undergraduate transcripts, and placed them on file with the Civilian Institutions Division of the Air Force Institute of Technology at Wright-Patterson Air Force Base in Ohio. So, my application was pre-loaded in the system.

That pre-work turned out to be very fortuitous since an announcement came down from Headquarters AFOSI for a fill of five slots for any AFOSI Officers to the MSU graduate program, and the students had to be there by mid-June, just days away. I applied and was soon accepted. Four other AFOSI officers were selected as well, and we all met up later that month in East Lansing.

Pat and I cleared our military housing unit in record time. From the date of notice until we thoroughly cleaned the house for inspectors, it was something like three days. Then, there was a quick trip back to

Southern California to say goodbye to family, and then we were off. We fixed up a mattress in the backseat of our 1964 Chevy Malibu hardtop for Ryan, then about seven months old, and headed straight for Michigan. I don't recall we had much in the way of freeways, and I definitely remember going though Iowa on US Highway 30. It was a two-lane cement roadway traversing hills and endless upon endless fields of corn. The car tires recorded every bump (again, every bump) in the road, and I was never so glad to be through with that part of the trip. We arrived in East Lansing in a Sunday afternoon. HELLO! Everything was closed; totally the opposite of wide-open Las Vegas. We found a roadhouse restaurant, the Coral Gables, just to the east of campus on Grand River, and had dinner there, but no beer—it was Sunday! This is Michigan! Anyway, as a college joint, the place was jumping. Playing loud was Johnny Rivers' song "Seventh Sun" and a number of others by him of the era. I've checked, and the restaurant is still there. Oh, yes, there was another Johnny Rivers song that I really liked that came out later, but I could never figure it out as the song title didn't seem to match the lyrics, "Secret Asian Man."

Then we found a two-bedroom apartment near campus by the golf course just off Grand River. Pat was a housewife again and spent her spare time golfing, usually with other military wives. I set up my office in the basement and spent most of my time there or at the library.

All five AFOSI officers met up and enrolled for a full load of four classes for the summer. That was interesting. Together we took an undergraduate course for graduate credit in political sociology. We all studied very hard, and I recall we all made A.s in that class. However, the young professor was somewhat wary of us, all announced Air Force officers. and so older than the average student, and former special agents as well. The professor was gone some of the quarter to the South to participate in Freedom Rides. That was the summer a Michigan woman

Freedom Rider was killed down South, and that received a lot of attention. It was pretty scary stuff and a lot of grist in the field of political sociology. Those were the beginning years of the Civil Rights Movement and the Vietnam War was starting to heat up. I had another class with a woman psychology professor in abnormal psychology who was also a very experienced practitioner. She promoted a Marxist orientation to her instruction. Although I never engaged her in any serious and/or out-of-class conversation, I think she was a bit wary of me, too, because of my status. Never mind, I was there to get a degree and not make any problems, so whatever she dished out on Marxism, I recited back on the exams. How would anyone think I would ever get contaminated by Marxism?

The five of us all took almost the same classes and studied together. We all dedicated ourselves to our studies, and a couple of us socialized with our families. We enjoyed being college students and going to the MSU football games. Duffy Daugherty was the football coach and took the team to the Rose Bowl in 1965. That rivaled my Cal Berkeley Bears winning the Rose Bowl in 1959, a game I attended.

All five of us were keen on making A's. In this one graduate class in police-community relations (a hot topic because this was the year of race riots around the country and in Detroit), groups of students were assigned to subjects and required to assemble and provide the instruction. In essence, we created the three-hour lesson plan and did it. So our team got together and scripted a full three hours. Everything was under our control. We scripted each person's introductory remarks and then created questions to be asked of us by our colleagues. Our answers were also scripted. We even had some Army MP Officers in the class act as shills, and so they got into the act. The class was arranged in a square of tables with everyone facing the center. To pull off instruction, we used the old Commie "diamond formation," where each of us sat spread out at a different table. That way, we could control the action and make it all look more extemporaneous. I don't think any of the other students caught on to our machinations, and we left the room really proud that we had pulled off that stunt and that the professor liked what we had done. It was a real academic coup that we had staged. We all got an A in that class.

Our professor of Police Administration was Ray Galvan, and he had attended the University of Southern California in LA in the School of Public Administration as a doctoral student and was ABD (all but dissertation). Our textbook was *Administrative Theory* by Frank Sherwood, later to be my professor of same at USC. That book made a very good impression on me, and I memorized much of it for the class. The book was well written and made sense. Frank was every bit as good as his book.

Ray was also our graduate advisor in the program. I needed another four units in the forty-eight unit MS requirement to graduate, so I signed up for four units of Directed Study and did an approved paper on the topic: "Sizing Up Suspects and Subjects Using a Psychoanalytic Profile." I had had a number of criminal psychology classes in my AB Criminology degree program at Berkeley, including by two different instructors who were psychiatrists as well as lawyers with significant practical experience, and still had the first edition of *The Technique of Psychotherapy* (New York: Grune & Stratton, 1954) by Lewis R. Wolberg. Using the book, I developed a composite of key factors in a psychoanalytic profile and then did a massive amount of research to fill in the blanks.

Recall that this was way before Internet, so all these citations were books I had checked out of the library. I really got into the subject matter because it interested me, and I believed I could use it in the field later on when I got back to AFOSI duty. I wrote a thirty-five-to-forty-page paper and covered all the various aspects. I especially got into non-verbal behavior, particularly of the eyes. The eyes are the window to a person's behavior and soul. It is not possible to fully mask true emotion with the eyes. Hundreds of emotions can be registered with the eyes; always watch the eyes. The eyes do not lie. They are spontaneous and cannot be controlled well. For that paper, I read a book or two by noted scholar Ray L. Birdwhistell. I believe I used his earlier edition of the book *Kinesics and Context: Essays on Body Motion Communication*. Ray Galvan received my paper well, and I got a good grade on it. But, more than that, I had created an invaluable investigative tool which I used extensively and daily in my next assignment in England as a counterespionage case supervisor and afterwards. Over the years, I actually internalized the profile components such that they became second nature and natural to me. I destroyed that paper somewhere in our rather frequent military moves.

We all graduated in June 1965 (with an overall 3.77 GPA, myself). The graduation ceremony was held in Spartan Stadium—what a happy day! We were glad to be done and move on with our careers. I received orders for a three-year accompanied tour to DO 62 (England) as a Resident Agent (one-man operation) at RAF Upper Heyford, Oxfordshire, wherever that was. After we had cleared the apartment, we drove back home to California to see family for about two weeks and then drove straight back across the country to McGuire AFB, New Jersey, for air departure to England. Every time we crossed the nation, we took a different route to see more of the country.

So there were three of us, Pat, Ryan and me, going to England. En route to England, Pat asked me how I would recognize our sponsor, Captain (Special Agent) Dave McKenna, whom I was replacing as he was separating from the Air Force to go to graduate school at North Texas State University in Denton. "Simple!" I replied. "He's going to be about my age, will have a crew cut, and will be wearing Air Force sunglasses, a suit, and a trench coat." Sure enough, we got off the plane, and there was Dave. "See!"

Lessons Learned at MSU:

- I learned the importance of teamwork in academic coursework.

- The paper on psychoanalytic profiling was extremely valuable, and I was always glad I did it. The paper enabled me to size up any persons under any circumstances. I could and would detect any kind of elicitation interviewing of me as did occur to me later on in 1971 by "the strangers" (more on this in Chapter 10.) I have never seen a similar paper published anywhere, so it was quite unique. I've checked the Internet and can find no similar paper subject. For anyone interested in this, it would be best to create his or her own research product from scratch. It would be time well spent if the need is there.

- Professors can play a very powerful role in shaping a student's understanding of the world. That is their job. The psychology professor was a case in point. I always wondered what impact she made on younger students with her Marxist philosophy. Students, especially the younger ones, are very vulnerable to the enacted philosophy of the professor.

- Regarding the police-community relations class: I have never really welcomed the learning approach or technique of students creating their own lesson plans and teaching them on their own without input from the professor, before, during and after. Later after becoming a professor myself, I considered this practice a BS form of education. The professor for that class was well versed and accomplished in his subject matter, but students filling instructional hours on their own was not appreciated. Later on, becoming a professor, I learned that some professors are forced to research and author peer-reviewed articles for publication in professional, often obscure journals, under the "publish or perish" rationale. Who knows, maybe that was going on here; there may have been competition for time with the classroom and students losing out. Students beware!

Chapter 6:
RAF Upper Heyford, England
Assignment:1965-1968

*****

"We'll Meet Again"

*****

We'll meet again
Don't know where
Don't know when
But I know we'll meet again some sunny day

Keep smilin' through
Just like you always do
Till the blue skies drive the dark clouds far away

So will you please say hello
To the folks that I know?
Tell them I won't be long

They'll be happy to know
That as you saw me go
I was singing this song

We'll meet again
Don't know where
Don't know when
But I know we'll meet again some sunny day

When I look back on that three-year tour of duty in England, I think of that British ballad "We'll Meet Again" that was so popular and comforting during the depths of WWII days. I think of the Brits now.

****

We took off in a contract airline, World Airlines, from McGuire AFB, New Jersey. We got a late start, and the airplane was full of military families, and we were all sweltering aboard for a couple hours while something got fixed. It was close and muggy, and there we were, trapped in the aircraft on the tarmac. It wasn't fun with kids crying and everyone cranky. It was late evening when we finally took off and then flew all night into the morning and landed at RAF Mildenhall, England. Dave McKenna, whom I was replacing, was there. He got us cleared through customs and loaded on a civilian bus to RAF Upper Heyford. Pat, Ryan, and I spread out, listened to the pop radio coming through the bus speakers, and watched the plush, green English countryside go by, driving on close two-lane roads most of the way. I don't think any one of us had slept on the plane on the way over.

When we got to RAF Upper Heyford that late July afternoon, Dave got us settled. The next few days were hectic, getting on-base military housing and meeting with Dave for a two-day turnover before he headed to the states and discharged out of the service. This was a Resident Agency, meaning a one-man operation, because Heyford, (also known as Upper Haystack, as it was in sheep country in the Oxfordshire Cotswalls) was a "Dispersed Operating Base" (DOB) because it had no active mission there. It was a backup for other air assets in event of hostilities, so there were less than five hundred Air Force personnel on base.

Dave filled me in on what had happened in his two-to-three-year tour there, and he kept me in stitches most of the time. Most of the humor had to do with the prior Colonel base commander and his antics. Among the stories, I remember that whenever an aircraft would be taking off from the base, he would shadow it on the adjacent runway and get up to speed with it; this was all highly unusual. This turned out to be unsafe, too, when on one occasion at night the Colonel flew off a loading ramp going full speed and totaled his staff car. Another story was about how they had aircraft in on short missions, and the crew members would stay at the Officers Club and go to weekend dances there, too. Most of these crew members were married men, and the Colonel would stop them on the dance floor with local women and say, "Major, aren't you're a married man, and don't you have a family back in the states?" That didn't go over well with the troops.

I soon discovered that there was one unit on the base with a real active mission, and that was Detachment One of the Fifty-Fifth Strategic Reconnaissance Wing out of Forbes AFB in Topeka, Kansas. The Det's mission was to support RB-47 aircraft coming in for short operational missions. (RB means reconnaissance bomber.) The crews consisted of pilot, copilot, navigator, and three "ravens," which were officers, who operated electronic monitors on their missions. Their onboard positions were in the converted aircraft bomb bay. At the time, all was classified, but it has since been known that they flew reconnaissance missions up into the Barents Sea in international waters for the purpose of electronically detecting signatures of enemy (Soviet) radar, fire control systems, and aircraft launched in their honor. This was for what is called "order of battle" information, used in case of hostilities when and if the B-52 bombers would go on their nuclear targeting missions. Those missions were considered very dangerous. There had been prior instance in 1960 of aircraft being shot down with the loss of four aircrew. The RB-47s were usually there for less than two weeks. I seem to recall that they would take off and land at night. The RAF Upper Heyford runway was quite long as well as secluded, so it was possible to conduct operations without any public attention. The motto of reconnaissance aircraft on missions I learned was "Alone, Unarmed and Unafraid." Well, they would go out alone, but the RB-47s had a 20mm cannon at the tail (nothing else). As for unafraid, I doubt it. In air, they could be met by one or more Russian MIG fighter jets flying alongside. That would create a "pucker factor" for sure.

I needed to contact the local British Police, especially the detectives, known as Detective Constables. Since the RA served nearby USAF Communications base, RAF Croughton, this meant I needed to contact British Police in Buckinghamshire as well as nearly Oxfordshire for RAF Upper Heyford. This I did one by one. A basic rule in any foreign enterprise is to get to know your local agencies and personalities. For me, that meant the regular detective Bobbies as well as Special Branch (local intelligence) detectives from jurisdictions all around. In getting around, I found during the first two months that I always seemed to have a half-second time delay from between the Brit's words and my comprehension. That went away, and I could comprehend most accents readily, except that of Scots.

I came to know the nearby detectives at Bicester very well. There was Detective Sergeant Robert "Ginger" Wilson, a Korean War Navy veteran (enlisted at age fourteen), Detective Constable Paddy Neffsie from Ireland, and Detective Constable Jock Conway from Scotland. It was an all-UK team. They took me to various pubs and introduced me to the local culture and customs, such as Double Diamond, Whatney's, and Guinness, even "black and tans." I also met the Oxfordshire crew at Banbury Police Station such as Detective Inspector Bill Boughton, himself a British Naval veteran whose ship had been torpedoed and he rescued at sea. There were about five other detective constables at that location, and over the next three years we all did business with each other.

One time while at Banbury Police Station, I observed a uniformed Police Inspector Weedon give a young British punk what's called "an official caution," authorized by law. In this, the Police Inspector pulled his police notebook from his jacket pocket and proceeded to tell the punk everything the police knew of his known or suspected illegal actions. He was then told in this official caution that if he were to be subsequently charged with an offense, the caution would be brought up with the magistrate, and it would likely result in heavy sentencing. I had never seen this done before and it seemed very effective to me. I don't think American jurisprudence would trust American law enforcement with this power.

I also went to RAF South Ruislip, near London, (Third Air Force Headquarters) to meet my immediate commander at AFOSI District 62, Colonel Robert Wayland, as well his staff in counterintelligence and general (criminal) investigations. I soon met and was briefed by Major Forrest Singhoff (later Colonel and Director of the Office of Special Investigations). I told Forrest that I wanted to get involved in the counterintelligence mission. One of the things he emphatically cautioned me on was the British Official Secrets Act, which is quite extensive and ambiguous. Even though I was in American intelligence, I could get myself as well as a British police person in great trouble by soliciting anything even appearing to be sensitive and/or classified information.

I needed to be super discrete; otherwise, I might be PNGd out of the country as well as damage the career of a local. I listened hard and well to this admonition and took it all very, very seriously.

I went back to base and started setting up my local sourcing network of Air Force persons similar to what I had done in OXCART. This meant monthly meetings with between twenty and twenty-five people.

The criminal caseload was light, perhaps one or two cases per month. At the base, I reported to the Base Commander and at RAF Croughton to the Unit/Base Commander. We got along very well.

Sometime in 1966, the base became more of a regular operating base after FRELOC, which meant France Relocation. France had quit NATO, and all USAF units there were kicked out. The Sixty-Sixth Tactical Reconnaissance from Laon AFB was reassigned to RAF Upper Heyford. This consisted of two squadrons on RF-101, Voodoo, and single-seat reconnaissance aircraft. This meant a large influx of aircraft, personnel, and material. The complexion of the base changed rapidly. Colonel Kendall Young came in as Wing Commander, and he was later replaced by Colonel Robert Holbury of 1129th fame. In my new position of AFOSI Detachment Commander, I reported to Colonel Young and then Colonel Holbury. I also reported to the base commanders, who were in charge of support operations on base.

In June 1967, an informant told me that there was a U-2 spy plane in a hangar on base. I got as much detail as possible and went directly to Colonel Young's residence at night. Colonel Young greeted me, and I could see five to six civilians sitting in the living room. I figured those guys were CIA. Colonel Young took me to his office in his home, and I gave him all the information I had. In the next day or two, I met with some civilians upstairs at the room in the Officers Club. I told them who I was and what I knew. I offered to cooperate with them on their on-site security mission. At that point in time, it was not known just how long this unit was going to be doing its work there. A couple days later, a man appeared at my AFOSI Office and wanted me to sign a CIA security-briefing statement. There was a project code name, which I don't recall. The man didn't show me any CIA credentials or explain to me what the form-signing was all about exactly. I went ahead and signed the form, mainly because I didn't want to create a problem for Colonel Young. I figured the U-2 was there to support strategic reconnaissance missions related to the Six Day War in Israel. In a week or two, the same guy returned and had me sign a security-debriefing certificate, which I did.

That whole experience did not impress me with the CIA. The administration of the security briefing and debriefing was inept, likely purposely so. They likely had consulted with CIA Headquarters after my initial contact with them and decided it was best not to get Rogers and/or the local OSI office involved—it was way too secret. Plus, this AFOSI entity was just a little piss-ant operation. The best course of action was to silence the son of a bitch, and that will seal that deal. It did because I didn't even tell my own commander what went on. I didn't direct any attention to their situation. However, had anything come to my attention, I would have gone directly to Colonel Young with it, not any so-called CIA people. Had he asked me why I was coming to him, I would have given him an earful. I figured I never knew what the so-called CIA mission was about because I was never officially briefed on it by a bona fide CIA agent displaying CIA credentials. As I thought about this then and later, I thought this was an expression of arrogance of mission. There was no reason to officially silence me because I was well performing my job in doing the reporting and serving my commander. People actually on the ground know much more than headquarters types. What was missed here is that the British Ministry of Defense Public Works workers on base who were everywhere on the flight line, near hangars, and on the rest of the base could see what was going on. Most of these Public Works blokes were WWII vets who knew what was going on, having worked at the base for many years, and they posed no threat whatsoever. There will be more on the U-2 matter below.

With the mission accession came another OSI Special Agent, Technical Sergeant William "Bill" E. Keown. Bill came in from an OSI Detachment in France. This was my first time really supervising anyone, and Bill soon informed me how he wished to be supervised. I learned, and we had a great working and personal relationship. Bill worked the criminal cases, and I worked the counterintelligence, special projects, and some criminal cases.

Operations-wise, we had one big drug bust, concerning the sale, use, and possession of marijuana involving about eighteen airmen. That was a major operation, and we brought in OSI agents from all over England to participate in a simultaneous five a.m. individual room and barracks search. It didn't yield much, and I think only two or three airmen were really seriously into it. I had an airman informant. He was in possible personal jeopardy, and I had him sent to the Wing's offsite training location at Moron AB in Spain, near Seville. That was done to keep him safe. Naturally, I had to get myself sent over there to interview him. And, naturally, while there, I just had to check out the City of Seville.

We had the usual thefts and lead running from other AFOSI units around the world. Another criminal case I worked on was an alleged incest case. It was difficult to prove. The young daughter seemed so vulnerable, and the wife/mother was absolutely devastated by it all. I felt so very sorry for her, and it was difficult for me to maintain a professional demeanor about it. In another instance, a sergeant was stopped at night by British police on a road back to base and found to be wearing women's clothing. That resulted in a barracks search with a search authorization (warrant) of his room and the finding of all sorts of women's clothing and weird self-photos. I believe he was medically discharged from service. On another case, I had to testify in British Court in Coventry. The barristers were wearing white wigs, and I took the stand on a pulpit-style witness stand suspended about twenty feet off the ground floor. It was an interesting experience!

One of the criminal categories we investigated was black-marketing, or "flogging." Here authorized American personnel were afforded duty-free cigarettes and alcohol purchased at the BX or Commissary as well as Class VI store. To sell any of these duty-free items on the economy was a very serious offense because it was a privilege to have such a concession by the British government. Occasionally, we would receive information that a certain British National would have possession of such contraband, sold or given by a USAF person, at a civilian dwelling. We would immediately notify agents of Her Majesty's Customs and Excise (HMC&E) office in London. They always responded immediately, and the allegation was turned over to them for action. Action was swift. An investigative tool of HMC&E was a "Writ of Assistance," which is an actual printed writ on a large parchment paper, folded down to fit into a shirt-pocket carrying case. The Writ permitted search based on mere suspicion only, not probable cause. There was a provision in the Writ that in hours of darkness, a constable had to be present. From US history, I knew that such writs were part of a basis for the American Revolution with England. I did accompany HMC&E to the offender's dwelling, usually at night, but I never stepped over the threshold. I didn't feel comfortable participating in such a search; plus, I didn't want the media to pick up that an American agent was associated with a Writ of Assistance search. Can you imagine how that might have hit the fan?

One of my contacts was at the military post office where the APO mail comes and goes. The contact informed me that a certain major, a pilot type, along with his wife, were sending antiques to the US, and he believed that due to the volume, it was for purpose of sale. That would be a violation of military postal regulations and, if proved, could result in the major and his wife being in major trouble. For him, it could mean courts-martial that might result in unfavorable discharge action, fines, possible imprisonment, and certainly relief from flying duties and/or return of both to the US.

I thought through this case and decided to go to the Base Commander with it with a recommendation. A really fine officer, Colonel "Scoop" (I don't recall his last name) listened to my approach: Call the officer in and say that the post office was noting this behavior and that the major might be engaged in illegal use of postal facilities and this could result in drastic disciplinary and/or administration. The major should stop it immediately. I strongly believed that I, along with OSI offices at various locations, could prove the case and that it would be brought before military judicial authorities. I told Colonel Scoop this. I felt I could make such a case. But it would really disrupt wing operations, and Colonel Scoop and I would need to bring this before Colonel Holbury for a decision for AFOSI to pursue investigation since the officer was assigned to a flying squadron under his direct command. AFOSI did not do investigations like this without the written authorization of the Commander. I felt that Colonel Holbury would ask me for my recommendation, and I would recommend squelching it. The major was a combat pilot. The Vietnam War was still raging, and we needed experienced pilots. The Air Force had a lot of money into him. But it was true that his actions were really stupid.

Colonel Scoop agreed with my suggested course of action: Call the major in, read him the riot act, and then see what happens. I asked Colonel Scoop to keep any mention of AFOSI out of it, which he did. Sometime later, Colonel Scoop gave me the wink and nod that he had taken care of the matter. In doing so, I don't believe that Colonel Holbury ever knew about any of this. Even the hint of it could have ruined the major's career via OER. Colonel Holbury was a compassionate, fair, and no-nonsense commander (all the things I liked in a commander). I figured Colonel Scoop and I had saved one each, pilot and officer, from disaster so he could live to fight another day. I don't think the pilot/officer ever knew how this whole thing went down—which is just as well. Did I do the right thing here? You might ask where was the justice in comparison with the Cookie Crumble case at Nellis AFB where the airman went to Leavenworth.

On another occasion, Colonel Holbury called me to his office to conduct a certain type of investigation. It was about 1967, and there were racial incidents at the Base Airman's Club. It revolved around racial sensitivities/insensitivities between black and white airmen as well as issues related to music played, food served, and companionship with the local British girls. I told the Colonel that indeed AFOSI and I were capable of conducting such an investigation, but it would be just that. I strongly recommend NO AFOSI investigation for several reasons. For one, under AFOSI investigative case classification, the matter would get all around the Pentagon; it would get very, very visible. For another thing, no one in the Pentagon had any capability to really resolve the issue, including at the base level. Generally, AFOSI did not get involved in conflict-resolutions measures (we could investigate and find probable causes, but it wasn't our business to get involved in solutions). That incident could have been handled at the Wing level by getting the squadron commanders, senior sergeants, and base chaplains involved, working as a team.

I convinced the Colonel that this was the best way to handle the matter, even though I don't think he was quite satisfied. I may have told him to check with my Colonel at Ruislip if he wanted to. I always tried to give it to the Colonel straight out, perhaps giving him information he didn't want to hear. I was no "yes man." I figured that was my job as part of the Air Force Inspector General organization. Colonel Holbury did not press for an AFOSI investigation, and I believe the situation got resolved. Several years later, the USAF created an entity called Social Actions with the job of dealing with race relations. Several years later at the Pentagon on other business, I met the Social Actions founding general officer. I didn't share any of this information with him at that time.

A funny story on Colonel Holbury: On a Friday after-duty Happy Hour at the pub lounge at the Officers Club, Colonel Holbury was a bit buzzed, and one officer prankster faked a phone call from Third Air Force Headquarters. "Hey, Colonel, that was Ruislip on the line. They said for you to disregard the first message!" Can you imagine the confusion?

I did varying counterintelligence operations, some on my own initiative and some directed. I decided to study "the subversive situation" at RAF Upper Heyford and RAF Croughton and to do counterintelligence collections. To help do this, I read the Oxford City newspaper daily as well as had daily subscriptions to the Birmingham City newspaper and the *Daily Worker*, an arm of the Communist Party of Great Britain. The Communist Party of Great Britain is a legal entity and party. Also, I was looking for any indications that peace activists might protest at the base. This never happened the entire three years I was there. I read the *Daily Worker* daily and did cut and clipping of letters to the editor of any persons living in vicinity of the bases. At the end of three years, I had quite an inventory assembled of Communist Party members located nearby. I think I was the only AFOSI agent in Britain who was reading that newspaper throughout those three years. I came to the conclusion that the CPGB posed no threat to my bases or to the Air Force in England.

Just before my three-year tour was up in June 1968, I self-initiated a report entitled, "The Subversive Situation at RAF Upper Heyford." This was largely based on numerous EEIs (intelligence reports) that I had prepared over the period. The overall conclusion was that there was NO subversive situation at Upper Heyford. There were, however, a couple potential problem areas.

Under Air Force Regulation (AFR) 205-57, there was a requirement that all USAF personnel be briefed annually on its provisions. This regulation had to do with reporting any suspect or unusual contacts with any known or suspect foreign intelligence services. The regulation was very specific that all such contacts needed to be reported. There could be military, judicial, and administrative sanctions if not reported. AFOSI had a super fifteen-minute color movie that depicted the threat and how USAF personnel might be approached and/or cultivated for recruitment by foreign intelligence services, even under the guise as innocent friendship or feigned third-country identification. I did countless briefings to on-base units during the three years I was there. We felt the greatest threat might come from personnel going to London and getting targeted at clubs, pubs, social events, and the like. I told the troops this and requested that they report any suspicious activity and let the professionals in AFOSI evaluate the matter…no individual choice. These sorts of briefings were routine and regular and were conducted throughout the Air Force worldwide. Other branches of service did the same thing. Bottom line: ALL military personnel had a clear requirement to self-report any suspicious contacts, especially of a possible intelligence nature.

In a directed operation, my job was to debrief an Air Force person after a personal tour and trip to the Soviet Union. Forrest gave me the tasking with strict instructions that in contacting this person before the trip, I was not to give him any instructions whatsoever on what to look for and report on later. That could put him the category of an espionage agent. I didn't but just wished the person a nice trip and a request to see him when the trip was over. Upon his return, I met with the Air Force person about three days total and completely debriefed him on his day-to-day itinerary, sometimes hour-by-hour. This pertained to places visited, persons met, any unusual events, and anything of an intelligence nature. The end report was extremely detailed and covered page after page, including photographs. This was my first experience in doing such an intelligence debriefing, and all seemed satisfied with the final product. Even the Air Force person was impressed. I had totally "wrung him out." I learned a tremendous amount about the Soviet Union.

The three-year tour in England was very enjoyable, both professionally and personally. Professionally, I came to know many British Police. That also included detectives at Oxford City Police: Inspector Brian Boyt, Detective Sergeant Tom Cooper, and Constable Alf Smith. Sometimes, usually on Fridays, Bill and we would be visited by the Bobbies of the Midlands Crime Squad from the north. These were big, hulking blokes, and we would go over to the NCO Club where they loved to scarf up on the American food and cold beer. These blokes always came with big hunger and big thirst. On other Fridays, by prearrangement, Ginger would roll out to base in his red Austin Mini, and the three of us would take off on a special mission with Ginger to look for and "nick villains" at various rural pubs. Ginger would be careening on narrow countryside backroads whilst we were doing the villain-hunting thing. I never knew where we were or where we were going, or that we ever saw a villain to nick. Ginger took care of all that. Amongst the pints of ale, the conversation went something like this:

Ginger would holler, "Stan, barkeep! Draw a pint of brew for the lad." And then to me, he said, "You bloody Yanks."

"You bloody Yanks from the Colonies!" I would reply. "You bloody British Nationalists!"

"They should send your arse to Australia as a bloody POME (Prisoner of Mother England)!" Bill caught on to the socializing rapidly. I was once invited to meet him and the Biscester CID ¦blokes at Stan

Judd's Pub in downtown Bicester to hoist a pint or two. I had trained Bill well, and here he was liaising with the Bicester CID on his own. I was just an invited guest. Bill just loved Stan's bitters, and Bill told me later than I had trained him well in doing official liaising. Did he utilize this training in his Air Force retirement when he was with US Customs in Washington State and he liaised with Canadian RCMP and others? Me, a party trainer? Bill and I attended many British Police balls. This was fun but also necessary for the police to know us as a resource and point-of-contact. There were many Air Force personnel, including dependents, frequenting as well as living in the communities, and we wanted to be called first if there were any problems. Also, if any of our commanders wanted to know something quick, we could get the answer quick. I found just one eating challenge at those police balls: a solo slice of cucumber straight on a slice of bread, with no dressing. This would need to be chased with a pickled egg and half-pint.

One of my choicest memories is an Air Force Dining-In at the Officers Club. All of us were in our Mess Dress uniforms, and while sitting at a long table, I heard this man's voice behind me lumbering along with effort. The man was our guest speaker for the evening, Group Captain (later Sir) Douglas Robert Bader, of WWII RAF fame. I found out later that in 1931, he had had an aircraft accident where he had both of his legs amputated, one above and one below the knee. He had attempted low-level flying, and his wing touched the ground. Bader made the following entry in his logbook after the crash: "Crashed slow-rolling near ground. Bad show."

After extensive recovery, he returned to active duty in the RAF in 1932. In the Battle of Britain in 1940, he flew numerous combat missions in his Spitfire fighter plane, with *no* legs. By August 1941, he claimed four German planes shot down. He was shot down himself in 1941 and spent four years as a German POW. He tried to escape many times, and the Germans threatened to take away his prosthetic legs if he kept it up. He was a special person to have as our guest speaker. What spunk, charisma, and humor he displayed.

After the formal part of the Dining-In, everyone adjourned to the Informal Dining-In, which was held in the large dining hall at the rear of the Officers Club. There, squadron pilots and personnel had created a funky rides-and-games carnival. Plus, it got wet back there. Group Captain Bader was on one of the funky airplane rides and fell off. As he struggled to get up flat off his back, he was laughing uproariously, in the moment and enjoying the whole thing so much. What a sport! Jolly good show, Group Captain! That's a special memory in my book.

In doing current research I've found two quotes by Sir Bader that deserve citation: "Don't listen to anyone who tells you that you can't do this or that. That's nonsense. Make up your mind. You'll never use crutches or a stick. Then have a go at everything. Go to school, join in all the games you can. Go anywhere you want to. But never, never let them persuade you that things are too difficult or impossible," and "Rules are for the guidance of wise men and the obedience of fools."

Wikipedia says of him, "Bader is upheld as an inspirational leader and hero of the era, not least because he fought despite having lost both legs in a pre-war accident. His brutally forthright, dogmatic, and often highly opinionated views (especially against authority, both British and German) coupled with his boundless energy and enthusiasm inspired adoration and frustration in equal measures with both his subordinates and peers."

What also struck me about the British while there in the 1960s was just how close the WWII experience was to them, as if it were yesterday. There was a television program aired during our time there called "All Our Yesteryears." The British went through absolutely punishing times well before the USA got involved: Dunkirk, the Blitz, the Battle of Britain. I came away with a better appreciation of the special character of the British People, one of tenacity, perseverance, loyalty, and indomitable spirit.

During our assignment at RAF Upper Heyford, Pat taught elementary and middle school at the DoD Dependent School on base.

Family USAF Photo for ROTC duty 1968

That gave us extra spending money. I came to realize that one of her students was the son of Colonel Scoop. So during social occasions, Pat would have informal teacher-parent conferences with Colonel and Mrs. Scoop. Pat also served as a Girl Scout executive volunteer for the two bases, so she had frequent occasion to go to Colonel Scoop's office for support needs, so she had her own thing going with Colonel Scoop. I'm sure her activities had a lot to do with the favorable evaluations I received from him and from my own AFOSI Commander Colonel when he visited my operation.

We went to London on a couple occasions and once saw the stage musical and play, *Man of La Mancha*, staring Richard Kiley. I found this especially interesting since I had read *Don Quixote* in original Spanish in a UCR Spanish class as a freshman. We took in the Queen's Birthday Parade one time. Absolutely no one, no country does parades better than the Brits with all the pomp, like the King's Troop, mounted horse cavalry, and Royal Horse Artillery, with other historic military units like Coldstream Guards, Royal Welch Guards and Fusiliers, the Black Watch (Royal Highlander Regiment) Dragoons, marching bands along with Royal Marine buglers, and horse drawn carriages. (In November 2005, Judy and I saw the annual Remembrance [Armistice] Day Parade with at least a mile-long line of be medaled veterans marching, many in traditional fashion with arms swinging, through the streets of London en route to the Cenotaph Veterans Memorial where the Queen and other royals met them. What a sight!)

We saw a Shakespeare play at Stratford upon Avon and one summer drove to Scotland, seeing Edinburgh, Firth of Forth, and Loch Ness. After base chapel on Sunday mornings, I would often spend Sunday afternoons on "junking missions," scouring the rural village antique shops for treasures. I had a secret route and routine on this. We often went to Oxford where Pat shopped at Marx & Spencer for clothing that she liked. During Easter 1968, we traveled to Paris. It was bad timing because there were student protests and rioting going on. We couldn't go into the Left Bank because there was tear-gassing going on, and we found many, many police in riot gear assembling around Notre Dame Cathedral. I stupidly traveled on my USA Official Business (Red) Passport. Shortly after depositing the passport at the hotel desk, our nice room was changed to a not-so-nice room that had a phone instrument right over the headboard. Go figure! We still managed to go to the Sacré Coeur, the Eiffel Tower, the Louvre, and Moulin Rouge. At another time we traveled to Barcelona, Spain, on vacation. While there, we visited the Black Madonna at Montserrat, which did seem to be a special "power spot," a very special holy site. I could feel it while there.

Final story: In 1968 before rotating back to the states, I was invited by colleagues at Oxford CID to join them in hearing Senator Bobby Kennedy speak at the Oxford Union at Oxford University. This is a large, square meeting hall, and I sat in the balcony with the British Bobbies. I felt conspicuous wearing my short military haircut and civilian clothes. Kennedy's speech was well received, and it was apparent that the crowd was in great respect of him and what he had to say. I left the hall with the police and was standing out on the street curb. Kennedy appeared with his entourage from an alleyway unto the street. He was wearing an electric blue suit, with his signature Kennedy locks, tan, and white teeth. He was "Mr. Charisma" in motion, and that scene in fixed in my memory because it was just him in full color against a backdrop of black and white.

Brooke, or "Brookie," was born at RAF South Ruislip Hospital in February 1966. The delivering physician was supposedly sixth in line to deliver royalty. He was very effective with Pat in facilitating delivery by having her consume large quantities of half-pineapple juice together with half-castor oil. You could say that Brookie slipped into the world.

Before returning to the States for reassignment in 1968, I really wanted to earn a doctorate and thought my best chance was to get an Air Force ROTC instructor assignment at an American university where I could do it part-time. I then applied, unsuccessfully, for AFROTC duty. A part of the application package required a full figure photograph of our entire family. In the photograph of Pat, Ryan, Brooke, and I please notice the not-so-subtle choke hold by Pat on Ryan's neck. Poor little tyke! But he was definitely under his mom's control. Also notice the priceless expression on Pat's face.

I never returned to the States from 1965 through 1968. During that time, I picked up some English vocabulary which has very specific meaning, and I use it occasionally when the situation calls for it.

"Uhmmm": a non-committal reply to a statement. Make it sound like a cross between a question and statement. Persons wanting to hear "yes" will hear "yes," while people wanting to hear "no" will hear "no." It's very ingenious, I think.

Vetted: To vet; to screen, to clear by investigation; to check for accuracy.

Seconded: to loan an employee out

"Spot on!": a very accurate, correct assessment.

Mandatory: pronounced "man-DAT-ory"

Schedule: pronounced "SHED-ule"

Buggered: …no explanation needed

Cheeky: impertinently bold; impudent and saucy.

"Have a go at it!": Do it with vigor.

Chequered: as in chequered career; many unrelated jobs or career positions.

"A man is assisting the police in their enquiries": They got'm!

Also, during those three years, my civilian clothes wardrobe changed as I "went native." That included cavalry twill tan trousers, Harris Tweed sports coats, checkered dress shirts with different pattern vests, and non-matching ties. There were also boot-type shoes that zipped up the insides and tam caps of different design, not matching with the rest of the garb. It was a sort of subdued yet loud look.

Some Lessons Learned:

- On dealing with government agents: On first contact, you should be shown official governmental credentials, usually carried in a dress shirt pocket. They all have them. If one cannot be produced, don't go any further. After display of the credentials, ask to see to see another form of photo identification such as a driver's license. Take your time, and write down all the information from these forms of identification. From the government credentials, take down the agent's number or credential number. Some also have badges. Ask to see that, and write down the badge number. In the post-9/11 world, you can't be too sure and or safe enough.

- Before the interview starts, have the agent write down the name of their office's chief supervisor. In the case of the CIA, it is the Station Chief; for FBI, it is the Field Office, such as Los Angeles Field Office.

- It is a criminal offense to lie to an FBI agent. Be very sure and careful what you say to any agent, and always cooperate and tell the truth.

- Ask to know the specifics of the visit or contact. Don't agree to hear any form of classified or sensitive information unless you are comfortable doing so. Never sign a secrecy agreement without knowing beforehand what it is about. Once it is signed, you may be legally bound to maintain silence, or else!

- If you ever feel that your phone is being bugged, say every foul, outrageous thing you can think of; no person or group of people is exempt from any topic whatsoever. If you speak a foreign language, use that, too, along with slang. Be very inconsiderate of those persons who are monitoring your conversation, taking notes, or creating transcripts. Have some fun in your outrage.

- Re: Group Captain Bader and his flying injured status: I recall, going back to Nellis AFB days, that there was a major on active duty who hobbled around on a cane because one or both of his legs were crippled. I believe that this was due to a Korean War injury. He flew an F-86 SaberJet fighter as an instructor pilot to foreign pilot trainees, such as from the Iranian Air Force. He would hobble out to the aircraft, get assisted up into the cockpit, and be belted in by the crew chief. His cane went into the aircraft with him, and I believe he flew the aircraft aided by the cane. If the Group Captain and the F-86 major could fly handicapped, why can't other wounded, otherwise perfectly capable, Air Force people stay on active duty and continue to serve in capacities best able?

- Do use common sense in foreign travel. Don't bring attention to yourself. Read up on customs and habits well beforehand.

Based on my three years of service at DO 62, Colonel Arthur Dressler recommended me for an Air Force Commendation Medal, which I received from Colonel Free, Deputy Commander AFOSI, in his Washington, D.C., office.

Song: **There'll Always Be an England!** Vera Lynn, singer

Chapter 7:
Headquarters AFOSI Assignment, 1968-1969
Counterespionage Operations

WE ARRIVED IN MID-SUMMER 1968 and rented a house in Alexandria just south of the Beltway from the retired military parents of a military couple stationed with us at RAF Upper Heyford. Coming out of England, I thought that my first Washington, D.C., assignment with AFOSI Headquarters would be with the AFOSI Inspections Division. Bill Keown and I had worked hard to prepare for and receive the AFOSI Inspector at our Detachment Office. Everything went well, and we were rated Excellent. Somehow in conversation with the inspector, it came up that I should get on the inspection team on my next assignment. I knew also that I needed to go to AFOSI Headquarters in my next assignment for best career progression purposes. The inspector job had great career progression possibilities because that meant as a mid-grade officer, I would be traveling around the world on an inspection team and inspecting foreign headquarters and field operations. Plus, I would be meeting many, many people in the organization, including senior members. I would get to know the politics and the players as well as how a unit was excellent in fact. That would be useful later on because down the line, I would want to be a District Commander at senior lieutenant colonel or colonel level. The downside of the job was a whole lot of family absence due to official travel.

I don't recall how it happened, but I was selected for assignment to Headquarters Counterespionage Operations (CE Ops) Branch of the Counterintelligence Division. Being at what I felt was the core of the organization, it seemed like a very good career move for me. As a senior captain, I was assigned to the Western Hemisphere Section of the CE Branch and soon came to know the players. Colonel Heston C. "Tony" Cole was the CI Division Chief; Lt Col (later Colonel) Leo F. Olson, "Leo the Lion," was the CE Ops Chief; and my immediate supervisor was Major (later Colonel) Ray Marin. In our section were about four to five of us. The key old hand going back to Army Counterintelligence Corps (CIC) days was CWO-4 Jesse McSwain. The rest of us in the section were experienced but not in counterespionage operations. Chief of the Pacific Air Force (PACAF section was Major (later Colonel and AFOSI Director) Roy C. Tucker

I met Colonel Cole soon after I arrived. As it turned out, there was a major at AFOSI School who was lusting for my CE slot, and he was arranging for my transfer to the school. I found out about this and got permission to talk with Colonel Cole myself. I was upset at the transfer machinations going on, and I told Cole just that. I told him I wanted to remain in CE Ops for the betterment of my career and that I wanted to "work for him." I think he liked my pitch and spunk and he let me remain in CE Ops. As a result, I think I became one of "Tony's boys."

I was given a bunch of CE files to read because I would be taking over those cases and operations. But before I could really get into such, I needed to complete the four-week AFOSI Advanced Counterintelligence Course given right there in the building. That course was super with a nice mix of theory and classroom with practice and field training. The whole program had been designed with the care and attention of

Lieutenant Colonel Olson. As I came to learn, Lt Colonel Olson was the wizard extraordinaire of Air Force CE Ops. He was the one who designed, produced, and directed the CE instruction. He was the one who brought talented experts in from within the organization and from other organizations to provide instruction and who had designed and got funding for the AFR 205-57 training/briefing films that were seen by all Air Force troops. He was indeed "the main event." Within the course, there was a nice balance of lectures and speakers with great war stories and a variety of training films, including related recent movies— all to review and critique under guidance. Lt Col. Olson was also the CE evangelist who talked with many people, including AFOSI District Commanders and District CI Division Chiefs as they came through the building, and encouraged thought towards counterespionage operations to be created and undertaken. He also had a circle of contacts within the FBI, CIA, and other military intelligence organizations.

Though I couldn't know for sure, I believe Lt Col Olson had an excellent grasp of what was going on regarding espionage against the USAF and what the threat was. We were all players in the game. Sometime during this period, Lt Col Olson told us his view of the field of CE—that of a collage of windows and doors, some closed, some open, some halfway. You may be able to look through and out them. You may not be able to control the openings and closings. Behind the first line are other windows and doors, opening and closing, so in that case, you never really know what's reality. Several years later, another colleague and I created a window and door collage with pictures from magazines mounted on a display board and gave it to him as a retirement or transfer present. He was surprised that we had so well compromised his model. With my later experience, I would add to Lt Col Olson's model smoke, mirrors, all-around lighting, sounds/noise, and varying odors.

From the Advanced CI School I learned many valuable lessons for later on:

- <u>Photography</u>. Major Bob Wardell from the AFOSI School was a wonderful instructor, and he had practical experience, including in CE operations. He had the students take available light (like that inside an office) photographs of documents using a 35mm camera with high-speed film. This was to simulate what a spy might do in covert photography. Part of his lesson was counterespionage techniques. (Take a photograph of a suspect covert search area in order to record the exact position of all items. If no camera is available, make a memory record of it. Compare before and after pictures to see if anything has been disturbed.) This technique came in handy later on.

- <u>Covert Entry Detection</u>: I learned how to make detailed measurements and notes of objects juxtaposed to each other and to photograph, if possible, the arrangements before and after. (To detect penetration through a doorway, affix a human hair at the door opening and set it such that it will fall away if the door is penetrated.)

- <u>Clandestine Surveillance</u>: We did surveillance and CE counter-surveillance practice operations in downtown Washington, D.C. We did personal meets and surveilled such and located and loaded dead drops (including by limpet magnets).

  We learned how to shake surveillance by doubling back, driving or walking, checking reflections in large panes of glass windows for action all around, ducking into shops and stores having many exits, and changing outer apparel quickly and out of sight.

- <u>Espionage cultivation techniques</u>: There was depicted in a rather old, but useful, training film a senior American agent slowly cultivating a young Iranian student or government employee up through and including the "soft pitch" to commit espionage against his country. From all of that, I learned that there is no such thing as a friendly country, or even a friendly, allied intelligence service. It's all just war out there. It is a crazy war out there!

Sometime after I graduated from CI School and was at my CE Ops desk, Lt Col. Olson informed me that I was to go out to a District Office in the US for the purpose of assessing a sergeant for prospective use in a CE operation. The Candidate had been identified and preliminarily screened by the District Commander and his CI staff. They thought they had a good candidate. In preparation, I read his file and reports in detail. I then flew out to the District Office, and they set an interview for me with the Candidate. I asked a lot of questions of the Candidate and revealed to him, as permitted, the true nature of his use in a CE operation. The operation would involve face-to-face contact with a member of a hostile intelligence service. In role-playing, I then portrayed the hostile agent in a threatening interview situation, getting angry and pounding my fist on the table to put him under pressure. I thought the Candidate did well in it all. However, I asked him the million-dollar question: "Do you think you can do this?" He replied "No." I then terminated the interview, went back to D.C., and wrote up a detailed blow-by-blow account of what had happened and shared that the Candidate had said he didn't think he could do it. It was my recommendation in the final sentence that the Candidate not be used based on the fact that he said he couldn't do it. It was my opinion that the best person to ask about a challenge is the person himself; what better source?

I later learned a couple things:

- They did use the Candidate as planned. I don't know how it all worked out. I think the District Commander and staff convinced Lt Col Olson that the Candidate was viable. I never knew anything about the Candidate's use, mainly because there was a considerable amount of compartmentation in the CE Ops Branch. Too, maybe they didn't want to hurt my professional pride. Furthermore, they would not assign the Candidate to me for case supervision since I would likely be biased because they had countermanded my recommendation.

- Lt Col. Olson told me that the Candidate believed me to be a psychologist or shrink. Thinking back, I see that maybe I did come off that way. I had been using my MSU "sizing up" stuff. Perhaps in retrospect, I came on too strong.

At the section, I got to know Jesse McSwain and highly valued learning the ropes from him. At the time, he was working on a certain espionage investigation. An Air Force person had volunteered to spy for the Soviet Union, and Jesse had acquired a phone conversation of this. In his work he would play, replay, and replay the tape, listening for nuances in the interaction. He would consult with Lt Col Olson, and the two pros would compare notes and figure things out. I listened to that taped conversation one time, and the treachery of it sickened me. Jesse pursued the craft with diligence. I recall him sitting at this desk and leaning back in his chair with hands clasped behind his head with face to the ceiling and eyes squinting, searching for answers and angles.

On another occasion, Jesse took me to a Soviet dead drop location in the rural environs of D.C. I drove, and we went on a cleansing operation upon leaving the building to make sure we weren't under Soviet surveillance. Jesse was a complete expert at observing everything;

nothing was missed. It took us about an hour to arrive at the site. The dead drop was near a road sign on a country back road.

I learned in CE Ops the absolute necessity to read and reread every word in reports, to make notes for comparisons and contrasts. Everything needed to be checked out. Whatever was missing needed to be detected, too. Detail is everything; no small morsel of information can go unnoticed. As a counterespionage case supervisor, instructions to the field counterespionage case officers must be clear and unequivocal. Sometimes I would check out my written instructions with others in the section. Then, I would send my completed staff work on to Major Marin (later Colonel, now deceased) for his chop, and then it would go on to Lt Col Olson for signature and dispatch to the field. These were no solo operations, and everything was thought through before approval.

I really liked working for and with Ray Marin. With a great sense of humor, he truly loved the craft of counterespionage, and in retrospect I realized that to do the work well, one needed to have a divergent mind with appreciation for even the minutest detail. One needed to look at situations very macro through very micro lens, to zoom out and zoom in, to look for figure and ground, then simultaneously. I mused that Ray would have made a great bookie, maybe even a stage actor in *Guys and Dolls*—"Got a horse right here…"

One time, Ray asked me to create counterespionage instruction for the CI and CE courses. He wanted a sequential scenario of espionage-counterespionage actions from beginning to end. In training terminology, this is called the "critical incident technique," involving problem-solution. I developed a fifteen-to-twenty-incident scenario involving a hypothetical Soviet agent. Ray liked what I had written except for the "covert search" (surreptitious entry and search). He told me to take it out of the scenario because as he said, "It's illegal and is not done anymore." I took that part out and then had the experience of being the instructor employing the instruction on special agent students in the school environment.

Lt Col Olson had gained the moniker "Leo the Lion" somewhere along the line, and I came to understand why. On occasion, he would really get upset about some operational matter and would blow up. To visualize what this blow-up was like, imagine the MGM lion roaring, only fast-frame the action and increase the volume by three, with the background breaking apart. When that happened, you ducked and covered or headed for the exit. I could understand him. He was brilliant in his field, did not accept sloppy work, and always demanded excellence. He never got on me. I respected him greatly and was afraid of him, too. He was also a great teacher, even a "counterespionage guru." One time he called me up to his office and talked me through one of the cases I was working on step-by-step. "Okay, what would you do next, now?" It was a great learning experience. One time he called me up to his office and introduced me to the FBI agent who was lead in the counterespionage investigation of famed Rudolph Abel, the Soviet Colonel deep-cover illegal who had operated in New York. The spy swap involving Colonel Abel and shot down American U2 spy plane pilot Francis Gary Powers is depicted in the movie *Bridge of Spies*. The FBI agent is probably Edward F. Gamber whose very interesting interview can be accessed on the Internet; Google "Edward F. Gamber." I sort of had the impression that Lt Col Olson was grooming me for bigger things. I don't really know for sure because I was assigned there less than a year.

In January 1969, I learned that I, along with about fifty other headquarters special agents, was going to be seconded to the Secret Service for the Inaugural of President Nixon. So then we all assembled in a large classroom and were given an initial briefing by SA John Stahl, a senior agent in the Headquarters Special Projects Office.

So when question-time came, I asked a very pregnant question: "What about Posse Comitatus?" This involves the use of Federal troops in civilian law enforcement, which is against the law. I wasn't being a smartass as it might have appeared in asking this question because I wanted to be protected from any form of civil action should I have an unfavorable incident with a civilian anywhere out there.

John got himself off the hook quickly with an answer along of the lines of "Do as you are told, and shut up." I did and did what I was told.

A couple days before Inaugural festivities, our fifty AFOSI agents assembled at a large auditorium at the US Commerce Building. There were slews of other agents from all sorts of other federal agencies. It seemed like a cast of thousands. We received a briefing by a Secret Service official and were then given more detailed information about our individual assignment venues. At all venues, I was paired with another AFOSI agent, and together we reported to a Secret Service agent—that made sense.

We were all issued our regular Smith and Wesson Combat Masterpiece .38-caliber six-shot revolvers along with holster and no extra bullets. A much better choice for this kind of work would have been low-profile automatic pistols with nine or ten shots. Most of us had no special training in doing what we called Distinguished Visitor Protection, so we were warm bodies used to convey an impression of overwhelming force. Here are the venues that I worked (we had no say in which venues to which we were assigned):

National Art Gallery: Reception for Vice President Spiro Agnew. The Secret Service agents were right next to him in shifts the whole time, and I was impressed by how professional they were in doing their job. Others of us were standing around in the background and to the side. This went on for no more than three hours.

<u>Inauguration Day Parade</u>: This was January 20, 1969, and I was assigned to a block long stretch on the north side of the parade route on Pennsylvania and Third Street right in front of the USO Building. With the other agent and the Secret Service agent, our job was to watch the crowd, especially in the bleachers, for any threatening behavior. We also spot-checked bags. It was all uneventful, and I was so glad that I wasn't stationed a few blocks up further at the Justice Department because it got ugly up there with demonstrators throwing smoke grenades at the motorcade. I was out there on the street for about six hours total that day. It helped that it was a bright, sunny day, though a bit chilly.

I did not see President Nixon pass by on the parade route because I was busy looking at the crowd in my sector. I did get a glance of Governor Reagan as he passed by standing in an open convertible, waving and wearing a big, big smile. What impressed me most were the military ceremonial honor guards at the start of the inaugural parade. They all seemed about six feet, four inches tall in their finest parade service uniforms and carrying the US flag and all of the five military service flags. They were accompanied by rifle-carrying troops on either end. They walked with resolve as they came down Capitol Hill on Constitution Avenue, and it is another sight I will never forget. It was awesome!

<u>Inaugural Ball at the Shoreham Hotel in Washington, D.C.</u>: I don't know how many agents total were assigned here. There were three other Inaugural Ball venues. This one was different because the only invitees were Medal of Honor awardees and their guests. That was really a surprise to me as I walked around and witnessed all these Medal of Honor winners with their MOH decorations adorned around their necks. It seemed like there were about a hundred of them there, mostly WWII types, I thought, and some bore facial scars from burns. While

I was just simply there on assignment, I felt much honored to be just among them. Later on, I established a position in a mezzanine balcony and stayed out of the way, near a wall and in the shadows. I recognized Sgt. Joe Rodriquez on that floor accompanied by his wife. I knew of him from his hometown in San Bernardino, California. He was awarded the MOH for action in the Korean War. While at the balcony, I decided to move my revolver from my right side to the center of my back. It was less observable there, more comfortable, and I thought that no one would create a problem that night among all these honored men. It was a quiet, dignified ball.

As we two AFOSI agents were awaiting pickup at the end of the ball, we spotted in the hallway Dinah Shore as well as Harlan Sanders (Kentucky Colonel of fried chicken fame) in his signature white suit. Looking back, the MOH Inaugural Ball was the highlight of this Washington, D.C., tour.

We all went back to work the next day, tired and with various stories to tell our buddies. The Inaugural wasn't the only event where I was seconded to the Secret Service. The other time was in late March 1969 when along with many other agents, we were detailed to the funeral of President Eisenhower. My station was one block on Virginia Avenue NW, near E Street NW near the US State Department Building and along the route of travel to the National Cathedral. My responsibility included a high-rise apartment building with windows and balconies facing the Virginia Avenue route where the dignitaries would be transiting. I kept praying, "Dear Lord, please don't let anything happen while I'm out here!" When the entourage came back from the National Cathedral and passed by near my post, all the some two hundred balconies were filled with people, and I was never so happy as when the motorcade passed by.

Other agents had been used to augment Secret Service venues such as the 1968 Democratic National Convention in Chicago. That convention was quite chaotic and violent with Vietnam War demonstrators. I heard about it as I checked in for duty in August 1968. AFOSI agents also were secunded to the Republican National Convention in Miami in early August 1968. I heard about that one, too.

In about April 1969, I received a call from a UC Berkeley fraternity brother and also a fellow criminology student Bryce Hill. Bryce was administering a criminal justice program at Armstrong College in Savannah, Georgia. He needed me to come down and present a lecture on techniques of burglary investigation for about one hundred local law enforcement officers as part of a LEAA professionalization effort. I told him that I wasn't in that line of business, but he insisted. I got permission from my supervisors to do the lecture and gathered a whole lot of instructional materials from agents on the burglary desk. That included pictures of break-ins and the evidence likely to be found and analyzed. My burglary lecture went on for nearly two hours. I carried on like I knew what I was talking about, and it seemed like it went over well.

Shortly after arriving to the Branch in 1968, I noticed this stranger working at a desk near our section area. I learned that he was a script writer for another AFR 205-57 troop film. He was reading closed cases to create his scripts. Someone told me that he was creating an AFOSI agent main character based on me, English squire clothing and all. I never saw the completed product.

Even when arriving in D.C. in 1968, I was considering my career options. I was thinking further if I should get out of the Air Force since I was approaching the critical ten-year point. I had no further service obligations and could separate at any time and use my GI Bill for education. Also, I could possibly continue on active duty and attend one of the D.C. universities at night. I discovered that the Air Force Security Police, headquartered in our building, had one PhD slot in criminology and that it had not been used. I went to Staff Sergeant Eric Holt in AFOSI Personnel and asked to see if we could get that slot transferred over to AFOSI. He took action and shortly informed me that he had the slot transferred over. I then competed in a pool of one for the slot and, guess what, got selected. The result was that I was going to thirty months of graduate school at USC in Public Administration; it was a Permanent Change of Station (PCS) move. We left for California in June or July 1969.

Word of this got around in the shop. I specifically recall a conversation with Major Roy Tucker. With his characteristic granny glasses perched on his balding head, he asked me in his soft Southern voice, "Now, Jerry! HOW are you going to r-e-l-a-t-e?" (meaning when I got on a college campus). I didn't have an answer, but he saw the issue that I would be facing. Oh, how many times over the years did I think of that question!

That question got me thinking. How WAS I going to relate? Here were some of things I considered at the time:

- A fellow captain in AFOSI Analysis and Acquisitions (CI Collections) told me that the FBI had a program going on for the AFOSI to identify separating Air Force personnel returning to college for prospective recruitment as campus informants. He said, "Now there's a program you ought to get involved in." I think he was joking, but it was no joke to me. I decided I wanted no part of such a program and that if I was approached, I would go immediately to Col Cole in complaint. To get involved in such a program would destroy my integrity as a student as well as possibly jeopardize the status of the AFIT Civilian Institutions Division, under whose auspices Air Force personnel were attending civilian institutions.

- The Vietnam War was being waged, and feelings were running deep against the military. I would have to find some way to cope with this when I got to campus. I would need to prove myself as a student. I would need to immerse myself in studies and become a true scholar. During those thirty months at USC, I never wore my military uniform in order to avoid any problems at campus.

- For the thirty months, I would need to sever my ties with AFOSI. I was actually and technically out of AFOSI on AFIT assignment as a student officer during that time. I would need to insulate myself and make no contacts of any sort with Headquarters AFOSI or any field office agents who were associates or friends. In this manner, I could truthfully say I had no contact and was not an informant any way.

- Thinking things through, I considered a very, very remote possibility that I might encounter a suspect foreign intelligence person while at USC, and I would need to make an AFR 205-57 report. I thought that should the encounter occur in a classroom, I would need to go to the professor about my reporting it. If I didn't get any resolution with the professor, I would go to the college dean, getting approval for reporting if necessary.

- There was a danger in severing ties, being out of sight and out of mind, and that was not career-healthy. But the justification for the AFOSI PhD slot was for a Senior Instructor at the AFOSI School at Headquarters, and I would be returning for duty there after USC. In addition, I would be incurring a seven-and-a-half-year service obligation in return for the thirty months of AFIT education. That would take me up to twenty years for earliest military retirement.

- Also, I had not served a Vietnam combat zone tour, and this thirty months would take me off the line. All this could jeopardize my future promotion possibilities because I was out of the mainstream.

During that one-year period of time, Pat got an elementary school teaching job in Woodbridge, Virginia, near Quantico Marine Base. In Alexandria, Ryan went to a nearby elementary school, and Brooke went to a preschool which was on the way to Woodbridge. I carpooled with a veteran AFOSI agent who worked in CE Ops section. Overall, it was a busy year for us all.

Ray Marin put me in for an Air Force Commendation Medal (AFCM) for the CE Ops tour of duty. This second award of the AFCM (also known as Oak Leaf Cluster) was received later in Los Angeles.

Chapter 8:
Retooling at USC

I HAD APPLIED FOR THE doctoral program in Public Administration at the University of Southern California in Los Angeles during spring 1969 after receiving notification from AFIT that I had been cleared for a doctorate educational program. This was the second university to which I had applied. The first was the University of California at Berkeley, my old alma mater, at the School of Criminology for a PhD in Criminology. I was very disappointed to receive a turn-down letter from Dr. Bernard Diamond, the Dean, since I believed my academic and work qualifications were acceptable and I was an alumnus. I was later to learn that the school's students, primarily graduate students, were at the core of the campus "radical-revolutionary thrust" at the University and were concerned about the Vietnam War, human rights, prisoner rights, freedom of speech, black/ethnic issues, and other social ills. I had heard that then-Governor Reagan, also acting in his capacity as head of the Board of Regents, had redlined the School of Criminology from the university budget, so it was disappearing. In recent research, I learned that the School of Criminology was disestablished in 1976, and it has never returned to campus. Had I been accepted, I would have landed straight into a hotbed of discontent and a program which was going to be disestablished. Too, I couldn't know then what the impact would have been on me with what else was to happen in the country: Kent State, the Cambodian invasion, the Democratic Convention at Chicago, and other social-political protests. One could include in that distain for the military and distrust of law enforcement as well as "the government." In retrospect, Dr. Diamond did me a great, great favor. It was another example of "things often happen for the best." Some of life's disappointments are blessings in disguise, and thank God for unanswered prayers. It was not to be, and at that time, I was very disappointed. I'd like to footnote that Dr. Diamond (now deceased), whom I had never met, was a forensic psychiatrist, with a law degree. I think he scoped out the situation pretty well for me and through his admission turn-down action ultimately saved me from great personal and professional discomfort.

Once we got to California in July 1969, Pat and I bought our first house, a brand-new three-bedroom home, in Los Angeles County with a Torrance mailing address. The home was a twenty-five-mile straight shot up the Harbor Freeway to USC, and I spent the rest of July and August doing the outside landscaping at our house since it was new and bare. USC started in September, and sometime after our California arrival, I checked in with Ted Thomas, the graduate program coordinator. We went over the schedule of classes that I would need to take to complete the program and prepare me for the doctoral qualifying examinations two years off. I was on a PCS assignment to USC for thirty months of graduate education, for which I incurred a seven-and-one-half-year payback service obligation. Although I had completed the masters of police administration at Michigan State University in 1965, Ted explained that I would need to start from scratch with masters-level public administration courses at USC. I arranged for a schedule of classes in four qualifying areas: organizational behavior, administrative theory, public administration, and criminal justice administration. The first year of the program was spent taking masters-level classes in those areas and primarily with the experienced, tenured faculty.

I was soon introduced to Dr. John Gerletti, a long-time tenured professor in the School of Public Administration, known as a "where the rubber meets the road" kind of guy, which he definitely was. Dr. John, as I was to learn, had the job of taking on those students who were sort of the "square pegs in round holes," those not fitting some profile of the average graduate student, if there is such a thing. Dr. John invited me to get involved with the Delinquency Control Institute, a nationally recognized program within the School of PA. I did and was introduced to several graduate student program officers, Steve, Bob, Ted, and Gary Adams. Gary, a life-long friend, was from Idaho, where he had been a deputy sheriff and also a staffer for an Idaho political officeholder. He was pretty well experienced and also taught graduate-level public administration classes at night.

I was anxious to get into the academic program, and during the first semester, fall 1969, got into the swing of things and received all As in the three courses taken: Introduction to Public Administration, Public Personnel Administration, and Statistic and Research Methods. I spent a considerable amount of time doing research, taking examinations, and writing research papers. I was especially proud of one I did for Professor Bob Berkov in Intro PA on the senior civil service. I checked out of the library every book on the topic and photocopied many journal articles for content reading. I wrote about a forty-five-page paper and had it professionally typed. Dr. John later commended me for my writing skills, noting that my researching was very thorough. I really appreciated that comment and, while I didn't tell him, all that could attribute that to my AFOSI investigations and intelligence operations experience, including report writing. In the masters-level public personnel class, I did a paper on the "assistant to," which was a follow-up to a paper I did at Michigan State University. This was all a good precursor to my SPA doctoral dissertation since it contributed to the literature review on the "assistant to."

Around April 1970, I was notified to appear before a doctoral-level screening committee of faculty and students. I was upset about this since not all students in the doctoral program were required to meet the committee. I sensed there were concerns about my presence on campus and in this program by student members. This was because of my military status, which was clearly a matter of record on my university paperwork and on my application forms. I had been truthful about my last military assignment: "counterespionage case supervisor, counterintelligence division, Air Force Office of Special Investigations, Washington, D.C." On the other hand, while attending classes, I purposely took a very low profile amongst the students and didn't try to attract attention to myself other than to do as well as I could as a student. The statement of my work experience above was no doubt high profile. I was very anxious about the meeting of the screening committee because a turn-out from the program and a forced return to regular duty would be overall unhealthy for my career and financially ruinous because of the house we had just bought.

Prior to meeting the doctoral screening committee, I needed to complete a "My World View" paper, a requirement not uncommon in graduate level programs. The paper ran around four pages and I gave a lot of thought to it. It was a good task for me since it really focused my attention on what I wanted to do with my career, and that was to be a national security professional and leader. Too, I really wordsmithed the document, choosing every word and phrase very carefully. I wanted it to be a true and accurate representation of me, who I was, and who I wanted to be. Even though it was being submitted only to the committee, I realized that it would also be placed in my SPA academic personnel file, and so it was also an open and public document. I believe my copy of this document was in a file in my desk at home in Torrance.

Quoted here are the exact contents of my "My World View" paper:

MY WORLD VIEW
Submitted to
Screening Committee
School of Public Administration
University of Southern California
Percy G. Rogers
May 15, 1970

We live in a highly imperfect world—one which manifests and which is attributable to multiple realities. The imperfections and multiple realities seem to become more apparent as time passes due in large part to the disparities which exist between societies in their progress along a continuum of human development as well as science and technology. The inconsistencies and paradoxes of life, and to many the hypocrisies, are reflected in nations' failure to resolve the problems of war, starvation, and human existence in general.

These serious strains in the fabric of our as well as other societies have placed inordinate demands upon the social, political, and financial resources necessary for their resolution. A multitude of value orientations exist regarding the priorities which should be attached to each of these problems. In my opinion, there are two basic perspectives in existence today which are competing for primacy in what is essentially a scarce resource environment. One is the international perspective, which has been the dominant one since World War II. This perspective embodies the notion that the United States does not live in a vacuum and that this nation's interests and welfare are virtually bound up in the actions of other countries. Other nations' unilateral actions may and do have significant affects upon our way of life and freedom of action. This perspective holds that as the world's greatest power, we have no choice but to become involved in the affairs of other nations. Further, as the citadel of democracy and decency, we should champion this cause. We should take an active role in assuring the autonomy and integrity of other nations. What I term "the intranational perspective" presently holds that our nation is experiencing a deterioration, morally as well as physically, as a result of too much attention upon international activities. This perspective states that a nation serves the interests of its people and that its important asset is the quality of domestic life. It states that over the past three decades, the nation has been heavily preoccupied with the role of the world's greatest power, and this has resulted in the neglect of its societal responsibilities at an incalculable cost economically, morally, and politically to its national security. The economic costs are reflected in sizeable defense expenditures to the neglect of expenditures for education, welfare, health, and housing. The political costs are measured in terms of the discontent of the American people, particularly the youth.

The heightening conflict between these two perspectives is being reflected in a number of what I chose to call communities. These communities have also been termed establishments and systems at various times, depending again on one's perspective.

Each of these communities is presently undergoing a great deal of stress as a result of changes in societal values. For the reasons indicated, I feel part of and my value orientations encompass all three of the following communities:

1. The academic community—this being my sixteenth year in school

2. The national security community—having just attained ten years of service in the Air Force as an officer

3. The criminal justice community—having spent over nine of those years as an Air Force Special Agent.

I feel committed to affecting understanding and change within and between all three of these communities; however, it should be appreciated that accomplishing this in any one community is a difficult task indeed. The problem is that the day-to-day rush of events causes a narrowing perspective. One is committed, given the constraints of time and particulars of each of the various communities, to do the best he can with the task at hand.

I am hopeful that in the future I can attain a position of leadership with the national security community since this is my primary area of interest and where I feel that I can make a valuable contribution. I have become increasingly aware that the perspectives mentioned above must work together for a common purpose. I think it is extremely important that some sort of dialogue be maintained between and within all three of these communities. I feel that a meaningful dialogue can be affected more readily and effectively by persons functioning within and between these communities, and perspectives, on a person to person basis and within an atmosphere of mutual trust and confidence.

The above comments do not reflect any radical deviation from my previous views, although I must admit that over the past few months, readings and reflections have increased my perceptions and made my commitment clearer and more refined. My world view is not static, and I am confident that the future will provide more and greater insights and hopefully a way of dealing with the multiple realities mentioned earlier.

Upon completion of this academic program, I am scheduled to return to Washington, D.C., to assume the position of senior at the Air Force Office of Special Investigations' Training School. I feel available, however, to assume any other position at the federal level of government which will offer equal or greater responsibility, purpose, and opportunity for service.

I think Dr. John had done some one-on-one lobbying beforehand with the committee as I think they treated me pretty well. The big question was what was my commitment to public administration? I thought to myself that this was a pretty dumb question considering that up to that point, I had been in the armed forces for ten years, a major form and commitment to public administration, although considering the times, some would contest this. I got through the questions alright and also assured the committee, especially the one student member that I was not an on-campus CIA agent, if there were some sort of perception of that. I recall that I did tell or remind the committee that I was a bona fide Air Force student officer attending SC under a sponsored Air Force program and that this was known when I was accepted for admission.

After being excused from the above meeting, I waited around in the hallway for word of the decision of the committee. As I was awaiting the elevator, Dr. John stepped out into the hallway and waved me a big "okay" hand sign, indicating that I had passed. I waved back acknowledgement but wasn't smiling back at him when doing so. I left being upset about the whole deal while recognizing the SPA was operating under an open and inclusive system of governance. In this instance, it wasn't theory; it was reality!

This episode did not go over well with the family: Pat, her sister, and Pat's mother. From that time on, whenever I got home from school or started a phone conversation, it was often prefaced with "Well, did you get kicked out of school today?" I was so strongly committed to finishing the program that I just took it a day at a time and pursued the studies as conscientiously and diligently as I could. I also decided that for survival's sake, I would not report any of this matter to my AFIT career monitor/detailer Captain Jim Austin. It could affect my continuance in the program, questions directed from AFIT to the School of PA, and reports back to AFOSI, all of which could set up dynamics which I could not control.

The whole experience made me pretty insecure, and I realized that I had to find ways to make myself more transparent and "doctoral." Also, I needed to be more careful with myself in how I deported myself and I what I said and did. I felt under a microscope and not too safe. It was sort of schizophrenic, and Dr. John told me once or twice that I was paranoid. Anyone who has ever gone through a doctoral program knows how unsettling that can be. Plus, this was all with the backdrop of the Vietnam War and directly related issues impacting already mentioned. My solution was to really bear down in my studies, with that being the reason for my presence there in the first place. Also, I would need to find ways to fit in better. I would need to change and still be me. I wanted to graduate with a doctorate and do well in the process.

Chapter 9:
The Unexpected Class Visitor - USC 1971

IT WAS NOW SPRING SEMESTER 1971, February, and was nearing the end of coursework for the doctoral program. I was looking forward to the graduate seminar "Administrative Theory and Public Policy" taught by SPA core faculty member Dr. Bruce Storm. Well-liked and well-respected by faculty and students alike, Bruce was a graduate of the University of Chicago and had been an infantry officer in WWII. Up until that point, I had had no contact with Bruce, and we hardly knew each other.

The initial class meeting was held at the SPA downtown Los Angeles facility in the "OB room" (OB meaning organizational behavior). The room had no seats but rather was furnished only with a plush wall-to-wall carpeting that ran up the sides of the room about three feet. The idea was to make the environment hospitable to class discussions. This was a once-a-year-offered class and was required of me in the doctoral program. There were about fifteen of us doctoral students in the class, about five of them international students like from Jordan and Nepal. The first three to four hours of the initial class meeting entailed in-depth self-personal introductions. I called such sessions "groovy-groupie," and they seemed favored in the SPA classes, especially organizational-behavior-related classes. The idea was that in getting to know each other, openness and trust-building could help facilitate the learning process. I subsequently used such methods in instruction as a professor. But on that day, I think it was the eleventh of February, I wasn't delighted about going into my background with strangers, particularly in light of all that had gone on before with me at USC.

As we got into the introductions, about the third person up introduced himself by name, and I think Bruce introduced him as a friend of his, not as a registered student of the class. He was just visiting the class. He then began to get into his background, which was as a former member of the Iranian Secret Police, the SAVAK. Instinctively, I knew that I would have to report this contact back to the AFOSI since all service personnel were required to report any contacts with members of a foreign intelligence service, hostile, neutral, ally, or otherwise. Further, in the intelligence business, there is no such thing as a former or retired member of an intelligence service. Such contact reporting was part of the bread and butter of the Air Force counterespionage effort under Air Force Regulation AFR 205-57. I was bound by that regulation regardless of circumstances of contact. Too, I had given countless briefings on such reporting to Air Force personnel over the prior years.

Soon after Bruce's friend introduced himself, I got into my self-introduction. I gave the class a sanitized version of my work history. I told the class that I had a problem here, as I needed to report the contact. I told them that I faced military disciplinary action for failure to report. Failure to report could jeopardize me, potentially leading to a Dishonorable Discharge and imprisonment at Leavenworth. It was a pretty harsh statement, but I wanted to make the point that I needed to make such a report. There followed some brief discussion in the class about this, and then I turned to Bruce to request his permission to report the matter. I was in a difficult situation. I told the class that I would not report the contact if that was their wish. I felt that the classroom was a sanctuary for ideas as well as a protected place and that their privacy had a stake in it, too. The class voiced unanimous consent that I could and should report the matter. I then asked Bruce if I could report the matter, and he said, "Of course." About then, Bruce's friend told the class that I <u>had</u> to report the contact. That seemed to seal the deal. Then Bruce's friend wrote his name down on a slip of paper and handed it to me. In retrospect, I guess you could call that "professional courtesy." I asked the class to keep the matter confidential. The class then went on with self-introductions, and we finished out the semester meeting at the downtown LA facility and back at campus.

Bruce's friend did not show up to class anymore. I did see him on campus from time to time, and we nodded at each other. I was later to learn that the SPA had had an educational presence in Iran in years prior, and this was the basis for Bruce's relationship with the SAVAK guy. The incident got around the SPA grapevine, and the faculty helped by putting out the word: "Don't worry about the intelligence agents you know; worry about the ones you don't know." A fellow doctoral student in that class who was also a friend of Bruce's told me that Bruce was so upset about this incident that he was considering resigning from the faculty. I never spoke to Bruce about that matter subsequent to the first class meeting, and when I learned of Bruce's reaction, I was very concerned for him and felt regretful that the whole thing happened in the first place. But it was a turn of events over which I had no control. In retrospect of years, it was probably too much made over a small thing, but in the context of those times and circumstances, it was clearly the thing for me to do. The doctoral student later told me that some of the students in the class had appreciated how I had handled the situation with the Iranian.

When I got home from class that day, I told Pat what had happened in the classroom. She was mildly upset at me, saying, "Well, what are you, a student or an OSI agent? Make up your mind!"

I replied, "Look, it happened. I did what I thought I had to do, and I've got to make a report."

Soon after, I telephoned a Special Agent friend stationed at the nearby AFOSI District Office 18 at Norton AFB in San Bernardino for an appointment. On the ensuing Saturday, I drove over to his house in Grand Terrace and gave him the report while he wrote down the details. I didn't go through the punishment aspects but did give him the slip of paper with the Iranian's name. I didn't expect any other action on the matter at that time but realized that I'd probably catch some flak when I got back to Washington, D.C., for the next scheduled duty assignment.

Looking back over the years at the contact-reporting incident, I thought at the time that it was strange, thinking through the probabilities that such an incident might ever occur like that. Also, I felt strangely at peace with myself in the classroom and in doing the reporting. Question: Had all this been an accident? I don't know. I don't have the answer.

Chapter 10:
Strangers at the Doorstep and More – 1971

THERE WAS A SHUFFLING OF feet and murmured voices just outside the front bedroom window. For some reason, I was standing in Ryan's bedroom located to the front of the house and just next to the front door, and his window facing the front door was open for ventilation though the Venetian blinds were full down and closed. Also, no one could see inside into the room as it was dark inside the room, and it was daylight outside. However, persons outside could be heard from inside—and I did hear them. The doorbell rang with more quick shuffling of feet.

It was a new three-bedroom home in Los Angeles County with a Torrance mailing address with a two-car garage facing up front toward the street. The walkway to the front door was adjacent to the east side of the garage, and all was under one roof. Two rectangular stucco pillars helped to support the roof over the twenty-foot interior walkway. The landing to the front double doors was in an alcove, and so that whole area was shaded.

I had been studying that day, as other days, for the doctoral qualifying exams to occur in September and October 1971. It was August 1971 and seemed mid-day, and I was alone; Pat was out as were the kids. I opened the front door, and what I saw is etched in my memory. Here were two men, persons I had never seen before, standing shoulder to shoulder on a relatively narrow walkway adjacent to the first roof pillar and about ten feet from the front door. Again, the walkway could only handle one person easily at a time, and here were the two standing there, side by side. My antenna went up immediately because of how they were weirdly presenting themselves, and more instinctively than anything else, I think it was the shorter one on the left who seemed different in some way. Maybe it was some sort of apparatus that was situated just above his belt line. It was just odd.

I stepped out the front doorway and onto the walkway area, and a short conversation ensued, probably lasting no more than five minutes. The conversation moved to the front of the house to a point where the other roof pillar stood, just to the entrance to the walkway and next to the garage door. With the passage of years, I don't recall what the conversation was about, but I definitely had the impression then that this was an elicitation interview of some kind, drawing me out on something. During my investigative and intelligence career, I had had plenty of experience in doing elicitation interviews (like with OXCART), ones in which the target is not witting to the intended purpose of the interview, and the questions are intended to lead to some sort of spontaneous response that leads to some sort of confirmation or disconfirmation. The conversation broke off with me walking back into the house and the strangers departing to I don't know where. I was puzzled initially and then started to quickly pull the pieces together over what I had just experienced:

- Two guys appeared at the door and weren't right there in the doorway; they were ten feet away. Why ring the doorbell and then scurry around, leaving the entry to the doorway where a conversation could occur in a natural setting? This had never happened before, and the only time it happens now is when Mexican illegals come knocking at the door looking for work and then back off the front door so as not to alarm the resident. The only other two men who appear at the door are Mormon missionaries, but they are younger, and they stand near the front door, not away from it.

- The strangers were white men and seemed to be in their forties.

- They were standing side by side, shoulder to shoulder in a narrow walkway. Men don't naturally stand that close together, and it would be uncomfortable in that situation.

- The conversation didn't make any sense except that they were trying to elicit information from me.

- The conversation seemed official, not casual.

- Their manner of dress seemed out of place, more like east-coast clothing, definitely not California type.

- More importantly, their eyes were intense, very focused, almost glaring. Neither one of them took their eyes off me. The taller one of the right seemed most officious with his glaring eyes, like he was trying to penetrate inside of me. The shorter man at the left was difficult to describe, and that was puzzling.

- I didn't notice much else about them and their appearance, but their eye actions were most puzzling and alarming. I'd seen it sometimes before and probably had projected it myself in operations.

I had a strong urge to go back outside to see where the strangers were going and possibly see what type of transportation they had. My intuition told me there was more to this encounter than met the eye, and it strongly appeared that I was being investigated by this pair. While I thought I'd "made them," I decided not to go back outside. Otherwise, this may have increased their own suspicions of "being made." I didn't have anything to go on in terms of identifying who they were or what they were up to. If and should they have known my background, which I was sure they did, they would have been very cautious about a contact. Whoever they were, they must have found my location through official sources. That really concerned and angered me. <u>What were they up to?</u> I decided to wait and see what happened next. There didn't seem anything else I could do.

During the summer of 1971, Pat told me that we were experiencing problems with the home telephone, and I noticed the problems, too. We had problems connecting on the outgoing call and sometimes no connection at all. We called telephone repair servicemen, and they came out, but the problems didn't seem to be resolved. I noticed on about two occasions telephone repairmen working at the aboveground telephone utility box located about two houses down to the east. One time I picked up the telephone, and a man's voice came on right away and said, "He's on now." This was very strange, and I was rather disbelieving that our phone could be bugged, but I didn't relay my suspicions to Pat. I decided to do nothing and see what develops.

Sometime during the summer, I was standing in the opened garage doorway, and a man pulled up across the street and then walked up to me. He started a conversation, handed me a business card as introduction, and wanted to talk about the characteristics of the neighbors. Thinking back, I recall he may have presented himself as a realtor. It was just a strange encounter, particularly since I was starting to question things. The encounter may have been related to this matter and maybe not.

Pat and I did a lot of socializing with her sister Sandy, her husband Mike, and their two young children. We socialized at their house in Cypress in Orange County and at our house in Los Angeles County, about forty-five freeway miles away. They had a speedboat, and we went boating with them to the Colorado River often. We planned a river trip for Labor Day weekend September 1971, on which we went. Because of the strangers' visit, I became very suspicious of everything and began by setting up covert search traps in the home. This would include placement of knickknacks in exact measured placement to each other, such as on the bookshelves, and made periodic checks to see if they had been disturbed. I was the last one out of the house just before our departure for the river and made a specific effort to take a mental picture of the desktop of my desk in the master bedroom. The desk was the usual messy, but I took a good, long look at each item in juxtaposition with each other item. My USAF medical record file was in the right hand drawer. My informal personnel file was also in the drawer, and it included an unclassified Air Force memo which I had written to the DO 62 (England) Commander listing the official EEIs (intelligence reports) by number and subject matter that I had written when stationed in England. It was provided in partial justification for an Air Force Commendation Medal.

Two things happened of significance when we returned from the Memorial Day river trip:

- I made it a point to be the first person into the house and went directly to my desk. Things had been disturbed; they were no longer in the exact positions in which I had mentally recorded them before departure a couple days earlier. I checked my medical and personnel records but didn't notice anything unusual. It was definitely a concerning and puzzling situation, but there was nothing I could do about it. I was feeling so very vulnerable and helpless.

- Sometime early in the next week, my next-door neighbor, Ed, approached me and said that he had heard men's voices coming from inside the house when we were at the river. His house was just to the west of ours with the homes about six feet apart with identical floor plans but flipped 180 degrees, side by side, back to back. We had left the tiny bathroom upper windows open for ventilation. I immediately recognized the significance of Ed's disclosure and decided not to probe him for any further details, in part because I didn't want to alarm him. What he told he served to collaborate my earlier discovery.

All of this caused me to question how anyone would know we would be gone over the Labor Day weekend, and the only conclusion I could come up with was a bug or bugs planted in the home or a telephone tap.

Thereafter, I really watched for strange cars and/or persons in the neighborhood. Only once did I notice anything strange, and that was when I walked up the street in the neighborhood and observed what looked like a plainclothes police vehicle with a man sitting in the passenger seat, armed with a pistol. I didn't say anything and may have recorded the car license.

The last event that happened was when in the days later, a young woman, maybe in her twenties, knocked at my front door. She was a total stranger. She stood right at the entry, almost falling inside, and said in an alluring tone of voice, "They say that you wanted to see me." I was alone in the home as Pat was teaching, and the kids were in school. Completely astonished, I cut her off and closed the door. I thought the action was a continuation of the other actions, above, and some sort of move to sexually compromise me in a crude extortion attempt. Oh, how upset and confused I was. Exactly, who was doing this and why was unknown, and this was very concerning.

Once I closed the door, I went into the living room hallway and bent down on one knee in prayer. I said something to this effect: "Lord, I don't know what is going on here or why. Something is very seriously wrong. Please do everything to protect my family and me from all harm. You know that I have always loved you. Please help!" I concluded with the Lord's Prayer. After that, I did devise some home entry traps but never employed them.

With regard to suspected telephone taps or home bugging, I decided not to tell Pat. It was only a suspicion, and I didn't want to upset her in any way because that upset would get to her family, including her mother, Beryl, who would have gone absolutely ballistic over it (she such a loyal Canadian as well as a US citizen).

I did not want to telegraph to whomever an awareness that we were on to them. Let them hear what was going on in our household. The conversations were totally innocent and included:

- Discussions I had with fellow doctoral students about our studies. I had detailed conversations with fellow doctoral student, Mike Sparks, about books and concepts of the so-called radical British psychiatrist R.D. Laing. This included Laing's books: _Self and Others_; _The Divided Self: An Existential Study in Sanity and Madness_; and _The Politics of Experience_. Mike was well read in R.D. Laing and explained his theories of meta-communications analysis theory to me, which I incorporated into my doctoral dissertation. These were weighty, technical conversations that would have blown the mind of any layman, provided they could be understood. Mike saw the application of Laing's study of individual and family madness (psychoses and schizophrenia) to organizational behavior (our field) in terms of organizational sickness and health. Mike (now deceased) was a real solid guy and brilliant.

- Conversations with our neighbor, Bob, an aerospace machinist from Muskogee, Oklahoma, about the relative merits of country western music by such artists as Buck Owens, Merle Haggard, and Marty Robbins. Later we would listen to the music over beers and carry on.

- Coordination conversations with fellow USC Air Force officer student about the content of our YMCA Indian Guides newsletter (we were the Sandpainters) and campouts.

- Conversations by Ryan and Brooke and their friends about their activities.

- Conversations I had with Pat, usually from school, to coordinate our family activities and my status on coming home. Pat usually started the conversation with "Well, did you get kicked out of school today?"

- Conversations Pat had with women neighbor friends that involved juicy gossip. Pat would relay some of it to me, and I found it incredulous. It was an earful.

- Lengthy conversations Pat had with her sister Sandy about their respective school teaching day. For two and a half years, 1969 through 1972, Pat taught at Century Park Elementary School in South Los Angeles as a sixth-grade teacher. This LA Unified District School was all black: students, teachers, and administration. Pat was the only white teacher on staff, and each day presented a different challenging experience to be coped with. The principal, Birdie Lee Bright, was an "old school" disciplinarian type of both faculty and students. She didn't tolerate any sort of nonsense and demanded educational excellence in her own style. Everything was regimented, including strict positioning of student chairs and no decoration of any sort allowed on classroom wallboards, totally contra Pat's teaching style. No parent teacher-conferences were held during hours of darkness, only on afternoons when conditions were considered safe. There would be outbursts in the classroom that Pat would have to deal with. Pat said that the kids were basically good but that about ninety percent of her time was spent on control versus education.

Sandy taught fourth grade at a LAUSD school in Carson, California. Both of their jobs were very stressful. Every afternoon when they got home from school, they would talk on the phone for an hour or so about what had gone on during the school day.

The "debriefings," aided by martinis, were very lively and often involved renditions/reenactments of student-teacher interactions in the classroom. Listening in, I found some of them quite entertaining because Pat was such an actor. They both needed those afternoon sessions to get through it all and to prepare for the next day. They were each other's best friend and counselor. Pat was so stressed out at the last week of each school year, she was also taking tranquilizers. Pat would often tell me, "You ought to try doing what I do every day!"

Pat told me that on her last teaching day at Century Park, Birdie Lee called her into her office and gave her the all-time commendation of her entire twenty-plus years of teaching: "Pat, you've taught here, and you can teach ANYWHERE!" Indeed, she had "been there, done that!" She was a pro!

Lesson learned: Being a LA Unified School District teacher is super tough duty. My hat is off to any LAUSD teacher!

I bring all this up because both Pat and I were under absolute tremendous emotional and mental pressures. I found no justification for telling Pat any part of what was going on with the strangers. She had enough on her plate. I think I also felt she might have an emotional or mental breakdown because of overload. It was a risk I didn't want to take, even though Pat was strong. Too, I didn't want to disturb or destroy our family in any way.

I thought then and now that anyone who may have been listening to, transcribing, and reading, our household conversations and lives would get a real earful. Question: Were tap transcribers affected in any manner, particularly taps which were illegal in the first place?

During the remainder of my USC doctoral days and the strangers' actions, it was difficult to keep my spirits up. When driving to USC on the Harbor Freeway, from the Sepulveda Boulevard onramp, I would sing American patriotic songs. I couldn't do this very often because I would get so emotional that my eyes would tear up. I was afraid of running off the road or getting into an accident.

Author's Note: The strangers' actions against me (and my family) involved

- A surreptitious elicitation interview to assess me.

- A covert, clandestine, and illegal search of my/our home and personal effects.

- A believed crude and unsophisticated extortion attempt via sexual compromise.

- A believed illegal electronic surveillance of our home and/or telephone tap on our home phone.

All of the above seemed to me to be totally unwarranted as I had done nothing wrong. I was a loyal, trusted Air Force officer, and the strangers' conduct was an assault on my personal and professional integrity. It was evident that some persons considered me a traitor or enemy of the state, a serious threat to national security. The acts done were irrevocable, irreversible, and clearly criminal. I felt victimized and vulnerable. I questioned who was doing this and who had authorized it.

I doubted that the perpetrators were aware that they had been detected at any stage. I felt that the perpetrators would eventually be caught based upon my previous experiences that there is no such thing at a perfect crime and that the truth will out. The totality of the circumstances were horrific, and I believed the perpetrators acted in the belief that I was some sort of disloyal, naïve, incompetent professional with no skills or redeeming qualities. I was a stupid dumbass. Apparently, I needed to be assessed, discovered, compromised, and destroyed.

Chapter 11:
Enemy of the State:
Making Difficult Choices – 1971

COMING UNDER INVESTIGATION BY SOME unknown entities could not have come at a worse time for me personally. I spent the summer and fall of 1971 getting ready for the doctoral qualifying examinations. I, as well as other doctoral students taking the exams, were to complete lengthy, day-long written essays in three areas: organizational theory, organizational behavior, and public-personnel policy. Characteristically, there was tremendous insecurity amongst the doctoral students, some twenty of us, at this time because the examinations were the crux of continuation in the program. While the doctoral coursework was supposedly preparatory for the examinations, the questions as prepared by the professors were far ranging and sometimes far out. To cope with this situation, doctoral colleagues Gary Adams, Mike Sparks, Ron Bates, and I formed a study team with a fourfold mission:

1. Individually pick off the professors with whom we were on good terms in order to get clues as to the study areas and/or possible examination questions

2. Gather information on questions in previous examinations

3. Find out what the other doctoral students were doing in their preparation

4. Gather study material used previously as well as currently

We met periodically at the Tyler Building, home of the Delinquency Control Institute, to consolidate our findings and commensurate with each other. We purposely kept a very low profile in order to keep our findings as confidential as possible. As a result of our collective effort, we decided to publish our notes immediately upon completion of the written examinations as some kind of "tour de force." This we did in about a one-hundred-page document we called "Notes and Quotes," and the release took place the day after the last written qualifying examination was given. We stuffed all the faculty mailboxes with the booklet, and the four of us took great delight in this mini-coup as the document was unnerving to the other doctoral students and some faculty because we had come right out and released to the world coveted study notes. These were closely held secrets to getting through the qualifying examinations. The booklet was a hot seller for awhile amongst the doctoral students.

I thought I had done well on the written examinations; however, I was informed by my doctoral faculty advisor, Dr. John, that a fourth professor was going to be added to the oral examination to ensure integrity of the process. As a Doctor of Public Administration degree candidate, I only needed three on the committee as opposed to five. Dr. John was one of the three. I met the oral examination and got through it, although Dr. John later told me that one of the faculty members told him I was weak. Looking back, I probably was.

The events of that fall with the strangers were debilitating, and I was experiencing a great deal of mental and emotional distress. My motivation for success in the doctoral program was flattened. Maybe I was suffering from depression. During the fall, I was taking a class in Comparative Public Administration from Dr. Guerreiro-Ramos. My mental and emotional state must have been evident because at one point, Guerreiro questioned, "Jerry, what is the matter?" I really didn't know my state was that obvious, and he had read me perfectly. I replied to avoid any further complexity, "I'm alright, Guerreiro," but I wasn't. Somehow, I completed his course satisfactorily, thanks to Guerreiro.

Sometime during midyear, the Delinquency Control Institute had an evening reception and recognition event at the USC Faculty Club for the two actors who portrayed police officers in the television production *Adam-12*. I was standing by myself and Dr. Henry Reining, Dean Emeritus of the School of Public Administration, walked right up, faced in front of me, and said one word: "Integrity!" and then walked away. I was a bit astonished, but it was clear to me he was referring to my February 1971 report. I didn't know Dean Reining at all, but everything about him exuded competence and integrity. That one-word comment was very much welcomed, appreciated, and totally unexpected.

I wrestled over what I should do about the strangers' actions. Should I report what I thought was going on back to my organization, the AFOSI, or let it ride until something more definitive happened? I could never imagine an AFOSI superior or fellow Air Force officer doing what was done. It wasn't warranted by the circumstances, and my superiors and colleagues were honorable men. But somehow the strangers could only have identified me through the AFR 205-57 report. It seemed likely that there must have been some coordination at the national level with the Central Intelligence Agency as well as the FBI on the Iranian. Plus, my name would be flagged through my previous access to OXCART on file at CIA. I couldn't imagine either the CIA or FBI going to the excesses I was experiencing, yet these strangers were acting on official information and someone's authority. It did occur to me at the time that my reporting with all its circumstances might reach the attention of someone in the White House. I think I mentioned this in passing to Gary Adams at the time I turned in the SPH in May 1971.

The strangers were clearly involved in criminal behavior against me: an intelligence assessment, a covert search of my home, a probable extortion attempt through sexual compromise, and a telephone tap. It seemed that the sloppy operational security I was witnessing would only result in their being caught in some matter in time. Then, the authorities would find out the full scope of their activities, and the trail would lead back to me. I could corroborate events. It wasn't clear where the strangers were in their operational history. It seemed to be then and upon later reflection that the strangers had assessed me as some sort of incompetent dumbshit and had not really done their homework on me. It all seemed like a very slipshod, kneejerk operation. I couldn't fathom why I was being investigated some three months after the SPH turn-in in May 1971. Much later, when the Watergate and Plumbers story broke, it seemed apparent this was likely the first or second of their operations. It was all so crazy, yet I felt my integrity and honor as an Air Force officer was being severely impugned and that my good reputation was being trashed. Some persons were out to destroy me and, indirectly, my family concluded that I could not at that time report the matter because:.

- I had no solid proof of the events and could further damage my reputation with AFOSI reporting on such tenuous grounds.

- AFOSI was possibly witting to the authorizing of officials at the other end but probably not to what was actually going on in Los Angeles.

- If I reported the matter, it would be quashed because it involved higher-ups. Allegations would be denied, and I would appear as a careless and/or unreliable complainant. AFOSI would not want to get in the middle and destroy its own reputation.

- I wanted to complete the doctoral program and wanted nothing to interfere with it. If I were to complicate things with this report, I would likely be removed from the program altogether by the Air Force.

Due to all of the above considerations, I decided to do nothing and wait until I got back to Washington, D.C., to see what would transpire there. I was very concerned how and if my reputation with the OSI might have been blemished as a result of the February incident. I was concerned that when and if the strangers' actions did come to light, either soon or in the future, that somehow I needed a vehicle for preserving my innocence and protecting the reputation of the Air Force, the OSI, the University of Southern California, and the School of Public Administration as well as faculty and students, both current and future. During 1970, 1 had been acting as an unpaid research assistant for Guerreiro. He boasted to faculty and other students that I was the only student who had ever had unlimited access to his office and effects as I had a key to his office. (I was greatly honored by this privilege and trust since Guerreiro's actions to provide a safe haven in the eyes of others as well as access to academic materials generated from his classes were of use in my own studies.) In every graduate class, Guerreiro required analytical book reviews, which were generally about ten pages long and followed an exacting format. My own analytical book report was on Karl W. Deutsch's systems-analysis approach to examining political life, _The Nerves of Government_. A student could read the review and obviate reading the entire book—a great timesaver when one needed to read so many books to achieve mastery of the field. Guerreiro had accumulated some two hundred reviews, and I began a program of sorting through them to locate the best of the best. It then became apparent that I might be able to package a number of the better reviews into a book format and leave this as a legacy and indemnification of my attendance at USC. Again, I considered the book project as a defensive as well as offensive operation to protect me, the university, and the Air Force. I began working on a book, subsequently titled *A Compendium of Analytical Book Reviews in Organizational Behavior*. This edited book consisted of forty analytical book reviews, authored mainly by doctoral students and running three hundred pages total. I had absolutely no idea when or if things might blow up because of the strangers' actions, but I felt eventually it would sooner or later.

Over the period from September 1971 through January 1972, I obtained copyright permissions to publish from the students as well as the book publishers of each text and spent about six hundred dollars getting each of the manuscripts retyped and the volume printed and bound at the university print shop. I worked on this project steadily from the day the doctoral oral examinations were concluded until publication in January 1972. At the same time, I was working on my dissertation to officially complete the degree program, and because of the book project, which took first priority, I did not complete the dissertation by end of term, which was February 1972, or before returning to Washington, D. C. I donated the entire book project to USC and the School of Public Administration. I dedicated the book to the students and faculty of the USC School of Public Administration. The book proved to be popular with the students. The initial printing was three hundred copies, and I believe a second printing was done after I left for Washington.

I spent considerable time constructing the Introduction and Acknowledgement sections, which are quoted as follows:

Introduction:

Amitai Etzioni, one of the prominent authors on organizations and organizational behavior, has observed that our society is an organizational one. We are born, raised, and educated in organizations; we work and die in organizations. Organizations have been in existence for hundreds of years. They can vary in size from a sole proprietorship to a nation-state. In a sense, the world could be considered an organization.

Some argue that there is no such entity as organizational behavior. Rather, we should be talking of behavior in organizations. I find such discussions missing the point; the perspectives are mutually dependent. Organizational behavior is an extremely elusive and illdefined field of study. Once beyond some of the more noted theories, students of organizational behavior are often bewildered by the apparent lack of boundaries of the field. Also, one sometimes gets the impression that our knowledge of organizations has attained a high level of sophistication. The truth is that we have barely scratched the surface. It has only been within the past thirty to forty years that behavioral scientists, primarily psychologists, have systematically attempted to study organizations. Considering the history of organizations, it is apparent that there is still much to be learned and new theories to be discovered.

This volume may be considered a sampler of the scope and nature of the study of organizational behavior. This volume has been divided into five sections, each of the sections representing a level of analysis, an orientation, a perspective, a layer. While one may find some arbitrariness in the divisions of the reviews, their placement is intended for purpose of continuity and transition. The analysis is begun with a selection of book reviews dealing with man and his nature vis-à-vis the organization. We come full circle back to this perspective after considering his behavior in terms of groups, bureaucracies, organizations, and societies. Additionally, this volume references several books dealing with change and change technologies.

The books in Section I, dealing with man and his nature, provide philosophical as well as psychological orientations to this subject. Douglas McGregor's celebrated Theory X (man is basically lazy) Theory Y (man does not dislike work, but is basically creative and desires growth) approach to organizational behavior is merely one effort to provide a philosophical/psychological view of man. According to Werkmeister, no single theory can accurately reflect reality or a view of man. The world to which a man responds and in which he lives is in a basic sense his own world, comprehended and created by him. He says, "Our existence as a person is essentially a project." There are many who will contend that the true unencapsulated man can never be achieved or realized within the confines of a single organization. Organizations are always functionally rational. Thus, the dilemma is presented: Man cannot live with organizations, and he cannot live without organizations. The solution, it seems to me, lies in the possibility of living a dialectic. Rollo May uses the dialectic in noting that psychological growth lies in the capacity for an individual to see himself as both a subject and as an object. It is in the process of living between, actually integrating these two poles that lies the development, deepening, and widening of human consciousness. I see a similar dialectic between life within as well as without the organization. In speaking of the subject-object dichotomy, Rollo May has observed that freedom always involves social responsibility, that in this age of uncertainty to be free means to face and bear anxiety. To run away from anxiety means to automatically surrender one's freedom. Freedom must be earned. It seems to me that his diagnosis/prognosis can be applied to organizational life. One's freedom in organizations is attained by engaging them.

Section II of this volume deals with bureaucracies and their nature. Along with the rise of the welfare-warfare state, there has been a collateral rise of bureaucracies, here as well as in other countries. A number of authors, Peter Blau and others, have commented upon their positive (someone has to be responsible for providing service and rationality) and negative (their unresponsiveness, uncontrollability, and self-centered irrationality) features. We transition to Section III on organizations by looking at the role of professionals and semiprofessionals. Section III contains reviews on several classics in the field, mainly Katz and Kahn's book *The Social Psychology of Organizations.* Section IV contains a selection of reviews on books dealing with planned organizational change and change technologies. Section V provides rather broad coverage of the societal perspective.

In my opinion, the primary and most increasingly viable analysis perspective will be that of society, the sociological perspective. No person or organization in our or any other country has escaped, but rather is increasingly affected by, forces of change in the world today. Our societies are becoming so interpenetrated through technological advances in communications and transportation that we are living, in the words of Marshall McLuhan, in a "global village." In this context, the notion that organizations are the primary unit of analysis seems inappropriate.

It occurs to me that the task in the coming years will be to aggressively and actively engage and live in a world of multiple realities rather than a mode of passive reflection and disengagement. The latter behavior, without a commitment to action, seems to lack authenticity. The notion of living in a world of multiple realities has been somewhat the ethic at the USC School of Public Administration. It is achieved in part by a continuous effort to integrate theory and action, a praxis if you will. In plain language, this means "walking your talk" in an effort to improve the lot of man.

Percy G. Rogers
Los Angeles, California
January 1972.

Acknowledgements:

This book was first conceived in early 1970 when I had an opportunity to take a graduate course in organizational behavior from Professor Alberto Guerreiro-Ramos at the School of Public Administration, University of Southern California. To satisfy part of the course requirements, students prepared and presented extremely detailed analyses of significant books in the field. A number of us spent considerable time in preparing these detailed reviews. It occurred to me that other students of organizational behavior might benefit from an integrated collection of these reviews. With Guerreiro-Ramos's encouragement and support, I began this project. The project is now ended with publication of this volume.

I am indebted to the various book publishers as well as student reviewers for permitting publication of the reviews in this compendium. The reader will notice that each of the reviewers is individually credited with his contribution. In a sense, this volume represents a collective effort on the part of a number of Guerreiro-Ramos's students over the past two to three years. In another sense, through the quality of the reviews, it attests to Guerreiro-Ramos's continuous demands for academic rigor and excellence.

This volume was produced during a two-and-one-half-year doctoral educational program at the USC School of Public Administration. Success in such programs cannot be achieved without the support and encouragement of a number of people. In addition to Guerreiro-Ramos, I particularly want to express my appreciation to the following persons: Dr. Henry Reining, Dean, Von KleinSmidt Center; Dr. Emery Olson, Dean Emeritus, School of Public Administration; as well as my friend and advisor, Dr. John Gerletti, Professor, School of Public Administration. I also want to thank the other two members of my doctoral guidance and dissertation committees (in addition to Dr. Gerletti, Chairman), Dr. Robert Carter, Director for the Administration of Justice and the Delinquency Control Institute; and, Dr. Lyle Knowles, Assistant Professor, School of Public Administration. The assistance and support of the following members of the Delinquency Control Institute is greatly appreciated: Dan G. Pursuit, Associate Director; Ted Wilson and Ray Olsen, Program Officers; as well as Freddie DeVega, Sharon Ellison, Pat Smith, May Pedersen, and Carole Shebroe, staff members. Special thanks to my doctoral colleagues Gary B. Adams, Senior Program Officer at the DCI; Frank Adshead, and Mike Sparks. The typing services of Ruth Kaplan and much of the actual physical production of this volume by Bill Pittenger are greatly appreciated.

I am also indebted to the United States Air Force for making this educational opportunity available to me. The Air Force Institute of Technology (AFIT) at Wright-Patterson AFB in Ohio has provided such meaningful educational experiences to countless USAF personnel. Special thanks to my program monitor, Major James Austin, Civilian Institutions Division. I also want to express my appreciation to the USAF Office of Special Investigations (OSI); Brigadier General Joseph Cappucci, Director; and Colonel Heston Cole, Deputy Director for Operations, for initiating this educational effort. My special thanks to career-motivation specialists Major Elmer Holt and Technical Sergeant (how hopefully Lieutenant) Robert Smith.

Last, but first, educational programs of this nature are successful to the extent that one is encouraged and supported by his family. The support and patience of my wife, Pat, and children, Ryan and Brooke, are deeply appreciated. Degree candidates should be ever mindful that the names of family members should really also appear on any diploma received.

In February 1972 before returning to Washington, D.C., I sent a copy to each of the Air Force persons cited in the acknowledgements with a cover letter. I also gave a copy to every USC person mentioned. It was a major, time-consuming project, and I felt a tremendous relief to have finished it and to have contributed some sanity to the whole situation.

Chapter 12:
Back to Duty in Washington, D.C.:
The Good, The Bad, and The Ugly, Very Ugly
1972-1974

MY AFIT TOUR OF DUTY at USC was up in March 1972, after thirty months of full-time graduate studies in public administration. For the educational tour, I had incurred a seven-and-a-half-year military service obligation, so that would take me up to twenty years (1980) for minimum military service retirement. I approached the return to AFOSI with apprehension and trepidation. I knew I was supposed to return to Washington, D.C., in the capacity of Senior Instructor at the OSI School, later called the AFOSI Academy. The apprehension was that I would likely face questioning about my conduct in making the AFR 205-57 report of February 1971 and perhaps some questions about the strangers on the doorstep. I had no problems with the first issue but didn't want to go into the strangers issue, particularly since I had no way of corroborating what had gone on.

We had difficulty selling our house in the LA area through a realtor. He had the house for a ninety-day contract with few possible buys. We were getting very anxious to sell because we were definitely leaving the state. Pat and I talked it over and decided to sell the house ourselves. We bought sales flags and made up sales flyers as well as held open houses. We finally located a buyer and arranged financing through our lender. I finished up my business at USC in February, and in March, we drove back to D.C. towing our camper trailer. This time, as usual, we took a different route across the US.

I remember that sometime while we were selling the house, we were contacted and visited by a middle-aged woman. Both Pat and I talked with her in our living room. I don't recall the exact reason for the meeting; however, I felt suspicious about the woman and the purpose of the meeting. I didn't voice any apprehension to Pat at the time, but in thinking back on it all, it was very suspect. The conversation was off-center, and when we mentioned we were returning to D.C., she stated something to the effect that she had worked in D.C. for the government. With her eyes, she seemed to take an interest in my book collection at the nearby bookshelf. There were about three hundred books dealing with various aspects of intelligence. It was my professional library. I felt her comments were intended to get us to open up more in order to volunteer information, which we didn't. At the time, the woman seemed very sharp and skillful in the handling of herself and her remarks. It wasn't until years later upon reading Howard Hunt's book and also the news release of the Chicago aircraft accident killing Dorothy Hunt that we discovered the pictures of Mrs. Hunt in the book and newspapers seemed to be that of the woman who had visited us. It was also very strange, and all this was then and now a very strong hunch.

Towing our travel trailer, we went to Colorado Springs, Colorado, to visit a former OSI counterespionage colleague who was then a faculty member at the US Air Force Academy, his alma mater. I was interested in seeking an appointment to the Academy as an instructor. There my friend arranged for me to meet another major on the faculty with the PhD in public administration and also the chair of the Behavioral

Sciences Department. I met with the colonel and expressed my interest. We left it that I would pursue the assignment upon return to D.C. and would see if I could get a release from the OSI assignment to do so. I was very keen on getting the AF Academy assignment. It was a place where I could use my newly acquired education as well as get out of AFOSI and an ugly situation. I just wanted out! Again, I felt I had been betrayed and egregiously violated.

We arrived in the D.C. in mid-March, and I reported in by phone that we had arrived. Staying in a motel on Route 1 in south Alexandria, we started house-hunting and eventually found a very nice home in Collingwood Springs Estates, just behind Ft. Hunt High School. However, Pat and the family couldn't move in right away and had to stay at the motel.

When I reported in to AFOSI School at AFOSI Headquarters in the Forrestal Building on Independence Avenue in downtown D.C., I was informed that it was mandatory that I attend the USAF Academic Instructors School at Maxwell AFB, Alabama. I wasn't very keen on this or motivated to attend since I was "schooled out." I didn't think it would help that much; plus, I needed to get my family settled. Mr. Michael Ross, GS 16 USAF civilian employee and Commandant of the AFOSI School, told me that I would not be permitted to teach at the school without attending AIS. So in mid-May 1972, I left for Alabama with another officer who was to become an instructor. I found AIS to be a wonderful experience. The five-week hands-on school was taught by military and civilian professionals. It was not a graded exercise, and the students were encouraged to just dive in and learn. I took a special seminar in curriculum development and in the seminar met and teamed up with a Navy commander on a class project. The commander was on the staff of the DIA Defense Intelligence School. This contact proved to be useful later on in getting an assignment at Defense Intelligence School.

Back to AFOSI School: My apprehensions about being called in and questioned regarding my USC AFR 205-57 report were soon realized. Sometime in April 1972 within a week or two after my reporting in for duty, Mr. Ross told me that that I needed to talk with Lt Col. Glenn Cox (later Colonel, now deceased), but he didn't amplify on the purpose. I didn't pursue this right away, and in a couple days, Mr. Ross again instructed me to talk with Glenn. It wasn't stated then why I needed to talk with Glenn, whom I had previously known when we were both stationed at the AFOSI District Office in Los Angeles. We maintained a very cordial relationship. I met with Glenn in one of the offices in a very informal, conversational manner, no table between us. He went right to the USC AFR 205-57 matter, and I went over the details of it just as I had reported it back in February 1971. I immediately sensed from the elicitation orientation of his conversation and questions that he was fishing for something. It occurred to me then and later that he had been selected to question me because of our friendship and rapport, the interview being conducted in a non-threatening manner. I decided then and there not to go into any apprehensions I had had about the strangers because, for one, he didn't ask me any questions that directly related to the matter, and I had no independent verification of what had happened. I was protecting myself from harm, and Glenn was not offering anything to which I could respond. I immediately suspected that there was more going on here than presented on the face of it since he was not disclosing anything. Thinking back, I believe had Glenn been more straightforward with a statement like, "Jerry, something is strange going on here. This is what happened on our end," I would likely have disclosed to the extent that he disclosed. It didn't happen.

I felt then and many times later that the whole interview was carefully arranged by higher-ups who wanted to elicit my version of what had happened in California. Glenn's talk with me was clearly an elicitation interview and proof that unknown persons/higher-ups had concerns and/or had possibly had guilty knowledge of what had gone on. So when I detected an elicitation interview under these circumstances, I decided to say nothing. Again, I felt then as well as many years later that had Glenn leveled with me, I would have told him everything I knew. My assessment at the time was that the strangers had been in contact with AFOSI somehow either directly or indirectly through the CIA and/or FBI, and the AFOSI was likely not witting to the strangers' total agenda(s), other than that I was a person of interest or was suspect in some way. That, in and of itself, would have been very prejudicial to my situation, definitely not career enhancing. I felt at that time that AFOSI officials were trying to figure out what was going on and what was my connection and/or rationale with the strangers, assuming direct contact. At that point, I just didn't know. I had no further meetings with Glenn about this matter, and as we passed each other in the building, our greetings were cordial.

I was really feeling very perplexed about this situation and became more so when soon thereafter, Mr. Ross called me in to talk directly with me about the USC AFR 205-57 report. In his initial conversation with me, he said, "You shouldn't have done it." I told him that he wasn't there and that if I had to do it over again, I would do the same thing. He called me in another time a few days later, and we went over the same grounds, and he became aggressive and insulting. I said nothing further and didn't react to his insult. It was apparent that he was engaged in elicitation interviewing of me in the form of a hostile interrogation and that he wanted to incite me disclose more.

The Cox and Ross meetings caused me to believe that something more serious and grave had occurred and that I wanted nothing further to do with it. Too, Mr. Ross was in my OER rating chain, and I was very vulnerable to getting a bad OER as matters prejudicial to me were abounding. I was clearly in a no-win position. So I went off to AIS in Alabama very confused with feelings of being damaged and betrayed. I hadn't done anything wrong.

It was in mid- to late June 1972 at AIS break room when I read a short story in the local newspaper about the break-in of the Democratic National Committee Headquarters at the Watergate complex in Washington, D.C.

I followed the story further when I got back to Washington, D.C. I had a daily subscription to the *Washington Post* delivered to my home in Alexandria, Virginia, and read the daily, continuing developments in the DNC break-in case. Early on, there appeared photographs of Hunt and Liddy in the newspaper and explanations of their association with the White House. I didn't recognize Hunt from his photograph but believed that Liddy was the person who was one of the strangers who had appeared at my doorstep in summer 1971. I started to become very, very alarmed. The White House asserted that the DNC break-in that involved Hunt and Liddy was a "third-rate burglary." I wondered.

I became very discomforted by all this and also very unhappy with my assignment as an instructor at the AFOSI School. Mr. Ross supported me with a written letter of recommendation to the US Air Force Academy, but it didn't work. I called the AFA Department Head lieutenant colonel, and he stated he had been informed that I no longer wanted the assignment. I had never voiced such a position and felt then that someone in the hierarchy was purposely defeating my plans and desires. I thought that perhaps that there was something going on in the background on me that had created a view and position that my assignment at the AFA would be prejudicial to the Air Force and service academy.

I also visited the Federal Executives Institute in Charlottesville, Virginia, for a faculty position. FEI is a governmental school for senior civilian employees of the federal government. I arranged a visit and evaluation for a position with Dr. Chester Newland, FEI Executive Director, who had been a former USC SPA professor of mine in public-personnel administration in the doctoral program. Chet arranged for me to visit one of the FEI's Executive Learning Teams. The team consisted of about ten senior execs, one of whom was said to be chief of the technical services division of the CIA, and the other was Stuart Knight, Director of the Secret Service. I mentioned in the seminar that one of my goals was to "humanize intelligence agencies." This grabbed Knight's attention; however, we didn't have enough time to explore the topic further. Chet and I left it that I would find out how I could get myself reassigned from AFOSI when I got back, and Chet would check on it from his end. Sometime after the FEI visit, Mr. Ross told me he had heard I was disenchanted with my AFOSI assignment. I think that report came from Knight as about a year later he appeared as the featured guest speaker at a graduating class of AFOSI Basic School. We met in a reception line at the school and recognized each other. Sometime after that, I followed up with Chet on the FEI assignment, and he told me he had heard that I no longer wanted the FEI assignment, so it was off. That wasn't the case, so it appeared that I was again being defeated.

I made a third attempt to get myself transferred out of AFOSI and into something more career-rewarding. While at AIS, I met another officer who was a new faculty member at Air Force Command and Staff College there at Maxwell AFB. I needed to complete this mid-level officers professional educational school to make myself promotable and thought I could do double duty by being on staff and also completing the program. The officer introduced me to department head, but again I had no success.

Upon return to AFOSI in March 1972, I had signed up for the correspondence school of the Industrial College of the Armed Forces (ICAF). As I was out of military channels attending USC, I needed to find ways to enhance my promotability, and this could be achieved through a senior professional military education experience. I commenced studies in late summer 1972 but began to become demotivated as the Watergate disclosures and hearings came out. I further began to believe that my Air Force career was in jeopardy and that the taking and completion of the ICAF course was not going to mean anything. I was later withdrawn from the correspondence course by ICAF for non-performance.

When I came back to AFOSI School, I was assigned to be primary instructor in these areas: interviews, interrogations, and counterintelligence collections. Like other instructors, I was assigned to a seminar section of between eight and ten agent trainees in the AFOSI Basic School in a ten-week training program. I dressed up my seminar room with replicas of the US Constitution and US Declaration of Independence and tacked them on the wall panels. I considered it a form of silent protest. At the school, I introduced some content enhancements in my teaching areas. I was also assigned as the Course Monitor of the four-week-long Advanced Counterintelligence Course and went through two or three iterations of it while at the school. There I helped the Counterintelligence Division staff put on their instruction, so I was essentially a coordinator.

As I got into 1972 and into 1973, I became much more dissatisfied with my plight at the school. When I complained to Mr. Ross that I was not placed in the position of Senior Instructor, he replied that it was because I had not completed the doctorate, even though another instructor was filling the position without the degree. So it was a specious position and very discouraging. Added to that was that Watergate was looming and very much on my mind.

By January 1973, I wanted out of AFOSI and was very frustrated with the whole situation. One day I noticed that my annual OER was laying on Mr. Ross's secretary's desk, and it was a "9-4" numerical rating, the highest possible. I thought, erroneously, that it was firm, but it had not been processed through the system. At that time, I wrote a letter of resignation from AFOSI, in very tactful terms, and sent it directly to Brig General William Temple, AFOSI Director, in the building.

Here is the text of my letter:

29 January 1973
To: CC (Brig Gen Temple)

Sir,

I request release from AFOSI duties. I am making this request for the following reasons:

Since returning to AFOSI from AFIT-sponsored doctoral studies in March 1972, I have been serving as and rated in the position of "Instructor" at the OSI School. However, the position for which the doctoral slot was justified to the AFERB was "Senior Instructor," a position with different and greater responsibilities. No one is currently filing this position.

More importantly, neither my utilization nor the "Senior Instructor" position adhere to the position justification and utilization criteria set forth in Paragraph 5-4 AFM 36-19, a copy of which is attached.

On the basis of the above, I believe that I have been greatly underutilized. No effort is being made to correct the situation. This has resulted in an increasingly demotivating and career de-enhancing condition. It is a situation which I can no longer accept, professionally or personally. I therefore request, with your approval, release from AFOSI. I would appreciate your extending me sufficient time to locate a more suitable position elsewhere in the USAF or DOD. This matter in no way detracts from my overall, longtime affinity for AFOSI.

Respectfully,
Percy G. Rogers
Major, USAF
Instructor

Mr. Ross was very upset when he found out about it and wanted me to retract the letter. I refused. Shortly thereafter, I reported in to General Temple at his office and went over the grounds for my request to resign from AFOSI. He told me that he would not approve such an action until I had completed the doctorate. He told me that once I had completed the program, he would release me. I thought it was unusual when I talked with General Temple that he was very nervous and that his hands and fingers were trembling at the outset of the meeting. I have often wondered what he thought I was going to tell him.

I was devastated by his position and even more so when I learned that the "9-4" OER was changed by my raters at an "8-3," which was very non-competitive. Especially damaging was Mr. Ross's written comments as the endorsing officer:

"I concur. Major Rogers is an ambitious, aggressive officer who seeks to apply the knowledge gained in the academic world toward bettering the Air Force. However, he has had difficulty in readjusting to the disciplines of a military organization. When this adjustment is achieved, he could become an absolutely superior officer with unlimited value to the United States Air Force. (7 Feb 1973)

This was the ultimate "kiss of death" OER because it implied I was something less than full military, and it would come back to haunt me the rest of my military career. I believed the "8-3" OER was retaliation for surfacing my plight. I made a complaint on this to Colonel Hector DeLeo, Deputy Director AFOSI, and he supposedly conducted an investigation which he later told me was inconclusive; he believed both parties. However, it seemed he had failed to interview Mr. Ross's secretary, Annie, who had typed the "9-4" as well as "8-3" OERs. Col DeLeo was the second endorser, and his comments were weak. General Temple made no endorsements on this OER or on any others while I was there. I considered Col DeLeo's investigation a faux investigation and thought that he was just covering it up. So the OER stuck, and I was stuck. A while later, I contacted a lieutenant colonel in the Headquarters of the Staff Judge Advocate who was also in the Forrestal Building. I knew him previously as a JAG at Nellis AFB in Nevada. He concluded that I had no legal grounds to go on. I asked him to keep the contact confidential; however, it seemed that within days, word got out that "Rogers has seen a lawyer." It later occurred to me that the "9-4" OER I had seen was not signed, so it was not final or official. I was then very concerned that the non-competitive "8-3" OER would cause my non-promotion to permanent grade of major, which would force my separation from the Air Force prior to completion of the minimum twenty years of active duty service. I was very relieved later on when I did get promoted to permanent major. The following two annual OERs endorsed by Mr. Ross were competitive at "9-4" and were strongly endorsed by two other front office colonels, whom I knew. He also funded a very nice going-away party for Pat and me and other instructors with significant others at the Ft. McNair Officers Club. However, that "kiss of death" EOR did contribute to my failure to be promoted to lieutenant colonel the first time around in 1976. At that point in time, the probabilities in being promoted after an initial passover were nil. I phoned Mr. Ross in 1976 to request that he assist me by withdrawing the OER from my promotion file, and he adamantly refused. That further sealed my fate.

During that period of time, my attitude was admittedly very poor, and I just wanted out. Mr. Ross once commented to me that I seemed to be destroying myself. He had a good point! I think I was suffering some sort of stress syndrome, like post-traumatic stress syndrome, from all that had gone on before. The acute hypertension episode mentioned below must have been associated with this.

About that time, two things came up that changed my direction. It certainly seemed like a lifeline was thrown to me. The first was that I received a phone call from Dr. Peter Lejins, Director/Dean of the School of Criminology at the University of Maryland with an offer to teach part-time in the criminology program. I accepted happily. Dr. John at USC had previously advised me that if I ever wanted to teach when I got out of the service, I should teach part-time during my time in the military. In this way, I could keep myself fresh and develop an academic track record. Thereafter, I taught various undergraduate and graduate criminal justice classes, both on and off campus from 1973 through 1977. One of my 1973 classes was the undergraduate "Introduction to Law Enforcement," with about fifty students. Early on, I told the students that they could earn extra credit by bringing in someone who occupied a significant position in the criminal justice system to act as a guest speaker. Soon thereafter, one of the students, Charles, mentioned that his father was a judge and that his appearance might be possible. I told him to pursue it. One evening I met Charles and his father at their car, and we walked to the classroom. I learned then that young Charles was Charles Richey, Jr., and that his father was Charles Richey, Sr., a judge on the US District Court in Washington, D.C. It didn't really register with me then that Judge Richey had been working Watergate cases and was a contemporary of Judges John Sirica and Gerhard Gissell. As we walked to the building, Charles, Jr. was behind us and out of earshot while Judge Richey was aided by a cane. Totally out of the blue, Judge Richey told me that if I ever needed any legal assistance, I could get it from a non-profit legal center in Washington, D.C. He mentioned the name of the center, but I didn't recall it because I was so shocked at this statement. I was completely taken aback by Judge Richey's advice because I thought I was an unknown and a nobody. Apparently, he knew me and knew that I could use legal advice and had no funds to defray such. I don't recall making any response as I was so taken back by Judge Richey's statement.

Judge Richey delivered a terrific extemporaneous speech, and he was well received by the students. I was so very appreciative of his efforts. At the end of his talk, he reminded me to award the extra credit to young Charles as he expected him to get an "A" in the class. Charles was an excellent student; however, I assured the judge that Charles would do well in the class. Actually, Charles, Jr. did exceptionally well in the class and never really needed the extra credit that his father had earned for him. I believe that Charles, Jr. later became a lawyer.

The second thing that came up to change my direction was a phone call in April 1973 from fellow doctoral student Gary Adams to the effect that Dr. John wanted us to finish up our doctorates and graduate in June. I was very overdue on the project, and so his call came at a good time. I had already done components of the dissertation: literature review, theory and research questions, bibliography, and had collected all of the raw data through respondent surveys in twenty-two California cities. I put completion of the dissertation on the top of my priority list.

I worked diligently over the next two months both at home and at work, when permitted. I completed the entire project by about June first and coordinated it with my dissertation committee. There were no issues with it.

I arranged for air travel by our family for my graduation. I still needed to defend the dissertation before the three members of my doctoral committee. With permission, I photocopied seventy-five copies of my dissertation, had them bound, and shipped them to LA. I also had the AFOSI Graphics shop make color 35mm slides of my research model and related content. I had heard that the good way to get through the one-hour defense was to take up all the time possible to cut down on questions and to get the committee members arguing amongst themselves and take the heat off me. The dissertation defense went off well. By design, it was a multimedia tour de force. I had a 35mm slideshow, prepared flip charts, and overheads on a projector. I also had a one-page agenda handout and copies of the dissertation at hand, ready to mail out to all city respondents. I also arranged the seating for the committee members. In organizational behavior lingo, it's called "managing the situation." One of my committee members, Dr. Bob Carter, was also a colonel in the California Army reserves. Instantly he recognized what was going on saying, "Military briefing, huh?!" He nailed me! What could I say? Each of the committee members asked a pithy question, and it was over. The paperwork was signed, and, I gave a copy of my dissertation to each of the SPA faculty and my fellow doctoral colleagues in addition to the city respondents.

On graduation morning, upon invitation, I was inducted into the all-university honor society of Phi Kappa Phi at a university auditorium. It was a lovely moment for me because I was indeed graduating with a DPA, finishing with a straight 4.0 GPA, and graduating with honors. I felt so very fortunate and relieved.

The all-university graduation was held outdoors at the plaza in front of Doheny Library. An SPA-only graduation ceremony was held later that afternoon in a school auditorium.

Later that day, we took photographs of our family and Gary's. That evening, Pat and I were accompanied by Sandy and her husband to some country-western 'tonk and had a tremendous hair-letting-down evening. The pressure was off. Our son Erik was conceived that night; he was born April 2, 1974. So Erik was our graduation surprise and present.

We returned to Washington, D.C., soon after graduation. Upon returning to D.C., I made an appointment with General Temple to arrange for my departure from the organization. He gave me permission to go job shopping. I began doing so but had no immediate success.

In June 1973, I was sitting alone in my AFOSI School seminar room watching the Senate Watergate Committee hearings. Howard Hunt was testifying on television. At a point in time, Mr. Ross opened the door, saw what was going on, and said to me "Well, I guess that's the end of OSI!" I immediately replied, "Well, we hope not!" He closed the door. There were no further exchanges or encounters that day. Looking back, we both disclosed to each other a significant amount of information in that brief exchange. He acknowledged some complicity by AFOSI with the Plumbers that would cause grave damage to the organization. I acknowledged a degree of knowledge of Hunt's activities with respect to me and the organization. It was a defining moment in my connecting the dots between the Plumbers, AFOSI, and me as well as the severity of matters. During that time, I also caught televised testimony by John Ehrlichman, Bob Haldeman, and John Dean. It was all disgusting stuff.

Sometime during late 1973 or 1974, Mr. Ross requested that I furnish him a copy of my doctoral dissertation and *Compendium of Analytical Book Reviews*. He didn't explain why he wanted them, and he seemed pleased at the time to receive them. I figured he had turned them over to unknown entities who could or should see them.

With regards to Watergate, I followed developments closely in the newspaper and on television. I followed White House statements, including those by President Nixon. I read much of the news developments cited here. I was in total agony over it.

I felt that at any time, my name might surface and that I might be called in for questioning by some authority or agency. I was drinking, heavily on some evenings, and feeling totally trapped with no way out. Over time, I came to the conclusion that if my name came out or I was exposed and/or if I were ever called in, I would make a full and complete statement as to my knowledge, and I would immediately resign my commission from the Air Force. The rule was that an officer does not embarrass the Air Force, whether through fault of his own or not. I would immediately go to General Temple or my commanding officer and request immediate separation from military service. So that was my mindset. On any given day, I thought that that day would be my last day. But then I had to perform to the best of my ability on that day or any given day. It was a challenge. I believe higher-ups may have surmised this. I recall seeing a newspaper article where it was noted that Watergate involved an extortion attempt and also that there was a concern about mass resignations. That really weighed on my mind.

In 1973, I took a routine, periodic physical examination. The doctor told me I had excessive high blood pressure and referred me to an internist at Malcolm Grow USAF Hospital at Andrews AFB in Maryland. I met with Dr. Popper, the internist, and he discovered that I had life-threatening, stroke-range hypertension. He yelled at me, "Do you want to die?! Do you know that this is a silent killer?!" He gave me a sedative shot immediately and prescribed medication for the condition. Thereafter, I reported in twice a day for blood-pressure readings at the

Army dispensary in the Forrestal Building. I knew what was causing the problem but didn't disclose it to anyone, including Dr. Popper. I believe that AFOSI officials knew of my medical condition. My medical appointments were no secret, and my military medical records were on file for authorities to examine.

Sometime in 1973 or 1974, before I left AFOSI, I saw a television news program where Liddy was driving a vehicle while being interviewed. I made a mental note of the make, model, and color of the vehicle and can still describe it today. Sometime later, Pat and I left our Alexandria home with another couple. It was evening and still light, and we were on our way to Ft. Meyers Officers Club in Arlington for dinner. While I was driving away from the house, I spotted this same vehicle parked near the front of my house at the curb in the direction opposite of traffic. I didn't spot the driver, but I immediately thought it might be Liddy. I started to become crazy with concern, knowing Liddy's reputation for violence and knowing that my children were still in the house. I thought of turning around to investigate and/or confront the driver, but I knew this might expose matters right then and there. I was very upset but didn't tell Pat or our friends.

Once seated for dinner at Ft. Meyers, I noticed two couples seated at a nearby table, one of whom was the FBI Headquarters Liaison Officer to AFOSI Headquarters. He was seated with another man who, from his looks, appeared to be another senior FBI agent. They appeared to be with their wives. These circumstances kept building the tensions inside me, and I became intoxicated. I needed to go to the men's room and passed by the table of the two FBI agents. While standing at the urinal, I felt a sudden and severe push in the middle of my back that pushed me further into the urinal. I turned to my left and noticed SA Friendly and his buddy standing right there looking at me intently. I had the presence of mind to avoid confrontation, finished my business, left the restroom immediately, and went back to my table. In retrospect, I see that what the two wanted was an altercation, which would have been totally ruinous to me on all accounts. It was a physical assault (assault and battery) that could have wound up even worse. I was still intoxicated when we left the club, and someone else drove us all home.

When I awoke the next morning, I was disgusted and alarmed at myself for my lack of control and shocked by how personally and professional dangerous the whole previous evening had been.

During the next workweek, Mr. Ross told me that I had been seen drunk at the Ft. Meyers Officers Club. I thought I detected mirth in his voice. "You screwed up, Rogers." Indeed, I had lost control but not enough control to lose it all. I didn't tell him the background of my behavior. I was sure the FBI Liaison Officer had generously spread the word around on me at the AFOSI front office since it was laughable and discrediting. I couldn't figure out why the FBI had targeted me. I was conflicted and alarmed. Perhaps it was some form of retaliation. It occurred to me later on that perhaps the FBI was somehow complicit with the Plumbers on me and that their actions were a revenge move. I have been left to wonder. Sometime after this incident, the FBI Liaison Officer (now deceased) was replaced by a new FBI Headquarters Liaison Officer.

In 1973, further news revelations seemed to tie me in to Watergate:

1. Special Prosecutor's stated that there was a sensitive **national security** matter that he would not go into nor be blinded by. He had agreed with the President on this.

2. Senators Irwin and Baker of the Senate Watergate Committee publicly stated that here was a sensitive **national security** matter related to Watergate that should not/would not be disclosed.

3. There was a newspaper article in the *Washington Star News* wherein Senator Baker asserted he had discovered "the missing link" of Watergate and had been unsuccessful in convincing President Nixon to disclose it. Interestingly, a record of this conversation could not be located in the Nixon tapes.

4. President Nixon made various public statements related to the above.

I left for a new assignment as an instructor at the Defense Intelligence Agency's Defense Intelligence School. I was absolutely delighted with the assignment and excited to make a fresh start elsewhere.

Chapter 13:
Defense Intelligence School, Washington, D.C., Assignment: 1974-1977

GOING BACK TO 1972, I had met a couple military faculty members of the Defense Intelligence School (DIS) while attending Academic Instructors School at Maxwell AFB, near Montgomery, Alabama. I learned that DIS was the joint-service professional intelligence school of the Defense Intelligence Agency. The school was physically located in decrepit wooden WWII buildings at Annapolis Naval Annex, adjacent to Bolling AFB in Washington, D.C. It was on the south side of the Anacostia River right across from the Washington Naval Yard and dock for the *Sequoia*, the Presidential yacht. I believe that the DIS school complex had been a Navy photographic center in its earlier life.

I had previously obtained Brigadier General Temple's permission to resign from AFOSI to seek another military utilization having completed the AFIT sponsored doctorate in public administration. Through the DIS faculty contacts, I learned that there was a position opening up for a management instructor as a Navy commander, holding a PhD in management, was being reassigned. I interviewed for the job and was accepted. I was thoroughly delighted at this outcome because I could now put into practice what I had learned at USC in the field of organizational behavior and organization theory. Instruction in this case would be embedded into the larger field of strategic intelligence to military and civilian professionals of the military branches as well as intelligence agencies. I would be a management instructor and would be primarily responsible for the annual summer, eight-week-long Defense Intelligence Management Course (DIMC). I really got into the course and its content, coming up with ways to modify it for beneficial effect. I also learned that I could be involved in three other courses: the Senior Intelligence Course (NSIC) (twelve weeks); the Postgraduate Intelligence Course (PGIC) (thirty-eight weeks); and the Civilian Intelligence Analyst Course (CIAC) (six weeks). I learned that the DIS had been established years earlier because there was a great need for intelligence professionals to become aware of how to coordinate and harmonize functional specialties. Previous crises had established the need for such. The DIS had an all-star board of trustees, including Lyman Kirkpatrick of CIA fame and Edwin Teller, father of the H-bomb. For most of my assignment, the Commandant of the School was Navy Captain Robert W. Bates, a Navy intelligence professional with vast experience. So, DIS was pretty much a Navy show; however, there were administration and faculty representing the four military branches. Interestingly, as an Air Force officer, I had a "skipper."

Everyone at DIS carried advanced security clearances, called SI (Special Intelligence, meaning signals intelligence) and TK (Talent Keyhole, meaning photographic intelligence). I needed to complete the paperwork for the clearance and filled out an updated DD Form 398, Statement of Personal History (SPH). I turned the form with request into DIA's Security Office at the Pentagon. Soon after, I was called to the DIA Security Office for routine questioning on my SPH. The security officer (whom I later determined with an AFOSI Special Agent on assignment to DIA) went over the form with me point by point, line by line. We got to item twenty, about "any other matters affecting suitability." I was dreading that item because I had answered it as N/A (or nothing). However, the form warns the applicant that all facts and statements are signed to under penalty of perjury with fines and/or imprisonment for falsification. So he got to that point, and I responded that yes, there was an issue. I then told him that I had previously made an AFR 205-57 report under unique and unusual circumstances. I went into no further details and suggested to the interviewer that AFOSI be contacted for further details. I was put into a very difficult position and had decided if I was to be re-interviewed, I would tell everything I knew. I also knew that that would be the end of my military career. The timing was also bad because of the US Congressional impeachment hearings. I felt strangely at peace when I told the DIA interviewers this, knowing that should it be pursued, I would be history. Also, I was not going to lie on anything or for anybody, including myself. I went back to duty at DIS.

Several days later, I received a phone call at my Alexandria, Virginia, home from a young Air Force captain, "Barry," known to be working in the AFOSI Headquarters front office. He informed me that AFOSI had no record of my AFOSI 205-57 report, so there was nothing in my record. I was surprised at this statement and told him my sole motivation was to tell the truth because I did not want to commit perjury. He again told me that there was nothing there. I felt relief at this strange course of events and that AFOSI was trying to save itself from destruction at this critical time. So, I felt, the system lied. Maybe they were trying to save me. I didn't know.

I resumed duty at DIS and was soon informed that I should go to the DIA Security Officer to clear in for my security badge(s). I was to go only in the company of a fellow faculty member, a Navy lieutenant commander. With him at my side, I attended the security briefings on the SI and TK clearance accesses and then got my DIA badges. We returned after that to DIS.

In the coming weeks, I was called in for discussion with the immediate supervisor and Air Force (Officer Effectiveness Report) OER rater, an Army Military Intelligence lieutenant colonel, and informed that I was "not showing proper respect." I was confused about this statement, and he didn't clarify it directly. He did inform me that earlier in his assignments, he had been stationed in Iran and that he also had current friends at the Iranian Embassy in D.C. So it was apparent from that that AFOSI had communicated certain information related to my prior AFOSI 205-57 report, yet it was only partial information and not the whole story. The information and the officer's estimation of it resulted in prejudicial action with respect to my next OER where I was not rated competitively—it was not a rating that made me competitive for promotion to lieutenant colonel. That rating was marked up on certain blocks by my endorsing officer, the next rater in the chain of command, but it didn't override the basic report. There is no way that I wanted to surface my Watergate knowledge to him as I wanted to stay in service and at that assignment. I was taking a major hit. As time went on, that officer and I developed a cordial working relationship, and later on, he wrote me a special favorable evaluation letter to get me promoted. That didn't work either.

In 1978, Air Force Colonel Onorio Aquaviva became the new Chief of the Career Intelligence Division and my indirect supervisor. Sometime later, he called me in for a chat. He told me that he had checked out my Air Force personnel file, and there was absolutely no record of any derogatory information or special holds on me. He intimated that he had also visited with General David Jones, Chief of Staff of the Air Force. I didn't know how to take that, but I greatly appreciated his efforts and concern. At that time, he did a critical comparative of the career strengths and weaknesses of another Air Force major in the organization. He lauded my officer presence ("Well, just look at you!") and writing skills but noted my intelligence-officer skills were weaker than those of the other officer. He told me he would support a promotable OER on the next occasion. I thought such would be problematic since I had not completed mid-career professional military education. I had enrolled in Air Force Command and Staff by correspondence and was making progress on it; however, my timing was late. Then, in 1976, I received the first of many passovers for the temporary grade of lieutenant colonel.

When I received the first passover, I phoned Mr. Ross to see if he would rescind the "difficulties adjusting to the disciplines of military organization" OER of 1973. He refused outright. I knew that the possibilities of being promoted on the second time were slim to none, even with a bad OER being tossed out. The percentages were against me. With all this, I stopped taking the AFCS correspondence course, worked on my DIS instruction, and continued teaching off campus at the University of Maryland. At that point in time, I realized that I would never be promoted and needed to start positioning myself for a post-Air Force career upon completion of my minimum twenty years in 1980. When Colonel Aquaviva called me in, I really appreciated his care and concern, but I thought to myself, "Thanks, Colonel, but there is NO WAY I'll going any further with this Air Force career. It's over!" Even with this plight, I committed to doing the best job I could. The OERs received in 1976 and 1977 at DIS were not sufficient to override the damage already done.

Going back a little, I really began duties at DIS in July 1974. We started the duty day at seven thirty a.m. and were off at four thirty p.m. In the mornings and evenings, I would read the home-delivered *Washington Post* and transcribed contents of the Watergate tapes. It was sickening, personally sickening! I watched the impeachment hearings in total agony for everyone involved. I came to believe my own days in the Air Force were numbered; it was a day-to-day operation. I was despondent and depressed over it all, and I felt that this did affect my overall duty performance at DIS. My driving route to DIS took me across the GW Bridge, through Bolling AFB as well as Anacostia Naval Annex. The latter part of the roadway paralleled the Anacostia River, and as I looked over to the Naval Yard, I would see the *Sequoia* in the river with two or three Secret Service boats ringing it. On a couple occasions, I could see a hunched over figure at the rear of the boat, and I took this to be President Nixon. I read somewhere that he did in fact seek solace at the *Sequoia* during those early days in August 1974. So I had a firsthand view of a broken man in a broken presidency. It was very sad and painful to look at.

All of us at DIS followed the impeachment hearings closely. On the day President Nixon resigned office on August 8, 1974, we watched it on the school televisions. We saw President Nixon depart from the White House in the *Marine 1* helicopter. Soon thereafter, an Air Force Captain, Jim, who had recently transferred to the Intelligence Community Staff at CIA Headquarters, came to DIS and visited. He had just come from the Executive Office Building at the White House and had seen the events on TV as well as the President's departure from the White House lawn. He gave a firsthand account of what he had seen.

Later that afternoon, a military faculty colleague came up to me and said, out of the blue, "Hey, Jer! Did you hear that if Nixon hadn't have resigned, there would have been a military coup?" My instant reply was "No! And it sounds like a damn stupid idea to me!" My colleague's comment caught me completely off-guard, through I took his comment with some credence since I thought him pretty well networked into the Pentagon. In another way and in afterthought, his comment didn't surprise me as I had been wondering the same thing during those final days, but I never verbalized it to anyone before, during, or afterwards. So in my subsequent Watergate research, I found some references along these lines. These are included earlier.

Rumors are rumors, and they often have a ring of truth to them. It is a horrific thought that we might have experienced a change in government that violated our great heritage of democracy over all the years. So I have questioned to what extent President Nixon resigned based on real or imagined threats to a non-democratic change in government. It's a chilling thought but one which I don't believe justifies any attention today. It would just be an attention-diverting witch-hunt with no conclusion, disruptive and damaging to the nation.

Other Interesting Happenings:

All throughout my DIS assignment, I kept no exact chronology of events, but here are some pertinent recollections in probable order of occurrence.

- In about 1975/6 the CIA Deputy Director for Plans (Clandestine Operations) was a guest speaker at the DIS PGIC before about 120 mid-grade students. I did not attend the presentation; however, sometime later that day a student officer came to me and said: "Do you know that that guy knows you?" I replied no and asked what happened and he told me that a student had asked a question about ethical conduct of intelligence personnel and the DDO replied to the effect: "The guy who knows about that is your own Major Rogers: check with him" What a surprise that comment was to everyone including me.

- In 1978, Mr. William Colby, CIA Director, was guest speaker at DIS to faculty and students. I was sitting in the front rows in uniform and had never met the man before. I was just part of the masses in the room. Mr. Colby gave an interesting talk and then, right in the midst and totally out of context of his remarks, looked right down on me and said directly, "The CIA apologizes." I was taken aback by this comment but did get the message. I don't believe anyone else in the room caught it, but I did.

• Sometime in 1978 or 1979, I attended a special one-day-only CIA briefing at the CIA Headquarters Building. The speakers were all senior CIA officials such as Deputy Directors. The legendary David Phillips gave a captivating talk; the guy was charismatic and had a silver tongue. One of the other speakers was the same DDO who talked about CIA clandestine services in general terms and was the same person who mentioned me to the DIS student earlier. This briefing was for DIA personnel only, both military and civilian, with about twenty-five of us attending. I was wearing my Class-A blue uniform. Totally out of the blue, the DDO said "OXCART" and then characterized AFOSI personnel approaching their intelligence operations in a convoluted manner (or words to that effect). No one followed up with any questions or comments on these statements, and they were said totally out of context of the rest of his presentation. He was looking directly at me when he said it, and I definitely got the message for whatever unknown reason he had. I'm sure that the term OXCART went right over everyone's head because it was still a classified codename and would have had no meaning to others in the room. The so-called AFOSI convolutions sort of rang true if I thought back to Col Leo F. Olson's characterization of counterespionage operations as being a succession of windows and doors opening and closing.

- By 1979, I had revamped and revised the six-week-long Defense Intelligence Management Course (DIMC) four times, such that it had well-honed sequential instruction that involved both process and content. We had adopted the Learning Team concept from the Federal Executive Institute Executive Learning Team. With my faculty colleagues, I wrote up the program and submitted it to the Washington, D.C., Training Officers Conference for an award of excellence.

We were successful in getting the award in competition with all other training entities in the D.C. area and Captain Bates, the DIS Commandant, went to the luncheon awards ceremony to receive it. None of us in DIS management instruction could attend because we were all attending a seminar on management instruction at the FBI Academy at Quantico, Virginia. Over my three years at DIS, I engaged in a lot of networking with staff at various agencies and local academia. I came up with ideas for a management trainers conference consisting of agencies under the umbrella of the National Foreign Intelligence Board. Those agencies included the FBI, CIA, DIA, NSA, and State Department Security. I organized a program wherein representatives of each agency gave a rundown on their training programs. I was really gratified by the results as were the other participants. This was a first as it had never been done before. There were pockets of excellence in each of the agencies. (I was very impressed with the FBI's description of the Assessment Center operation for identification and selection of first-line supervisors.) The event started out with a wine-and-cheese social on the Thursday night followed by a full day of presentations the next day. I had hoped that the conference might be institutionalized in the following years. I found it strange that the FBI veteran counterespionage agent of Colonel Able Soviet-spy fame attended the whole conference. This was the same guy to whom Colonel Olson had introduced me in 1978 or 1979. He was based at FBI Headquarters and had no management training duties, so I thought, "Why is this guy here? What is he doing here?" I never got an answer on that, and he never opened his mouth at the conference. I do recall that I made the statement toward the end of the conference to a group that I thought that intelligence work could be emotionally and mentally hazardous to the people who do it. A younger CIA officer totally refuted by assessment. I said my piece, and he said his.

- In 1976 and 1977, I participated in the following professional conferences:

  - o Speaker, "Organization Development: A Proposal for Improving the Organizational Effectiveness of the National Intelligence Community," Annual Conference, National Military Intelligence Association, Ft. Meade, Maryland (June 1977).

  - o Convener, "Organization Development Programs in the Armed Forces," Annual Conference, American Society for Public Administration, Atlanta, Georgia (April 1977).

  - o Panelist, "Professional Conscience: A New Synonym for Morality," Annual Conference, National Capital Area Chapter of the American Society for Public Administration, Washington, D.C. (1976)

- The DIS instituted a master's degree in strategic intelligence (MSSI), and it was overlaid on other courses. The MSSI was initiated by the DIS Academic Board/Trustees and was also fully accredited academically. There were about thirty students in the initial classes, including an FBI agent as a regular student. I taught two different classes: "Strategic Intelligence Management Systems" and "Intelligence Futures Research and Creative Analysis." The later course consisted of many futures research (futuristics) experts from the D.C. area as guest lecturers in a seminar setting. The course was mind-bending, one of the highlights of my DIS experience. The students liked the course, too, because there is a philosophical and operational relationship between futures research and strategic intelligence, especially intelligence estimates.

• The closest I got to being bodily harmed at DIS was when I pulled evening duty (security) officer. This meant checking to make sure the building's safes were locked and that no classified information was left out. I was sitting in one of the offices and noticed a mama raccoon walking down the hall with her babies. They were on a food mission, knocking over the waste baskets for lunch leftovers. She spotted me at the same time I spotted her. I froze, and she went on about her business. After a decent interval of time, I got the heck out of there. I filed a raccoon report the next day. I think the raccoons came from under the building's raised foundation and/or from the reeds lining the Anacostia River. That was my story of DIS hazardous duty.

• The DIS was an all-service affair and my first joint-service assignment. I gained an appreciation for the traditions of the other military services.

- A faculty Navy commander was retiring, and he was accorded a fitting US Naval ceremony. He was awarded a military decoration in the auditorium by Captain Bates with his wife and troops attending. Then, per tradition, he was "piped over the side." All DIS faculty and staff lined the passageways and outside walkways leading from the auditorium to the waiting car. (We assembled on deck.) All of us stood at attention, equally spaced out along the route. Then a bosun whistle was sounded, and Marsh and his wife were "piped over the side" walking the route. As an Air Force guy, I felt honored to be part of a proud Navy tradition.

- Marines attended DIS, and we had a Marine major on staff. The annual Marine Corps birthday is a very big deal for the USMC, and it happens every November tenth. I witnessed two such celebrations at DIS. Marines in full dress would slowly carry at the four corners a large, beautifully decorated sheet cake with numerous candles lighted on it down the hallway and into the auditorium. There the youngest and oldest Marines present would be recognized, and a Marine would give a short talk about the founding of the Marine Corps, which was at Tun Tavern in Philadelphia on November 10, 1775. This was followed by (sugary) cake eating along with a shot of rum (yuck!). I always wondered what that whole scene was like at Tun Tavern and wished I could have gone back in time to be there. Can you believe the tavern owner provided free beer in an effort to recruit two battalions of Marines? Beer? Marines? With Marine family friends and spouses, Pat and I went to the USMC's two-hundredth anniversary formal at a Washington, D.C., hotel, held on November 10, 1975. The major speaker was Marine Corps Commandant General "Big Lou" Wilson, who began his military career at Guadalcanal in WWII. It was an impressive ceremony.

- PGIC students held a roast of DIS faculty, myself included, in the auditorium, and no one was spared, including Captain Bates. It was all so brutally honest and insightful as well as very funny. (One of us faculty was called "half-tin soldier, half-Doberman pincher.") Nothing escaped the students' scornful attention, and as a military tradition it helped to round off any hard edges in military organizations; you might call it group therapy through outrageous humor. Even today, I still remember some of the other comments.

- I shared an office with Pat, a woman Air Force captain and fellow faculty member whose subject matter area was "the national intelligence community." One day, I received a phone call from CIA Director's secretary for Pat for a guest appearance at DIS by Mr. Colby. Pat wasn't there, but I told the secretary, "She's around here somewhere because I see her shoes over there." I caught myself too late, and the secretary and I had hearty laughs, she telling me I had made her day. So the inference was that Pat was walking around the place in stocking feet. How was I to know she had two sets of shoes? Pat was furious at me when I told her what had happened. I had put her shoes in my mouth.

Just before my PCS departure from DIS in June 1977, I was presented the Joint Service Commendation Medal by Captain Bates in the auditorium. Other persons received awards, and other troops were in attendance.

Chapter 14:
The World Turn'd Upside Down

If buttercups buzz'd after the bee,
If boats were on land, churches on sea,
If ponies rode men, and if grass ate the cows,
And cats should be chased into holes by the mouse,
If the mamas sold their babies
To the gypsies for half a crown;
If summer were spring and the other way round,
Then all the world would be upside down.*

*Legend has it that the British played the march, "The World Turn'd Upside Down," taken from a English nursery rhyme, when Cornwallis surrendered his forces to General Washington and the Americans at their defeat at Yorktown, Virginia, on October 19, 1781. This was the last battle of the American Revolutionary War. A mural painting by John Trumbull called Yorktown Surrender is displayed in the Rotunda of the US Capitol Building in Washington, D.C.

With Watergate starting to recede from daily consciousness, things started getting back to normal, and I was really enjoying my assignment at Defense Intelligence School. By early 1976, I had shepherded two iterations of the six-week-long summer sessions of the Defense Intelligence Management Course (DIMC) and had learned a great deal more about the field while putting the program together. Each of those courses had required considerable revision. Also, I was participating as a faculty member in a thirty-eight-week-long residential course, the Postgraduate Intelligence Course (PGIC). Each iteration of PGIC had about 120 mid-career military and civilian students, divided into twelve seminar groups of ten students each. We were successful in changing the course around such that the initial three weeks consisted of group/team-building activity based on changes experienced in DIMC. I felt we were making real progress.

In February or March 1976, I was aware from reading the press that President Nixon, still in self-imposed exile in San Clemente, was ill and possibly close to death with phlebitis. I was concerned about this situation and prayed for him from time to time. I was considering about sending him a Bible with possibly a get-well message inside. However, I didn't feel that I had any authority for doing so, and the effort would be self-serving.

Our family was now fairly regular attendees at Aldersgate Methodist Church on Ft. Hunt Road near Collingwood Road in Alexandria, Virginia. The church was several blocks from our home in the neighborhood. During our time in the neighborhood, Ryan and Brooke joined the church. Our son, Erik, born in April 1974, was baptized there. The church had a fairly large congregation with two regular services each Sunday morning. During the latter part of March and early April, I recall praying to the Lord about the meaning of Watergate and asking for answers as to why I had been involved. Questions I asked were: "Lord, weren't you involved in this? Wasn't this part of your plan? Why was this done? Why was I involved in it?" I would just become oblivious to the sermon or whatever else was going on and ponder these issues while gazing at the large cross mounted against the high stone wall at the Narthex.

About two weeks before Easter 1976, a voice came to me in the night while I was sleeping and said twice, **"The world turned upside down! The world turned upside down!"** The voice was calm, clear, and distinct. Hearing a voice or message like this had never, ever happened to me to me before. When I awoke, I really didn't know what to make of it and attached no special significance to the matter, saying nothing to anyone. So while I didn't forget it, I didn't dwell on it either, and during the coming days, I went about my life.

Easter Sunday 1976 (April 18, 1976) turned out to be one of the most memorable I have ever experienced. Reverend Jim Dooley, the senior pastor, whom I admired though I didn't know him personally, was at the pulpit. Early into his service, he stated something to the effect of, "There are people who are still suffering from Watergate and who are in need." In conjunction with that statement, either shortly before or after, he used the phrase **"the world turned upside down."** I was absolutely stunned considering the voice in the night that I had heard two weeks or so earlier. So the voice I had heard was that of the Lord, and this Easter Sunday was an answered prayer. I was indeed hurting on that day and also thought that others would be hurting as well. Reverend Dooley read Colossians, verses one through twenty-two, from the Bible, and I found the reading to be very comforting.

During the service two songs were sung by the congregation lead by Reverend Dooley. Both of these songs went straight to my heart and soul. They were affirming and calming. I was finding peace.

I Need Thee Every Hour

I need Thee every hour, most gracious Lord;

No tender voice like Thine can peace afford.

I need Thee, O I need Thee, every hour I need Thee.

O bless me now, my Savior, I come to Thee!

I need Thee every hour. Stay Thou nearby;

Temptations lose their power when Thou art nigh.

I need Thee, O I need Thee. every hour I need Thee.

O bless me now, my Savior, I come to Thee!

I need Thee every hour, in joy or pain;

Come quickly and abide, or life is vain.

I need Thee, O I need Thee; every hour I need Thee;

O bless me now, my Savior, I come to Thee!

I need Thee every hour, Most Holy One,

O make me Thine indeed, Thou blessed Son!

I need Thee, O I need Thee. Every hour I need Thee;

O bless me now, my Savior, I come to Thee!

During Reverend Dooley's sermon, he recited the story from scripture of the Good Samaritan and then said, "There are people out there who need the healing hand of the surgeon," and they should be assisted just as the Good Samaritan. I instantly thought of President Nixon and thought of his great physical and emotional need. Words cannot describe how moving this Sunday sermon and service was. The other song we all song we all sang was:

Eternal Father: Strong to Save.

Eternal Father, strong to save,

Whose arm hath bound the restless wave,

Who bidd'st the mighty ocean deep

Its own appointed limits keep;
Oh, hear us when we cry to Thee,
For those in peril on the sea!

O Christ! Whose voice the waters heard
And hushed their raging at Thy word,
Who walk'dst on the foaming deep,

And calm amidst its rage didst sleep;
Oh, hear us when we cry to Thee,
For those in peril on the sea!

Most Holy Spirit! Who didst brood
Upon the chaos dark and rude,
And bid its angry tumult cease,
And give, for wild confusion, peace;
Oh, hear us when we cry to Thee,
For those in peril on the sea!

O Trinity of love and power!
Our brethren shield in danger's hour;
From rock and tempest, fire and foe,
Protect them wheresoe'er they go;
Thus evermore shall rise to Thee
Glad hymns of praise from land and sea.

I felt all along that I had been cast upon a storm-tossed sea, and I found this hymn and its words totally comforting and calming. Towards the end of the service, Reverend Dooley mentioned, "I can see that this service has moved some people." I looked right at him when he said this, and I believe he back at me, but I wasn't exactly sure because we were seated about three-quarters of the way back in the church, and the church was packed with people. I did glance at Pat a couple times during the service, and I believe she was aware that something was going on, but we didn't talk about it then or later.

I continued marveling about this answered prayer and began to consider that I now had authority for sending a message to President Nixon. The thought of sending the Bible was back in my mind. Several days later while on my lunch hour at DIS, I drove over to a religious bookstore near the new FBI Building in Washington, D.C. I browsed around looking for the right Bible; it needed to be the same version that Reverend Dooley had used. I was kind of in a daze, looking without seeing, listening without hearing, and asking the Lord for help. I found the right Bible as well as a small packet of blank message cards with envelopes and took them to the cashier for payment. I drove back to DIS in deep thought and upon arrival back at Anacostia took the purchase to my office and placed it in my desk. I prayed long over several days about what the message to President Nixon should be. Once while I was in deep thought, colleague Commander Jack Moser, USN, barged into my office. Seeing me staring straight ahead in thought, he politely excused himself and left me alone. Finally, the message was:

Dear Sir:
May the messages in this Holy Bible fill you with peace, hope, and comfort now and in the future.
Sincerely,
Percy G. Rogers

Since my signature is illegible, I also printed my name under the signature and dated the short message, either 24 or 26 April 1976. I don't recall the exact date because I again kept no record. I inserted the short note into a matching envelope and inserted it at the pages beginning with Colossians and folded a small dog-ear at the page on the left side. No verses were marked. I then double-wrapped the Bible with brown wrapping paper and secured it with good tape. With a black marker, I printed on the outside:

President Richard Nixon
Casa Pacifica
San Clemente, CA

I then pasted a whole bunch of stamps in the upper right-hand corner of the package and placed no return address either on the outside or inside of the package. I carried the package to my car and drove around with it for several days, praying on the propriety of my actions. Finally, after a couple days, I drove to an outside mailbox located in a shopping center on Ft. Hunt Road on the way home. I had concluded at that point that the mailing of the Bible was a direct order from the Almighty. While sitting in the car with the wrapped Bible in my hands and praying, a loud, commanding feeling came to me: "Execute the order!"

With that, I got out of the car and, holding the Bible with two hands at my beltline, walked with deliberation directly to the mailbox located just outside the Port Office facility. I opened the swing door and rested the package on the inside of the door for a short moment, ready for the drop, saying, "Father, into thy hands, I commit!" I then released the package from both hands, and for some unexplained reason, I thought, *Bombs away!* The package hit with a thud at the bottom of the mailbox, and I thought, *Whenever this matter may become known, it will light up the world more than a thousand atomic bombs.*

I got back into the car, and the tears began to flow. I was crying uncontrollably, and my body was shaking all over. It took me awhile to get myself together, and I had to get home soon. It was pretty wet out there. I finally started driving home, but my eyes were so full of tears I could hardly see. The tears were dripping down on my uniform shirt. I am not sure if I drove home directly or drove around while trying to get myself under control. When I did get home, I opened the door and rushed upstairs to the master bathroom. On the way in, Pat said something to the effect of, "How did everything go today?"

I replied, "Oh fine!" I stayed in the bathroom for quite a while as my eyes were red from the crying.

It later occurred to me that the package I had mailed did meet some of the profile of a mail bomb: It was hand-wrapped, didn't have exact postage but was papered over with stamps in not the correct amount, and had no return address on the outside. I could imagine that the local office staff and/or Secret Service on the other end opened the package with caution.

During the next several months, Pat occasionally told me we were getting hang-up calls. I didn't pay any attention to this. Too, we were listed in the phonebook and information directory as Percy G. Rogers. About two to three months after the mailing, I picked up the home phone in the kitchen, and a voice said, "Is this Percy G. Rogers?"

I replied, "Yes."

The other party hung up, and I immediately recognized the voice as that of President Nixon. The voice sounded firm and normal, and I then knew that the package had been received, and this brief message was confirmation. I never expected nor received any other written or oral communication from President Nixon from that day to now.

After the Easter message, I was left to ponder over everything. Slowly, I began to become aware that the phrase "**the world turned upside down**" had more meaning and significance to it than I previously thought. On two or three occasions, I walked by the Turnbull painting of the Cornwallis surrender at Yorktown, on the wall of the US Capitol Rotunda, and became aware that the tune "**The World Turn'd Upside Down**" was played as the British and other troops marched past General Washington and his commanders in surrender at Yorktown, the last battle of the Revolutionary War and the beginning of America. See Appendix 10 for more information about the Turnbull painting and circumstances surrounding the bank playing "**The World Turn'd Upside Down**."

The Rotunda visits were with my family and/or with the Boy Scouts, such as on one of the Washington Trail medal walks with Ryan. I was further humbled that this tune and phrase was associated with Yorktown and the painting displayed in the US Capitol Rotunda, the symbolic center of the United States of America.

As a result of all of this, I was and began even further humbled and struck by God's grace.

In attending other Easter services in the ensuing years, I heard the phrase "**the world turned upside down**" by various pastors and at various locations. It was only during Easter Services and never at any other time:

1. Easter 1977: Aldersgate Methodist Church, Alexandria, Virginia
   Reverend (Dr.) Smith, senior pastor. Reverend Dooley had been reassigned.

2. Easter 1978: Post Chapel, Yongson Army Garrison,
   Seoul, Korea
   Chaplain (Lt Col) Hansen.

3. Easter 1984: Victoria Community Church,
   Riverside, California
   Reverend Gurden Henley, senior pastor. He stated that when
   they rolled the rock back from Christ's empty tomb it was a day
   that "turned the world upside down."

4. Easter 1985: Victoria Community Church,
   Riverside, California
   Reverend Don Foor, senior pastor. Reverend Henley had died.
   Reverend Poor stated that the early Christians were persons
   who "turned the world upside down."

   • Note: All VCC sermons during those years were audiotaped
     and sold at the Church bookstore.

5. Easter 1986: Liberty Baptist Church, on national television
   Reverend (Dr.) Jerry Faldwell sermon

On each occasion this happened, I was astonished and felt very
blessed. I have not shared the totality of these experiences until this
writing. I believe the messages in the above sermons can be independently
verified. I always felt, the Good Lord willing, that I would eventually be
able to share my experiences with the American people.

Chapter 15:
Korea Assignment: 1977-1979
Land of the Morning Calm

Korean National Anthem
Until the East Sea's waves are dry, (and)
Mount Paektusan worn away, God watch o'er our land forever!
Our Korea manse!

Refrain: Rose of Sharon, thousand miles of range and river land!
Guarded by her people, ever may Korea stand!

Like Mount Namsan armored pine, standing on duty still,
wind or frost, unchanging ever,
be our resolute will.

In autumn's arching evening sky, crystal, and cloudless blue,
Be the radiant moon our spirit,
steadfast, single and true.

With such a will, (and) such a spirit, loyalty, heart and hand,
Let us love, come grief, come gladness,
this our beloved land!

IN APRIL 1977 WHILE AT DIS, I received a phone call from my detailer at Randolph AFB that I was going to be reassigned. I was finishing a normal three-year tour at DIS. He stated that since I had not gone to Vietnam as a remote assignment, I was going to be assigned to Korea. It could be taken as a one-year remote assignment or as a two-year accompanied tour. In that case, my family could go with me. The assignment would be to Seoul, Korea, to the Intelligence Division of Headquarters United Nations Command. It was also Headquarters of US Forces Command and Eighth US Army. I immediately notified Pat of the assignment possibilities, and she was delighted with possibility of being posted to the Far East. We had had a tour in Europe (England) and now the Far East.

I was a bit anxious about taking my family to Seoul, Korea, because of the possibility of war with North Korea, which, as some said, was only three minutes by MIG border to city. I checked with military students at DIS who had had recent tours of duty in Korea, and they thought the threat was not as severe as imagined. So after a day or two, I called the detailer back and accepted the two-year tour of duty.

We leased our home in Alexandria and left on the PCS assignment for Korea, towing our travel trailer to California. This time we took a northern route via New Hampshire, New York, Canada, and then more northern states. The unexpected happened when our station wagon quit right on Las Vegas Boulevard in the heat of the summer one Friday afternoon across the street from the Sahara Hotel. It had been a long, hot drive that day. The wiring harness had shorted out and burned up. Fortunately, a good Samaritan helped us by towing our vehicle off the roadway and then towing our travel trailer to a nearby trailer park. Ryan and Brooke stayed with me for the week while a new wiring harness was installed at the dealer. Pat went on to California with Erik. We later sold the car and trailer in California.

It was very long airplane ride from Travis AFB in California to Osan AB, located south of Seoul, Korea. We were met by our sponsor Army Lt Col Chuck Grimes and taken to their military housing home near Yongsan US Army Garrison in Seoul, where I was to be stationed. We were fed a traditional Korean meal, complete with kimchi (highly seasoned Chinese cabbage made with cayenne peppers and garlic which could cause one to have a flame-out right in the mouth). It takes experience to eat the stuff, but after that it can become addictive. At that time, I became aware of the derivation of the GI expression of being in "deep kimchi." Years later as a professor of international business at Cal Poly Pomona, I would "offer" kimchi to my students, admonishing them to eat it at risk of offending the country host (cross-cultural sensitivity for future foreign postings). Pat also fed her elementary students kimchi. We all considered it a "character-building" experience of international significance.

I reported for duty and was assigned to J2 (Intelligence) Plans and Budget. There were seven or so of us assigned, Army, Navy, and Air Force. Our J2 Plans Branch Chief was a newly assigned Army major. That officer was experiencing severe marital difficulties, which resulted is his reassignment from the S2 (Division Intelligence) with the Second Infantry Division at Camp Casey near the DMZ. Within days, the officer became severely depressed and was hospitalized in the psychiatric ward of the Army Hospital. So as ranking officer in the Branch, I became the Branch Chief. My first official duty was to get the officer's wife and child air-evacuated back to the states and then him, too, about two weeks later. All this was very time-consuming and emotionally draining on me. The whole situation was so very sad. The officer was in very bad mental and emotional shape, and he was very appreciative for my efforts on his behalf.

The major task of our Branch was to develop intelligence scenarios for the two annual major all-forces (US and Korean) war exercises: Ulchi Focus Lens, a command post exercise, and Team Spirit, a command post and field exercise. Doing the intelligence parts right required considerable knowledge of the Korean peninsula terrain, combat units on both sides, war plans, and intelligence assessments of how the attack would happen, including for up to sixty days prior to commencement of hostilities. On my first assignment, I relied heavily on a US Marine Corps major with considerable in-country experience to develop the scenario. I didn't have a clue, and he saved my butt.

Other officers in the Branch worked on Team Spirit, and in all cases the intelligence scenarios were developed in partnership with officers in J3 (Operations). I was told before going to Korea that it was an Army show there. So the combined staffs were actually overlaid on an Army Headquarters, Eighth US Army, commanded by General John Vessey, a WWII veteran of Anzio who had risen to General from the enlisted ranks. The leader of the HQ UNC/USFK/EUSA J2-G2 was Colonel Jack Dodds, a thoroughly competent Army Military Intelligence officer. He was my supervisor one-to-two-times-removed. He reported directly to General Vessey.

Our other branch duties involved what we called "ash and trash." This was a catch-all for taking action on matters that didn't fall under any other functional area. During that time, the Carter administration wanted to reduce or eliminate US forces in Korea. One of the Army lieutenant colonel's full-time jobs was to work on planning documents for force reductions. It was an agonizing exercise for everyone, especially considering the threat from North Korea which never diminished.

During our first year in Seoul, we lived in a wealthy area of town called UN Village. We actually lived in the upper level of a two-story Korean home overlooking the Han River from the north, owned by the operator of a "Happy Mountain" (Korean cemetery). The second year, we lived in US government housing on the south side of the Han River near Yong Dong Po called RGH. These quarters were American-style with hot and cold running water and central air and heat. It was very pleasant living considering all the other alternatives there.

As an elementary-school teacher, Pat went to work at Seoul International School (SIS). This was an accredited K-12 school, and Pat taught the upper elementary grades. She really enjoyed the experience. Some of the students were embassy kids, and others were of mixed Korean heritage. Our social life revolved around the associations with other military wives working there and their families. Ryan was a student at SIS and studied Korean culture, history, and language. He also traveled throughout the country. By the time we left Korea, he was fairly proficient in reading, writing, and speaking Korean, skills which are still useful today in Korean restaurants and dry-cleaning shops. A blond-haired Korean speaker really fakes vendors out.

Over the two years, we hired Mrs. Lee as our maid. She was in her forties and spoke excellent American English, learned over the years through interactions with American GIs and families. When she answered the phone, she was often mistaken for Pat, and she became a member of our family. She helped with housekeeping, babysitting, and preparing meals. Mrs. Lee was a real take charge, can-do person and a wonderful Korean friend. She helped to make our Korea tour more comfortable, fending off this and that. Living in a foreign country can be quite a challenge, and one of us would often return home saying, "You wouldn't believe what happened to me today." Then we'd give it an arbitrary number, like "Korean experience number 451." During Christmas 1978, our family vacationed to the Philippines. During that week or two, Mrs. Lee moved into our quarters and lived like us. Mr. Lee got a nice bath and lounged around on the couch watching TV just like "Daddy" (me). All this was in dramatic contrast to their own dwelling in Bupion near Inchon in a micro-apartment with no bedrooms, individual kitchen, or lavatory. Our family visited them once and went away very humbled.

One of our memorable times was when we attended Mrs. Lee's wedding to Mr. Lee. She arranged for her marriage after living with Mr. Lee for many years and having a ten-year-old son, Sunjae, together. The wedding was held at a small Buddhist temple in Seoul, and Mrs. Lee was dressed in traditional Korean wedding garb. Her hair was done up in traditional style, and with her hand fan, she affected the demeanor of a young, virginal bride with soft-spoken voice and downward-looking eyes. She would turn her head from side to side, like on a swivel, and flutter her eyes in all innocence and with prayerful hands. It was quite an act and was totally opposite of her true essence. Pat and I got a real kick out of this. In years later, we would say, "Remember the time Mrs. Lee got married?" We would each give our mimicked renditions of her wedding day act and how she carried it off, swiveling head and all.

During our tour in Korea, Pat became the Girl Scout leader and arranged a really nice program experience for the girls. Pat did it for Brooke, owing to lack of volunteer leaders. Pat was also a supportive parent to the girls' swim team, and the girls and Pat travelled throughout the Pacific region on swim meets. At the same time, I was the Scoutmaster of BSA Troop 88, Ryan's troop. A highlight of Korea was when Ryan earned and received his Eagle Scout award. Four boys in our troop earned the award, and we arranged an Eagle Scout Court of Honor for all at one time at the Post Community Center. One of the dads arranged for General Vessey to pin the Eagle Scout awards on the boys, which he did. It was a very special evening, and General Vessey told me at the time that he, too, had been a Scoutmaster way earlier as a parent. That ceremony was a highlight of our Korea tour.

Humorous incident: Our scout troop of about twenty boys with leaders did an away-campout at Camp McNabb, an Army recreation site on Cheju-do Island, south of the Korean Peninsula, about twenty-five miles southwest of Cheju City. Over the weekend, a hurricane came up, and we all hurriedly packed up and traveled by local bus back to Cheju City. We arrived at a high-end Korean hotel, booked one large room for all of us, and then inventoried our food and money, all rather sparse. We then rearranged our return flights to Seoul. Thank goodness one of our younger scouts spoke Korean, and through him we got through the situation. I called Pat to let her know our status and asked her to call the other parents. When I returned, I found out that the Post Chaplain (whose son was with us), offered up a shocking prayer in the Sunday chapel service: "Pray for the Scouts in Cheju-do!" Mrs. Toner, wife of Brigadier General Toner, the J5, and President of Korea District BSA, was at the service and soon thereafter called Pat, asking, "WHAT is going on with the Scouts in Cheju-do?!" Pat gave her the answer and smoothed things over. This is one of my favorite Scouting stories. Ah yes, "Pray for the Scouts in Cheju-do!"—a cherished part of the Rogers family lore.

General Vessey saw to it that the troops in Korea got to watch NFL football games such as the Super Bowls on AFKN (Armed Forces Korea) TV. Due to time differences, this meant getting up early in the morning.

During 1977, television put on the David Frost-President Nixon interviews, and I got to watch the whole series. I was particularly interested in how President Nixon would handle national security matters and the Plumbers.

Here is a portion of the exact interview text which was made on May 19, 1977, and rebroadcast in Korea sometime later when we were there:

FROST: So what, in a sense, you're saying is that there
                                 are certain situations, and the Huston Plan

or that part of it was one of them, where the president can decide that it's in the best interests of the nation or something, and do something illegal.

NIXON: Well, when the president does it, that means that it is not illegal.

I was shocked and very upset at this statement as well as others in this interview and troubled over it a number of days while I considered my own experience. *So,* I thought, *any illegal (criminal) actions taken against me were justified because the President judged if he did it, such meant it was not illegal (based on* **national security** *and the best interests of the country)? So then, too, the President, in his role as Commander-in-Chief of the armed forces, could commit criminal acts in the name of* **national security***?* I prayed considerably about this and pondered what to do.

Finally, I decided to write a letter to the Chief of Staff of the Air Force, General David Jones, in the form of a complaint and the request for a comprehensive officer review for prospective promotion. It took me a couple months to gather the information including supportive letters and related documentation. I wrote a cover letter and shipped all off to the Pentagon in Washington, D.C., via registered mail to General Jones.

Here is the text of my letter to General Jones:

17 October 1977
General David C. Jones
Chief of Staff
United States Air Force
Pentagon, Room 4E925
Washington, D.C. 20330

Dear General Jones:

I am an Air Force Major currently assigned to the Headquarters, United Nations Command, J2 Plans and Budget Branch, Yongsan Garrison, Seoul, Korea. I have been passed over for Lieutenant Colonel on two occasions. My reason for writing is to request that you initiate a comprehensive officer review in my case in order to assess the validity of my non-selection. I believe that sufficient cause exists to seriously question the accuracy (both in content and context) of three different OERs which were critical in the selection process. As the enclosed material will reflect, I have unsuccessfully attempted to void these OERs in the usual manner. However, a complex set of circumstances surrounds these OERs, and I believe the issue can only be resolved by a fair and objective comprehensive officer review, to include a personal interview. Obviously, the promotion boards, including the one which just met, have not been aware of all of the information.

Lastly sir, in public statements, you have indicated that you want Air Force officers who are dynamic, aggressive, creative, innovative, and not "yes men." I firmly believe that any inquiry you initiate in my case will confirm for you that I met these criteria on and before the first instance of my non-selection.

Sincerely,

Percy G. Rogers
Major, USAF

In December, I received a November 1977 reply letter from Major General Svendson, at Air Force Military Personnel Center at Randolph AFB, Texas. The letter was empathetic and noted that the rating officers had not changed their ratings, and the ratings were what the system went by. He stated that I could appeal the ratings via filing with the Board for the Corrections of Military Records. It wasn't clear to me that the letter itself reported a comprehensive officer review. The request for a personal interview with General Jones was not addressed, nor were any other comments invited. It was my strong opinion that General Jones had to know something of my predicament and had elected to totally avoid it through the present actions. I continued to have the view that my military records were permanently blocked for any consideration for promotion.

So that reply was the end of any possibility of getting a hearing or making my case for promotion. My situation and fate were sealed.

However, sometime around the time I received the reply letter, I saw a short article in *Time Magazine* to the effect that there had been a mysterious situation in the Pentagon and that the Secretary of the Air Force decreed if anyone leaked anything about it they would be summarily dismissed. Perhaps my message got through. Also, after President Nixon's statement, both President Ford and President Carter publicly stated that a President has no right to break the law. Those affirmations were assuring.

We left Korea in June 1979 for reassignment to March AFB in Riverside, California. We moved out of military quarters and left Korea on an airliner from Kimpo International Airport in Seoul. Only Mr. and Mrs. Lee with Sunjae were there to see us off. I have a specific memory of Mrs. Lee admonishing Brooke as we left through the gate for the aircraft. She had the last word. She waived her finger back and forth, saying, "Now, Brooke, YOU listen to you mother! YOU behave!" (Brooke was a tad mouthy at that time.) When we left Seoul that day, it was overcast and rainy. Hours later, we arrived at Hawaii's Honolulu International Airport, and it was a bright, sunny day. There was the lovely smell and gorgeous view of Hawaiian flowers when we all got off the airplane and headed towards US Customs. We were back HOME! We were HOME!

Looking back, our family was deeply influenced and affected by our tour of duty in Korea. Korea is IN us. We gained a tremendous appreciation and love for the Korean people. Please take time to search out the music and words (in the Korean language) of the Korean National Anthem, above. Pat and I traveled around Korea on both long and short trips. We were hosted on a country-wide tour courtesy of the Korean-American Friendship Society.

Other Korea Remembrances:

- During a winter, our family drove to the popular ski area, Dragon Valley. On the drive, we saw Korean women squatted in the snow handwashing clothes in an icy stream. They smiled and waved. We did, too.

- On Saturdays, J2 staff usually showed up for morning office duties. On afternoons, I would go antique and clothes shopping in Etewon, just off post from Yongsan. The place was also laden with bars and strip joints to appeal to GIs. I bought a prized shoulder patch to commemorate it all: "1000 Missions over Etewon."

- We went to many Korean theater, dance, and cultural performances.

- We often shopped at Korean open-air markets, haggling over bargain merchandise. Most memorable was the large fish market at Inchon that smelled two blocks away. Going there was a character-building olfactory experience.

- During the first two months, we stayed in a Korean high-rise hotel due to lack of military housing. Upon arrival at the hotel, blond-haired, three-year-old Erik would run an obstacle-like route to the elevator to avoid Koreans touching his head and hair for good luck. Once in the elevator and alone, he would hit every elevator floor button to our consternation. Eventually, he would show up.

- Also, looking back, the Korea move was an excellent military experience for me, working with the various branches of the military in a field headquarters setting and with South Korean military colleagues. I applied myself to the job but knew all along I was just marking time with absolutely no prospect of ever being advanced. It was difficult at times to maintain a positive attitude. Just as at DIS, on some days I just faked trying to be excellent.

As far as I could tell, no one in Korea knew of my Watergate connection. My military superiors made a concerted effort to write outstanding OERs to make me promotable, but it was too late. I did receive an end-of-tour-of-duty military decoration: the Defense Meritorious Service Medal, which Colonel Dodds presented to me in his conference room with other J2 staff attending just before our departure from the country.

Chapter 16:
Last Assignment: Twenty-Second Bomb Wing
Riverside, California: 1979-1981
"Peace is our Profession"

THE TWO-YEAR ASSIGNMENT TO KOREA was chosen by my Air Force detailer (personnelist) at Randolph AFB in Texas. The final assignment was coming up in June 1979. I put in a "wish list" (assignment forecast) for California, especially northern California. There was nothing more specific than that; being long non-promotable and passed over for promotion so many times, I was not a choice selectee for anyone in anyplace. I would take whatever was available. I could retire with minimum service of twenty years effective on February 4 1980; however, I would need to serve a minimum of one year on a Permanent Change of Station (PCS) move in this last assignment, and that would mean sometime in June 1980.

I received orders to the Intelligence Division of the Twenty-Second Bombardment Wing (Bomb Wing) (Heavy) Strategic Air Command (SAC) at Riverside, California. So this meant I was being shipped back home, where it all started for me. Pat and the kids were happy since we would be located close to family in southern California.

The Twenty-Second Bomb Wing was indeed "heavy." Heavy meant heavy bombers which were B52Ds, sixteen in all with another sixteen KC-135 tanker support aircraft sufficient to refuel them on to their distant targets. March Field (Air Force Base) had a long tenure in Riverside going back to 1918 and the founding days of the Army Air Service. It was originally called Alesandro Airfield, and the Army Department had been lobbied for its Riverside siting by Frank Miller, founder and owner of the historic Mission Inn in downtown Riverside. In 1950, one of the Wing's B-29s was nicknamed with nose art "Mission Inn." The community honored the base and military with the "Flyers Wall" plaque at the Mission Inn. Many of aviation history's names appear on that wall. The Twenty-Second Bomb Wing also had a glorious history of its own going back to the Pacific Theater of Operations in WWII. March AFB was host to the first USO show by Bob Hope in 1941. The Wing had flown many missions in Korea and in Vietnam. In fact, one of its B-52s with all crew members was lost in Vietnam, and that was honored with a stone memorial at the entrance hallway to the Wing Headquarters building. Early on, I learned that the SAC motto was "Peace is our Profession." One SAC old-timer told me that the real motto was "War is our Business."

The Twenty-Second was indeed "heavy" since its bombers could be configured with conventional munitions, such as 108 five-hundred-pound bombs, as well as nuclear bombs (or special weapons, also known as atomic bombs) of fewer number. The crew of a B-52D (keyword: B-52D) Stratofortress consisted of a pilot, copilot, and electronics warfare officer, who were all positioned on the upper deck, and a navigator and radar navigator (bombardier), positioned on the lower deck. All were commissioned officers, and the sixth crew member was the tail-gunner, an enlisted man. He rode in his own special turret compartment as the very rear of the aircraft along with his four heavy-duty machine guns.

In later versions of the B-52, that manned position was abolished for an automated turret gun. It turns out that some of the aircraft were built before some of the aircrews were born. The Air Force took meticulous care of those airplanes to keep them all operationally ready. There was one aircraft, tail number 6666 (what an awful number!), that was a real hangar queen, and a sister aircraft is now on static display at the March Field Air Museum for all to see.

I was soon briefed into the Division by the Division Chief Lt Col Al Halloran. He was soon retiring after twenty-eight years of service, all of which had been in SAC. I took Al's job for a brief while after his retirement. Al went way back to the days when SAC did airborne alerts 24/7. During those years, there were always bombers in the air, "cocked" and ready to go on nuclear-bombing runs at radio notice. Those were the 1950s and the days of General Curtis Lemay. Al told me he had been a bombardier on a B-36 (keyword: B-36) Peacemaker, a very large and noisy bird with an aircrew of fifteen. Al told me of the interesting challenges he had of climbing into the bomb bay to fuse the weapons in air. He also told me of some pretty scary moments of aircraft accidents, mishaps, and crashes involving nuclear weapons onboard (keyword: US nuclear accidents). In one accident, there was a near catastrophe. An aircraft crashed in the US with live nuclear weapons on board. They were within seconds of detonation, but miraculously they did not detonate. As a result of that accident, the coded switch was created to allow the bombers to fly not fused until the aircrews armed the coded switch (keyword: nuclear weapons surety). The coded switches at March were programmed annually and were heavy, electro-mechanical devises measuring about eight inches square. I was assigned as a "coded switch custodian." Whenever aircraft were swapped out on alert, two of us (one from Intel and another from Ops) would go to the flight line (airfield aircraft parking area) at the Alert hammerhead to download and upload the switches. This involved the no-lone (two-man) rule, so neither of us could let each other out of sight with the switch. At the proper time, the aircraft crew chief would wave us in beyond the yellow no-lone zone line to deal with the coded switch. We would open a fuselage panel on the port side of the aircraft and together install the coded switch device onto its rack. We would then crawl up into the aircraft to the radar navigator and navigator positions and read off numbers/values to activate the installed switch in a certain way. One would read off such, and the other would come back with an oral echo to confirm the action. With this five-to-ten-minute procedure over, we would return to the step van and go back to the office. Whenever handling the coded switch or related materials out of the office, we were always armed with 38-caliber pistols. I was also designated as a "positive control custodian," which involved the handling of nuclear launch/authentication codes for use by aircrews. SAC procedure was that if one were threatened while in possession of these materials, we were to shoot first and ask questions later—no warning shots, just shoot to kill. There was absolutely no doubt in my military mind that I would have followed SAC policy to the letter if the occasion came up. I would shoot to kill.

Soon after assignment to the Intelligence Division, I was told of my assignments to Targets Processing Branch. I was somewhat awed by this job, I think mainly because it dealt with nuclear weapons, and I hadn't expected to be involved with such in Air Force or intelligence postings. I struggled with this a short while, asking the Lord, "Is this is where I am supposed to be?" I got no answer, so I took the answer to be yes. I said to the Lord in prayer, "Well, you have your reasons." I committed to doing the best job I could in the time I had with this final Air Force assignment.

This branch, located in a secure vault, maintained and stored all mission bags for assigned bombers and tankers. The branch consisted of another officer and two to three enlisted specialists. Our job was to issue and retrieve bags from aircrews who would come to the building to do target study. We would also do "bag drags" to the aircraft on the flight line. The bomber bags contained en-route-map displays (to get them to the target) and bomb displays (to show the terrain and target profiles.) The target displays were created by another branch called Radar Predictions, which drew topographical reliefs of how the target would look to the radar navigator while in en route and at the target, flying low level. Radar Prediction drawing was an art form and was created as a result of considerable experience. The third branch was called Combat Intelligence, which prepared daily as well as special intelligence briefings for the command element (Wing Commander) and operational aircrews, also known as "crew dogs." Aircrew combat intelligence briefings were done at the Alert Facility at one end of the runway. Here was a large briefing room with other breakout rooms. In the basement were sleeping quarters for crew members for their weeklong alert duty stays. They could leave the facility for on-base destinations only and only as a whole six-man team in alert trucks with lights and sirens. Alert duty was rotated amongst members of the bomber squadron. There would be four bombers and four tankers on alert on the "hammerhead" very close to the Alert Facility. Those bombers were always "cocked" and ready to go with uploaded nuclear bombs, fuel, and targeting materials.

When the klaxon would sound at any hour of the day or night, the idea was for crew members to race to their aircraft, get them started up, taxi off the hammerhead to the end of the runway, and take off. They never knew starting out if the klaxon was sounded for real or for practice; everything was real until called off. I don't think our assigned aircraft ever flew off operationally, but a work colleague, a radar navigator, told me that in 1973 at Pease AFB in New Hampshire, his aircraft flew off operational and was called back mid-air. He said the "pucker factor" was HUGE. The aircrews did practice MITOs, or Minimum Interval Distance Takeoffs. Here aircraft would take off one right after the other. The following aircraft would be in the jet wash of the other; the aircraft would fight to stay airborne on climb-out. It was quite a show and a feat of airmanship. Practice MITOs were not done with alert aircraft and were always done with no weapons onboard. MITOs were required because aircraft needed to take off immediately after warning because there were Soviet submarines sitting just offshore from California, ready to launch intermediate-range sea-missiles at the base. It was and would be a matter of minutes and seconds to evaporation time, making us all crispy-critters. We had no aircraft crashes or fatalities during my assignment with the Wing from June 1979 through September 1981. One of the B-52s did crash with loss of all aircrew members on October 30, 1981, while on a practice low-level bombing run near La Junta, Colorado. What a loss of some really fine young men.

I never got an indication that anyone in SAC or at March AFB or the Twenty-Second Bomb Wing had any knowledge of Watergate and me. My extensive intelligence background proved to be of interest in a brief meeting with Col John Fairfield, Deputy Commander for Operations. I thought he was curious how I could still be a major and almost out of the service with all that depth of experience. I just remained silent as there was absolutely nothing to be gained by going into it. I later discovered Colonel Fairfield had endorsed my last in service OER with these comments: "Major Rogers's vast, all-service intelligence experience identifies him as a critical resource in his profession. Promote of Lieutenant Colonel." (December 5, 1980)

With respect to Watergate, it did occur to me from time to time doing the coded switch duties that if the Wing Commander(s) knew he had a "**national traitor/enemy of the state**" hooking up these nukes, he would totally FLIP OUT!

In 1981, I was passed over for promotion to permanent lieutenant colonel for the second time and soon received a formal letter indicating that my tenure of service would expire on a certain date by January 31, 1982. I would then be involuntarily retired from active duty. Previously, I had been passed over for temporary promotion to lieutenant colonel the fifth and sixth times. My superiors at March AFB, including Wing Commanders Colonel Johnson followed by Colonel McDonald, made valiant attempts with firewalled OERs to make me promotable. These were controlled distribution markings of 1-1-1 (highest possible) on the last two OERs. It didn't work. Soon after the second permanent promotion failure in about July 1981, I received a phone call from my detailer at Randolph. He told me that if I did not put in my retirement papers before October 1, 1981, he would ship me on a remote assignment to Kadena AB. I immediately thought to myself, *Hell, yes! Ship my friggin' butt to Okinawa!*

If affected, it would be a very short tour because I could not be involuntarily retained beyond my mandatory retirement date. For a split second, it was an intriguing possibility: a third operational overseas tour, about a six-month duration, and I could and would make it fun even though I was on my way out and didn't know what the exact assignment would be. What could they do to me? Kick me out? I didn't fight it, though, because I was there to get out of the Air Force, so this was a force-out under duress. It would have been a big disruption to my family also. He told me to go immediately to Base Central Personnel Office, put in my retirement papers, and call him back when I had done so. I did so at once. It was a scare tactic, intended to free up a promotion slot for some other officer slot that I was tying up. I could see the logic of it, but the action did hurt very much, and a couple other officers in the shop thought the move was very shoddy and shabby. In essence, then, I was being "kicked out of the Air Force."

My last day in uniform was September thirtieth. My immediate supervisor, Director of Intelligence, Lt Col Sherwin "Brad" Simmons, asked me what I wanted to do for retirement. I replied, "Just walk out the back door." At that point, I had been passed over for temporary grade of lieutenant colonel six times and permanent promotion twice. I was not a good candidate to either request or receive an official retirement parade or anything else. Brad would have none of that, saying I must have had a reason for such long military service. He organized a very nice retirement party/reception at his lovely home in Riverside for Pat and me and invited the crew from the office with spouses or other guests. Brad and Carol organized a first-class event, which I have always appreciated. Brad presented me with an official Air Force retirement certificate and a special Air Force military spouse appreciation certificate for Pat. He also presented me with a US flag flown off the US Capitol Building with certificate, done at the request of Congressman George Brown (the flag and certificate were later gifted to a grandson). He also gave me a fancy silver plate inscribed with my name and dates of military service. I also received a colorful Twenty-Second Bomb Wing certificate of service and appreciation (gifted to another grandson) and a retirement military decoration, the Meritorious Service Medal (thanks to Brad).

I had been thinking of my last duty day. I decided to officially retire myself. I made sure my summer uniform (trousers and short-sleeve shirt) were in excellent order. I pinned on my military ribbon rack and shoulder boards. That morning after dressing, I practiced saluting before the bathroom mirror. I wanted to make sure it was a salute with straightened arm with no sort of "fighter pilot dip" to it. I also practiced running my salute hand up my "gig line" in front of my body at the buttons up to my forehead and the back down the same way upon completion of the salute to make it all very crisp and full military.

At the end of the duty day, I went to the hallway in the headquarters building leading out through the double glass doors to the front stairs and landing. I got there a little early, stood inside, and was alone, as I had hoped. I was thinking back to the three times I had taken the Air Force oath of office. There had been big, serious bumps along the way, some that I could have never imagined when I signed up. On that day, I had completed twenty-one years, seven months, twenty-six days, and a "wake up" of military service. It was a bittersweet experience. I was very, very disappointed, embarrassed, and humiliated that I had not done better with my Air Force career and felt that retiring in this way was a failure. I was retiring with a ten-percent VA medical disability for chronic hypertension (which could have killed me in 1973), caused by Watergate—a fact known only to me. So I was a bit shot up with the only visible wounds being hypertension. Far deeper and invisible wounds were psychic ones that have never healed and that have affected the very core of my being. Way earlier, Pat had once told me that she could have done better with a military career than I had. I didn't argue with her in the least; it was true, and she was right. Pat had the brains, looks, bearing and poise to be a flag rank officer. Navy would have been her choice. Imagine Admiral Patricia Rogers. Career choices were limited in her day: nurse, airline stewardess, or school teacher. She chose the latter and became a damn good one: Seven different school districts around the country and world (including England and Korea) with different working conditions and different kids and parents. On the plus side...

- Number one: Quietly, soulfully, I realized I WAS ALIVE! I WAS ALIVE! I had made it through in relatively one piece. I was very lucky!

- Number two: I had completed all my military obligations and contracts. I had faithfully lived up to my military oaths of office.

I had completed my military service honorably. This had been at costs to my military career and curtailment of service longevity as a result of prejudicial actions taken on me by the Nixon administration.

- Number three: I treasured the friendships and work associations with all the many great people I met in all five branches of the US military (and also foreign military and British police); I had come to know some truly unforgettable experiences and people! In my mind's eye, I can see them and also hear their voices.

- Number four: Stationed in Riverside, I had the unique privilege of serving and defending my country from home in a very unusual manner being in Targets.

- Number five (and beyond all other factors): My prayers and trust in the Lord had seen me through it all.

I waited for Retreat to sound. Just before the National Anthem started to play, I stepped out onto the stair landing and gave my best salute as the US flag was lowered on the parade field about a block away. I held the salute until the very end and made a specific mental record of the event. The salute practice that morning had paid off; it went off without a hitch. I then walked to my car, drove home, and took the uniform off. All I have left of the uniform is a blue overseas cap and a shoulder board from an Air Force mess dress uniform. Years later, I gifted my original military decorations to close relatives and replicas of them to another grandson. As I was driving home, it hit me that I had to get on with the next phase of my life in the civilian world. I had a family to support, and we had kids to put through college. It was time to start from scratch with a new career.

Major Percy G. (Jerry) Rogers
Official USAF Photograph ca 1980-81

<u>Author's Note:</u> March AFB was deactivated due to military-based realignment in 1993 and became an Air Reserve Base in 1996. The Twenty-Second Bomb Wing was deactivated several years after I retired with the B-52D aircraft sent to the aircraft boneyard at Davis Monthan AFB in Arizona. SAC never officially acknowledged the presence of nuclear weapons at any installation; however, it was well known that the B-52s were nuclear bombers at the time at March AFB. I always knew the special weapons at March to be in safe hands, mine included. All persons having access had special top-secret clearances with special access; all were covered by the Personnel Reliability Program (PRP) which continuously monitored individual suitability; and access to everything was compartmentalized and thoroughly controlled by personnel and procedures. More specifically, per regulation:

"Only those personnel who have demonstrated the highest degree of individual reliability for allegiance, trustworthiness, conduct, behavior, and responsibility shall be allowed to perform duties associated with nuclear weapons, and they shall be continuously evaluated for adherence to PRP standards."

The weapons were always safely kept. Now, with the bombers long gone, the weapons are long gone.

During the Vietnam War, Brad was a radar navigator on a B-52. He had been a crew member on a B-52 during Operation Linebacker II which involved the mainly nighttime bombing of Hanoi and Haiphong Harbor from December 18, 1972, through January 27, 1973. Brad told me the experience was a living death, and his world was just in black and white for the days he was involved. In later research, I learned that 150 B-52s flew Operation Linebacker, flying 729 sorties, with a loss of fifteen aircraft with crews. The bombing did help to bring the North Vietnamese to the negotiating table to end the war. Brad's valor helped to make that happen!

Chapter 17:
Winds Message – 1994

PRESIDENT NIXON DIED ON APRIL 22, 1994, at age eighty-one in New York City after suffering a stroke at his New Jersey home four days earlier. I watched the media and read the newspaper accounts of these events. Over the years, I had followed President Nixon's appearances and statements and had given scant thought to writing up my own experiences, especially while President Nixon was living. Sometime after this death, it occurred to me that perhaps it was time to write up and publish my experiences; however, I was busy in my career as a college professor and had no time or much inclination to do so. Throughout the years from 1974 to 1994, I had waited for "the other shoe to drop" with new revelations about Watergate. I felt fortunate that nothing ever came out that affected me.

Pat and I vacationed to Hawaii in summer 1994, visiting Oahu, Molokai, and the big island of Hawaii. We were there for about two weeks total; we rented convertibles and had a very relaxing time. While on Oahu, we shopped at a mini BX at Kaneohe USMC base. There on the bookstand, I noticed a somewhat obscure hardback book with an interesting title: *Betrayal at Pearl Harbor: How Churchill Lulled Roosevelt into World War II* (1991) by two cryptologic experts, James Rusbridger and Theodore E. Nave, an Australian Navy Captain. It was an excellent and informative book detailing intelligence experiences in breaking the Japanese diplomatic and naval codes shortly before the US entry into WWII in 1941. (I was particularly interested in Japan at this time, having just taught three classes on doing business with Japan, which included Japanese history, geography, and socio-cultural perspectives. I had previously read Col. Paul Tibbets account of his crew's bombing of Hiroshima on August 6, 1945, in the B-29 bomber *Enola Gay*. I had also followed the Pacific War of WWII in books and television programs.)

In Fall 1941, allied intelligence knew that the Japanese "execute" (go to war) messages would involve weather reports, or "winds messages." Japanese diplomats around the world were alerted to begin listening for such weather messages on November 19, 1941. The diplomats were instructed to monitor regular news and weather broadcasts from Tokyo, as always, and to pay special attention to the phraseology used to describe the weather

The words "north wind, cloudy" meant war with the Soviet Union.

"West Wind, Clear" meant war with the British Empire.

"East Wind, Rain" (or Higashi no kazi ami) meant war with the United States.

I recalled this aspect of the WWII "Go to War" codes from instruction in the area of "Indications and Warning Intelligence" at Defense Intelligence School, so the winds message code words were familiar. In history, the winds messages were broadcast several times from Tokyo on November nineteenth. The actual date of the attack was later broadcast from Tokyo on December 2, 1941, as "Climb Mount Niitakayama 1208." Mount Nitakayama was then the highest mountain in Japan and was the code word for the attack. 12-8 in Japanese time was 12-7 Hawaiian time.

As I read through the book slowly and carefully, I began to think that if I was supposed to write and publish my experiences, I needed a clear and unequivocal message from the Lord, some kind of winds message so that I could recognize it with absolute certainty. I would definitely not take it upon myself to do such a writing project. No way! I prayed, "Lord, if you want me to pursue this, I need you to send me a winds message. Otherwise, I will not do it. I need your clear, direct permission and authorization... I need an execute order; I will need a direct order."

I thought no more about this and did not dwell on it. I thought if I were to get direction, it would come, and there was nothing more I could do about it. I just put the matter out of my mind.

We returned to Riverside, and neither Par nor I were teaching the rest of the summer. I think it was a July day, and Pat was out of the house. I was being a couch potato and began watching the History Channel (or similar). The documentary program *The Red Bomb* started, and it was about the development of the atomic bomb by the Soviet Union. The video started out with a huge nuclear explosion, mushroom cloud, and the announcer said, "August 6, 1945, a day that turned the world upside down." With that I just ejected off the couch and was very, very upset, thinking this was some devil's ploy on the word. I said, "Oh no, Lord, this can't be it. This is terrible. There must be a mistake." I collected myself and turned off the TV program. I had about three pressing tasks to do that day and needed to get into the car right away. I was feeling very anxious because I needed to complete these important tasks to avoid getting yelled at. For some unexplained reason, I was drawn to the garage, which was a total mess. We couldn't park any cars in there because it was such a disaster. For some unknown reason, I started rummaging through a box of family pictures and stuff. I wasn't looking for anything in particular.

This was a box of materials which had previously been stored in my Mom's wooden hope chest, which I had carefully refurbished and given to Brooke at a wedding shower earlier. Stuck on the side of the box was a letter from Mrs. Edith M. Clarke (referred to in Chapters 18 and 19) written to me on my eighth birthday on January 21, 1946. It was dimly lit in the garage, so I took the letter over to the light over the washer and dryer. The letter was written in Mrs. Clarke's own handwriting, and it said:

"Jerry's Eighth Birthday"

Another birthday has rolled around.
They make you feel quite big.
Especially when you count the months,
For they are <u>ninety-six.</u>
A large number when you count the days,
Weeks, or even months, but years a very few.
Somehow you've accomplished quite a lot
For the time allotted you.
When <u>nine</u> years are ushered in,
Your clothes will be too small.
For you'll not only grow in width,
But be so very tall.
A party today with all your friends to play.
Congratulations extended for a <u>memorable</u> day.
I'm adding <u>mine</u> to the list of little folk assembled.
For Auntie Clarke wants <u>always</u> to be remembered.
God bless you, Jerry, in all you say and do!
Be good, kind, and honest through and through.

For you, dear boy, can make the <u>man</u>,
Either <u>bad</u> or good, it rests with you.

This little <u>game</u> I thought would teach you more about the world.
As you spin the wheel and watch it twist and hurl,
You may go to <u>all</u> these places via sea, air, or land.
My prayer: May God <u>direct</u> with <u>His</u> Omnipotent hand.

Written by Auntie Clarke for
Jerry Rogers
January 21, 1946

I could hardly finish reading the letter as I became very emotional. I was crying and shaking uncontrollably. Here was the winds message I had prayed and looked for, right in my hands. It was a very unique and defining moment for me. This was the permission and authorization order, delivered in two parts: the video and the letter.

The revisited letter from Mrs. Clarke was totally unexpected and astonishing. I had known Mrs. Clark for nearly twenty years during my childhood and youth. She was my Christian mentor, and because of her, I became a Christian youth and man. I truly believed then and now that she had a special relationship with the Lord. Her words were and are everlasting and have provided comfort through affirmation of me as a Christian, then and now.

I didn't tell anyone, including Pat, what had happened. Shortly thereafter, I began visiting the public documents section at the UCR library and began reading the US Congressional documents and the hearings on Watergate in many volumes produced by the US House of Representatives and the US Senate. Before that, I had never touched such testimony or read any of the many books written by principals at the time, including President Nixon. All that just turned my stomach, and I had not wanted to dwell on it in any way. Certainly, I had not wanted to dwell on Watergate in any way while President Nixon was alive. I had a tremendous amount of research do to, and I diligently got with it.

From 1994 to 1997, I spent a considerable amount of time researching in the library as well as reading at home. I began contact with the Presidential Materials Staff of the National Archives for documents. Pat was unaware of my research activities, and I then thought it best to tell her what was going on. I didn't want her to accidently stumble on to my work and papers. In early February 1997, I told her about Watergate, my (as well as our) involvement. Initially she was very angry that I had not told her anything. I told her that I had purposely decided not to tell her because there was nothing she or I could have done about it. Plus, I felt it would have totally disrupted our marriage and our raising the kids. I did it to protect our family. I then told my three grown children and Pat's sister and her husband. I didn't go into all the gory details, just the essence of it. After that, Pat, the kids, and I never discussed the matter in any way.

I do think that Watergate did affect our family. It affected my health, and my health affected Pat's health. In just over a year, on April 22, 1998, Pat died young at age fifty-eight. Her death affected us all. I suspended all my Watergate research efforts for several years while I repaired my health and life. I met Judy Casanova in late 1999, and we were married in August 2001. Early in our relationship, I told her about Watergate and me. I felt that eventually I would write up these experiences, but when was unknown. Judy has been my greatest supporter and partner in getting this research and publication out so that people can deal with it and make their own judgments.

Chapter 18:
Growing Up in Colton, California:
Management Lessons Learned

Presented to the Colton Joint Unified School District Management Conference at

The University of Redland Conference Center

August 15, 2002

By Jerry Rogers
Colton Union High School, Class 1955

Thank you very much John (Conboy) for the introduction. As mentioned, I'm Jerry Rogers, a 1955 graduate of Colton Union High School.

Actually, all of that early education was conducted in Colton at Lincoln Elementary School (that's the old location where City Hall is now), Roosevelt Junior High School (that's the old location which doesn't exist now but which is part of high school property), and the high school, some of which exists from that day and other parts which don't.

The opportunity for addressing you today came from a chance encounter with Mr. John Conboy when he was recruiting for staff at the Cal Poly Pomona campus where I teach.

Seeing the Colton banner at the recruiting table, I couldn't resist stopping by to chat. One thing led to another. Hence, here we are. During that conversation, we talked about various challenges, adversities perhaps, I had in growing up in Colton, and he thought it might prove of interest to you in covering how I got from <u>there</u> and <u>then</u> to <u>here</u> and <u>now</u>.

As an overview, I'm going to give you some autobiographical information about those days, and then I'll briefly tell what happened after I left Colton, including my current duties. I think that as one gets older, reflection on the early years as well as search for meaning in one's entire life takes on more attention. Since the invitation, I've done a lot of reflection on lessons learned.

Since I'm a management professor, I've chosen to call it "management lessons learned." Maybe it should also be called "life lessons learned." I'll conclude with some ideas for secondary education that might be adopted in the Colton school system that I think would prove useful to young people, young students.

First off, some of this story in the current context will not be considered "politically correct," but to tell you my story I have to be honest, authentic, and historically correct. Please accept my remarks in that light, and do not be offended by something I may say. I hope you will understand.

Also, please listen attentively to what I have to say. At the end, there will a test on points in my presentation and if you respond correctly, you will receive a reward.

———————————

Our family and extended families were dislocated from rural Wisconsin in 1940s, largely due to the economically debilitating results of the Great Depression. The family farm was sold off with the death of my paternal grandmother in 1940.

Three families lived under one roof and worked a bare subsistence on that farm in Clear Lake, Wisconsin. I was born in the farmhouse during a January blizzard with a midwife in attendance. The doctor struggled to arrive from town some two hours later. Can you visualize this 1938 scene?

One of Dad's sisters had earlier moved to North Hollywood. As a family of three, my folks drove straight through from Wisconsin to California on what was US Route 66. This must have totally worn my father out, but he was trying to make time and spend no money on lodging.

My mother was totally impressed with the scene and often told me later just how wonderful it was driving along Foothill Boulevard, seeing and smelling the citrus trees. She penned the family legend postcard back to Wisconsin saying, "I think I've died and gone to heaven." That postcard had an impact and dislodged others out of Wisconsin to California. That nice Southern California weather surely beat cold, hard snow-blown winters in NowhereVille, Wisconsin.

We lived at Big Bear Lake for two years. Mom was a waitress, and Dad was a woodchopper. He never really adjusted to not being a farmer. Mom was born in a log cabin in rural Wisconsin, and her mother had died at her childbirth, leaving behind a large family.

The family was broken up to live and be raised by various extended family members. Mom only spoke Norwegian until the start of grade school and went as far as eighth grade, when she had to go work to fully support herself at age fourteen.

Much of my early remembrances of growing up in Colton have to do with WWII. Looking back, I see it left a big imprint on me. Everyone was totally committed to the war effort—winning the war and beating the enemy. This applied to little kids like me, too. We were part of the war effort—it was outside and inside of us.

Probably it was 1943 or 1944. My parents would go to Brad's beer bar in downtown Colton to socialize just like they did in Wisconsin. My older cousin and I would position ourselves at the doorway to the bar and with our aviator caps beg the soldiers and sailors for money. This was my first experience in "cold calling," and we had success, particularly if you got them on their way out. It helped if you added verbal encouragement, something like "You gonna win the war, Mister?!"

On any given evening, we could make two or three dollars, which was good money! I still remember my favorite songs of that era: "Praise the Lord and Pass the Ammunition" and "Coming in on a Wing and Prayer." It came from the jukebox, which seemed to furnish the only light in the bar amongst all the heavy cigarette smoke.

I really hated Japs! Everyone hated Japs! There was a propaganda poster in a dark doorway of a shop a few doors down from Brad's that had a Japanese soldier bayoneting a baby underfoot with a rising sun flag in the background.

My cousin and his friend would grab me by both arms and drag me to the doorway, yelling and screaming. "We're taking you to see THE JAP!"

"NO! NO! NO! I don't want to see THE JAP!"

Then they would throw me into the darkened doorway. All this really reinforced my hatred.

As I said, little kids were part of the war effort. One time I went to the post office and bought a ten-cent defense stamp. War bonds were a way of financing the war effort, and with enough stamps you could buy a bond. I went to the sandwich shop where my Mom worked. My excuse for showing up there without permission was "Look Mom, I bought a 'fense stamp!"

Too, our little band of boys and girls fought the war all over the streets of Colton. See 1943 photo of Colton's band of WWII warriors. I can't tell you how many Japanese or Germans I killed with my toy rifle during those years, or how many times I died. We were good at making battle sounds with our mouths, like machine guns firing, grenades exploding, and people getting wounded and dying.

The troop convoys would pass right in front of my house on Eighth Street, now La Cadena. Eighth Street was US Highway 395, and I Street, now Valley Boulevard, was US Highway 99. This is way before freeways came on the scene in 1956. We just loved it when the trains would stop and back up the convoys. Our little band of warriors would surround the trucks and "encourage" the troops. We would get rained with candy. Were we part of some soldier's remembrance of going through Colton on his way to war?

Everyone had blackout curtains on their windows. When the air raid siren sounded, the curtains would be lowered, and we would sit around in the candlelight awaiting the next thing.

Thankfully, the worst never happened.

I have remembrances of V-E and V-J day. I found out while standing in front of Monty's Candy Palace in downtown Colton that we had won the war with Japan. I remember jumping up and down yelling, "We beat the Japs! We beat the Japs! We won the war!" Those were very different, difficult times for everyone. I believe I served in World War II even though a kid.

1943 Colton Band of WW II Warriors

But, for me there was another world-changing event in 1945. In April 1945, my Dad died of a heart attack at age forty-three. I was seven years old. This left my mother as the sole provider. For the longest time, she would sit at the kitchen table and sob and sob in grief. I felt very helpless to comfort her.

This was certainly a very difficult time, especially for her. We lived in a one-bedroom duplex apartment over a three-car garage at 122 West D Street.

I was an entrepreneur from an early age as mentioned. I sold the Sunday edition of the *Los Angeles Herald Examiner* at Eight and I Streets on Saturdays. I'd pick up the papers from a guy named Vern in the back of a shoe repair shop next to the Monty's.

I was supposed to have said while passing by the shoe shop owners on my way to see Vern, "Well, my Dad's died. Now I have to help my mother."

From that point on, I always had jobs. First there was Jerry's newspaper delivery service, door-to-door delivery of the *Herald Examiner* from downtown all the way to A Street.

This was followed by Jerry's shoeshine service, Jerry's lawn watering and gardening service, and Jerry's Christmas Card sales, followed by others I'll soon mention. I always made my own spending money.

In 1946, with the war over, Mom wanted to go back to Wisconsin to see family. When the war was on, there was rationing, and you couldn't travel cross-country as a civilian.

Mom didn't have enough money for both of us to travel. The summer of 1946, we left San Bernardino on the Greyhound bus. I sat on her lap all the way straight through to St. Paul, Minnesota, and back on that trip, with the occasional time she sat on a jump seat at the front of the bus.

Wisconsin had a really different feel to it from Colton. We made another trip in 1950 and way later in 1964 when I was going to university in Michigan.

I gained a real appreciation for a different life in Wisconsin on those trips. Mom said on a couple occasions, "I'm glad, being left, that it was in California." Me, too! What kind of life and place would I have been in growing up in rural Clear Lake, Wisconsin, with a 40-year-old widowed parent with limited skills, in 1945? With a 7-year-old boy?

I never thought that Mom and I were poor, even though you might say that in economic terms—but not in spirit. We had personal dignity. Her friends and work colleagues very well respected Mom. She was a meat-wrapper for Stater Bros. for twenty-five years and until her death in 1972.

I was later to learn about dignity in that 1964 trip to rural Wisconsin when Mom introduced me to the Aunt that she called her mother. With her headscarf and accent, she reminded me of "babushka lady." The lady, Aunt Lina, lived in a wooden house of logs and lumber. There was not a straight wall in the place, linoleum over dirt floors, a large wood-burning cook stove and oven, no running water—only a hand pump on a well, outhouse, and kerosene lantern for light. The humble abode was in a forest clearing and had springhouse as the refrigerator.

You can be dirt poor and have dignity! There was warmth, hospitality, good food and love at Aunt Lina's.

As Mom explained it, she was my mother and my father. She had me promise to tell her what was going on in my life and to tell her of any concerns I had. I did. So we had a very special relationship. When my father died, she hired a lady to watch after me when she was at work. That didn't work out as the lady couldn't keep up with me. She fired the lady, and I sort of grew myself up in Colton. Mom did not remarry. I was her "life's project."

Then there was Rose, the gypsy lady who worked with Mom at the sandwich shop. Her specialty was reading tealeaves, and Mom liked to have it done. Mom told me that Rose had foretold that my father would die at an early age.

Also, she foretold that Mom would be very proud of me because someday I would be somebody. I would travel the world and "be of (or in) the world."

THAT was very improbable to me at that age. I really didn't like Rose coming over to our place. She was weird! She would fix a gaze on me with those X-raying eyes that would bore holes right through my head. Rose was weird, and I really didn't like Mom bringing her over for those tealeaves sessions.

The 1940s and 1950s were definitely different than today, for better or for worse.

We didn't call it racial profiling them, but I think Mom exposed me to it. There was racial strife between the Mexicans (Chicanos now) and the Anglos. There were major fights between the Mexicans and the soldiers and sailors in LA.

One time, Mom held my little cherub face and told me sternly, "Jerry! Never, ever go into South Colton! The Mexicans will grab you and cut your balls off!" WOW! That got MY attention! I never, ever went into South Colton. Further, I was very nervous around Mexicans after that and for the longest time.

Then there was the matter of sex education. I don't recall we got any in school, but if we did, we got it too late. One of my very best friends, Bud, lived right across the street in the big house, now called the Ashley House for Bill Ashley, another Colton schoolteacher and my old Troop 46 scoutmaster.

Bud didn't have a dad either, and as childhood pals we engaged in a lot of self-education. When we were about eleven years old we spotted a book titled *Love Without Fear* on the bookshelf at Monty's Candy Palace.

Since we were too embarrassed to buy it, we shoplifted it. It was a daring operation!

We took the book back to Bud's room and spent many hours reading it. It had technical terms we didn't quite catch, but the various drawings and diagrams were interesting. Bud and I would enact the drawings. It was really quite funny with a lot of belly laughs as we learned. Each of us had our favorite passages in the book, which we would read to each other. The book was kept in a secret location in Bud's bedroom, available for sneak readings upon demand.

I outgrew my fear of Mexicans later on. It was about 1949, and there was Don, a Mexican guy from South Colton, who used to hang out at Bud's house. Martha, Bud's mom, a Colton schoolteacher and high school administrator, would hire Mexican girls as housekeepers.

This attracted Don to the house, and he was a super-cool dude who played a part in our sex education. Don was really clean, wearing white T-shirts, jeans, huaraches, and he smelled really good all the time. He was a really good-looking guy and told Bud and me about his various conquests, most of which had taken place in the back seat of his '34 Ford four-door, gray primered low-rider.

This low-rider was special; it had a purple rear window with rosary beads and knit dice hanging off the rearview mirror. Did you know that there's a lot of room in the back seat of the '34 Ford? Bud and I would get back there and with awe, reverence, and aspiration exclaim, "Gee, this is where Don DOES IT!" Looking back I think the rosary beads were there to help prevent unwanted pregnancies from back seat action.

Don was also our cholo-lengua and diction coach. He taught Bud and me every dirty, filthy cuss word in Spanish that he knew. We could create a full string of those words end to end and spew them out in one long breath. I practiced doing it again on the way over here today. But let's drop it at that!

It was a very special treat to take a spin in Don's low-rider. Don would sit back in his seat with his eyes on a level with the window ledge and arm cocked across the steering wheel. Bud and I scooted down in our seats, too, with the tops of our heads just visible in the window. I think we may have talked in Spanish with the limited vocabulary that Don had taught us.

Can you imagine two towheaded, crew-cut eleven-year-olds cruising around Colton in Don's low-rider and speaking Spanish? What an honor! What a thrill! Don still lives on in my precious memories of Colton. If anyone knows about Don, please let me know later on. (See after comments, below).

Mom was religious but not a churchgoer. She had been raised in the Lutheran Church and had had catechism in the Norwegian language. I have remnants of her catechism book in my belongings.

Mrs. Edith M. Clarke (Chapter 19) and Reverend Bill Jennings were big influences in my life as well as many of the folks at the Methodist Church. We had the same Sunday school class members for many years. As we got to be junior-high-school age, we were difficult to deal with, and we were proud of the number of Sunday School teachers we had run off.

THEN there was Mrs. Willard Sim. She was something else! She hung on to us like a pit bull and never gave up on us. I think back to why this was. She kept our attention by reading excerpts each Sunday of Father Flanagan's Boys Town. Were we like them?

Mrs. Sim was a Gold Star mother. She had lost one of her sons in combat on a Pacific Island in WWII. Truly, this must have been matter of great sorrow to her. Whenever you walked by her house on Edgewood Street, you could see the Gold Star banner proudly displayed in her window. Many years later, I visited her gravesite at Hermosa Cemetery. She had had her son reinterred alongside her gravesite some years later.

Sometime in 1951, I attended a religious revival program at the Orange Show in San Bernardino. I decided from that to join my Methodist Church and declared that intent. I think folks were skeptical about such a commitment on my part at that age, but I took the three or four membership lessons and became a member of the church in a formal ceremony. I was thirteen years old. Looking back, I understand I had arranged my own Christian version of a bar mitzvah. I had made myself a man.

By the way, my other jobs were as a newspaper carrier for the Colton edition of the *San Bernardino Sun*. My route was way over on Mount Vernon. On those cold, rainy Sunday mornings, I was overburdened with heavy newspapers, and getting to and delivering my route were a real challenge. I delivered way over on Mt. Vernon Avenue. I had to give this job up when I fell asleep in class too much.

I also worked for "Sug" Cooley at Cooley's Ranch picking cantaloupes one summer. Yes, there really was a Cooley Ranch. It wasn't always Wal-Mart and Giant RV or Interstate 215.

Later on, I was a soda jerk at, you guessed it, Monty's Candy Palace. Right on my sixteenth birthday, I went to work as a box boy at Stater Bros. in Colton, the old store. I was in Ray's face, the store manager, about this every time I was in the store the six months before I aged up. I think I wore him down.

Mom enrolled me into first grade at age five and half. There was no kindergarten for me; she needed me in school the full day because she was working. Early on, Mom had me on an incentive program for grades.

For every "A" on a report card, I would receive a shiny silver dollar. That was a real incentive, and I responded to it vigorously. My grades were excellent all through school including high school. With an exception of a "D" in Trig my senior year, I think all my other grades were "As."

A major message I have today is what a great education I received in Colton schools—committed and caring schoolteachers all. I can name just about each one from first grade on. I think it was about fifth or sixth grade that I really got turned on to learning. It was work, and it was fun. I really enjoyed making "As."

It was really a challenge not to mention the financial incentive plan I was on. Mom had her motives. Absolutely no one in our families had ever graduated from college. Every once in a while, Mom would stick her finger in my face saying, "YOU'RE GOING TO COLLEGE!"

That "D" I received was actually an "F." E. Ruth White gave me a gift. I just couldn't grasp the subject and could never get caught up. Plus, I was pretty busy. That senior year I was working near full-time as a grocery checker with Stater Bros. in Colton, was vice-president of the student body, was captain of the tennis team, and was going to school full-time.

Upon graduation, I went to UCR for one year. But, being really immature, I didn't do well and had to go back to Valley College for retooling. This was somewhat of a humiliating experience, but I found the best college instructors I ever had were there. I try to be like them as a professor at Cal Poly Pomona.

I graduated with a degree in criminology from UC Berkeley in 1959 and entered the Air Force into an officer-commissioning program in early 1960. Berkeley was a big growth experience both intellectually and socially. The Air Force was even bigger. I spent over twenty-one years on active duty and through the service received two masters degrees and a doctorate degree, all on active-duty time. For eleven years, I was an Air Force Special Agent involved with criminal investigations, counterintelligence investigations, and counterespionage operations. For seven years, I was a strategic intelligence officer.

Interestingly, my last assignment was with the Twenty-Second Bombardment Wing, B-52 bombers at March AFB. It was the unusual experience of defending my country from home.

I've been a professor at Cal Poly Pomona in the Management and Human Resources Department, College of Business Administration for the past twenty years and will be retiring to emeritus status in 2003. I wish to note that our President Suzuki is a Japanese-American who as a kid was an intern in a prison camp during WWII. This was a very painful time in his life, too. I respect him very much.

I also specialize in international business instruction and for the past twenty-one years have run a business called Global Risk Assessments, Inc., which specializes in international political risk consulting and publishing. It's an international business where I am "in (or of) the world."

So the question arises: What can we learn from this life and these experiences? Here are some ideas:

- If you have just one person in your life who lovingly cares for and directs you, it will be all right. A person can have punishing experiences and still survive. Blessed is Mom!

- If you have other or many caretakers in your life, that will help greatly. I can think back on Mrs. Clarke, Reverend Jennings, Vern, people in the neighborhood, and school friends and their parents. Hasn't it been said that it takes a village to raise a child? I think it happened to me.

- Caring and supportive schoolteachers as those in the Colton school system make a big difference. I'll never forget that!

- People learn when they are ready. Take my early sex education for example. The point is that when there is a thirst for knowledge, people will quench it. However, I think the regular curriculum may not motivate some. Whatever the curriculum, sometimes people are unable to learn except from concrete experiences and hands-on learning. Those experiences drive the thirst for knowledge to solve the immediate problems, like through math and reading skills.

- Just encountering all the various people in Colton in all the various endeavors I had. I thought in later years that if I were ever captured and thrown into solitary confinement, they would never drive me crazy. I could take a virtual tour of any duration around Colton, the streets and alleys, the parks and stores, and have countless visits with many people. Isn't that what a hometown is about?

- Praises to the citizens of California for making available free public education of the highest quality. Like Mom, I'm glad we were left in California. It's those generations before me then who created the opportunities I had for a successful life. Isn't it so that next generation stands on the shoulders of the generation before it? That was "the Greatest Generation" for me—the ones who won the war and suffered through the Great Depression.

- Someone once told me that there are two four letter words: plan and luck. Some say you can create your own luck. So many of things in my life were totally out of my control. An Air Force officer colleague once summed this up this way: On a mission, you may not have a full tank of gas or a full fuel load, and you may not have a full bomb load. But when the mission comes, you've got to go with what you've got! You may never have the optimum conditions; you have to have to make it (plan it) with what you've been dealt. Press on! Deal with it! Make it happen! Go for it!

Added note:

In 2010 in researching this book I had been thinking of Mrs. Sim and the agony she had gone through. I was awakened in the night with a voice saying "Mrs. Sim! There is a place of quiet rest" and then a burst of orchestra music to what I believed to be a hymn. When I got up I went to the computer and located the hymn, "There is a Place of Quiet Rest...Near to the Heart of God" This was a very special message from the Lord telling me exactly Mrs. Sim's status...She was Near to the Heart of God! This Gold Star mother's agony was over! She and her son were at peace. My agony for her was then over. Praise God Suggestion: Play this hymn on YouTube.

Chapter 19:
Mrs. Edith M. Clarke

I LIVED THERE AT 122 West D Street (phone: 1117M) in Colton, California, continuously from 1941 through September 1957 when I went to school at UC Berkeley. I returned home during summer 1958 and upon graduation in June 1959. On both occasions, I resumed my grocery checking job with Stater Bros. Markets. In 1959, I had already applied and been accepted into Air Force Officer Training School in San Antonio, Texas, and had to await joining the Air Force and attending the next class starting in February 1960.

All during those years, our landlady and occupant of the adjoining duplex was Mrs. Edith M. Clarke, previously mentioned. She was up in years then and was widowed, how long I never knew. With me she referred to herself as "Auntie Clarke" and was also known as "Mother Clarke." There were other families who lived in an adjoining house that was also divided up into rental apartments.

In a long-lost and forgotten photograph of Mrs. Clarke to her side is a table-top radio and on the wall a large, nicely framed picture of a beautiful young woman. The woman was Mrs. Clarke, likely in her late teens or early twenties with a white blouse, tight at the neck, and her hair done up to the top of her head as was the fashion in those days.

Mrs. Clarke told me she had been a professional singer in her youth and went by the name Edith Silverman, which I believe was her true name. I previously mentioned her singing with the radio. Mrs. Clarke was hard of hearing, so the radio broadcasts would be turned up loud, and I could easily hear them through the single sheet of wall board that separated the two apartments. I got religious instruction daily that way, ready or not. One time, she showed me some family heirlooms from a chest, which included what appeared to me to be Civil War military medals. I think she originally came from Arkansas, though she didn't have an accent.

When my father died in 1945, Mrs. Clarke appeared larger in my life, and she took on the role of surrogate parent. As mentioned earlier, Mrs. Clarke was my life and spiritual counselor as well as Christian mentor. She would often listen to religious broadcasting on her radio. Because of her hearing loss she would turn up the volume. Through the thin wall board that separated our adjacent apartments I would be listening too. She listened to a program called "Hour of Power" and sing along with the songs. Her voice would absolutely fill the rooms but occasionally fail due to age. I really liked it when they played and she sang "In the Garden." It was and is my favorite hymn. Suggestion: Play this hymn on YouTube.

She wrote other birthday letters to me. Here I have excerpted the most significant portion from January 21, 1949:

"Next year you'll be a real boy scout
Taking trips here and there about
doing a kind act day by day
Living up to your "Oath" in <u>every</u> way. *

God will use you in his plans
What joy twill be with His dear clan.

May you live to reap the goal
By blessing others less fortunate Souls
It's nice to go along earth's various ways
But you're learning that these are transitory days.
Make your foundation firm and sure.
By serving our God will make your eternal home secure."

Written for Jerry on his eleventh Birthday by Auntie Clarke
Jan 21st 1949

In 1964, Mom told me that Mrs. Clarke had been moved from Colton to a residential care facility in San Bernardino and that we should visit her. This we did, and I am so glad about it. At this time, she was also blind. As we talked with her, she was absolutely delighted that we had come to see her. She was so full of joy and the spirit of the Lord, stating she was just fine. As we spoke, she ran her fingers over my face and head and patted my chest and arms.

Sometime later when she passed away, we heard she had donated her body to science. I think she had told me one time earlier that such was her plan as someone else could use her body after her death. That was so Mrs. Clarke, that dear soul. There is no doubt that Mrs. Clarke was a strong force in my life. So as I read and reread her birthday letters, I wondered if Mrs. Clarke was sending me a message now, all these sixty years later, as well as then.

Mrs. Clarke lives in my heart always! Always!

Have I remembered Auntie Clarke?

Chapter 20:
Watergate Research and Actions Chronology as of March 2016: Due Diligence Research by Percy G. (Jerry) Rogers

All mail/correspondence was sent by receipted mail. Unless otherwise noted, **none** was acknowledge/responded to by the recipient.

Newspapers:
Comprehensive documentation for prospective publication; sending each copy of **Preface manuscript only:**

1. Mr. Bob Woodward, Watergate journalist and author, *The Washington Post*, April 12, 2012; March 8, 2014.

2. Mr. Dean Baquet, Managing Editor for News, *The New York Times,* February 4, 2014.

3. Mr. Nicholas Goldberg, Editor in Chief, Editorial Board, *The Los Angeles Times*, January 18, 2015.

The integrity and prerogatives of a free and independent press to publish or not to publish is NOT questioned whatsoever.

Persons/Principals:

Lost correspondence: 1994-2009

Correspondence and contact during 2009; all correspondence and records were lost at sea on Labor Day weekend 2009 when our sailing catamaran sank at Little Egg Inlet, New Jersey, and we were helicopter-rescued by the US Coast Guard, saving our lives.

1. Letter to Professor Archibald Cox, First Watergate Special Prosecutor. No significant information on sensitive **national security** matter. Two brief letters reply.

2. Letter to Henry Ruth, Third Watergate Special Prosecutor. In brief telephone call: no knowledge of sensitive **national security** matter.

3. Letter dated August 4, 1997 to General Alexander Haig, Former White House Chief of Staff and assistant to President Nixon during Watergate. Brief letter dated August 12. 1997 reply, furnished no significant information.

4. Letters to Senator Howard Baker, Co-Chair of Senate Watergate Committee, six letters. In last letter, I requested that he write a detailed statement re: this matter and place it in his estate personal effects. All letters sent to his law offices in Huntsville, Tennessee. Zero replies to all letters.

5. Letter to Mr. Samuel Dash, Democratic legal counsel, Senate Watergate Committee. Zero replies.

6. Letter to John Dean, Counsel to President Nixon. Brief letter reply, no relevant statements. Dean had White Plumbers office safe opened and removed three of Hunt's operation notebooks. The remaining contents were turned over to L. Patrick Grey, FBI Acting Director, with admonition that such should "never see the light of day." Disposition of Hunt's notebooks is unknown. Dean disdained revisionist historical research.

7. Letter to Leonard Garment, Counsel to President Nixon. In Watergate tapes, he refers to a **national security** matter which needed President Nixon's attention. In a brief telephone conversation, Mr. Garment told me, "There was nothing to the **national security** matter; it was all made up!"

8. Letter to Charles Colson, Counsel to President, Watergate Principal, and active relationship with Watergate Plumbers E. Howard Hunt and Gordon Liddy. Zero reply.

9. Letter to Lt General Vernon Walters, Deputy Director, Central Intelligence Agency. Watergate tapes reflect he expressed concern about of sensitive matter that if known would equal to a thermonuclear explosion. No further information on this concern has ever been disclosed or discovered. Zero reply.

10. Letter to Professor Stanley Kutler, University of Wisconsin, Watergate researcher and author. No relevant statements.

11. Watergate tapes and files collection at Archives II, National Archives, College Park, Maryland. Numerous research files and tape records.

Dated correspondence:

All mail/correspondence was sent by receipted mail. Unless otherwise noted, none was acknowledge/responded to by the recipient.

1. Letter to Judge Charles Breyer, District Court, San Francisco. Former member, Watergate Special Prosecutors Office. February 13, 2009; October 13, 2011. Zero replies.

2. Letter dated February 2, 2009 to Senator Fred Thompson, Republican legal counsel, Senate Watergate Committee, residence, Brentwood, Tennessee. Zero reply.

3. Letter dated May 1, 2014 to Senator Dianne Feinstein, Chair, Senate Intelligence Committee. May 1, 2014. Zero reply.

4. Letter dated March 5, 2016 to Senator John McCain, Chairman, Senate Armed Services Committee. He responded stating he had referred my correspondence to Senator Dianne Feinstein. Zero reply.

5. Letter to Attorney General Eric Holder, US Justice Department. May 3, 2014. Zero reply.

6. Freedom of Information Act Requests Based on My Name

7. Pages 58 and 59 FBI Watergate Summary Report. Redacted citations "B1" FOIA requested in 2010 and 2011 and each time denied based on **national security**. Citation relates to Hunt's Plumbers activity. See attached for details.

8. CIA: Classified information could not be disclosed. During the Congressional hearings, Senator Majority Mike Mansfield, directed the CIA to NOT destroy any Watergate-related files. It was reported that CIA Director Richard Helms destroyed such files the next day.

9. National Archives Watergate Grand Jury testimony cited as **national security** could not be released.

10. Other: No effort was made to contact Hunt or Liddy. It was believed neither would cooperate or make any statements against self-interests, making themselves vulnerable to criminal charges and/or civil consequences.

Afterward

To RECAP, RESEARCH FOR THIS book began in earnest following President Nixon's death in April 1994. That research involved countless hours in libraries: California State Polytechnic University, Pomona, and the University of California, Riverside. Research involved study of both US Senate and House of Representatives Watergate Hearings Proceedings as well as review of microfilm of the following newspapers for reports regarding Watergate and national security for years 1972 through 1974: *The Washington Post*, *The New York Times*, and *The Washington Star-News*. This all took almost three months of daily effort. This and other research was analogous to dumping a wheelbarrow of sand on the pavement and then examining each grain of sand with a jeweler's eyepiece. Research of this nature could not be done without foreknowledge of the subject matter in question. The scope and intensity of this research is similar to highly refined academic research and/or that in defensive counterespionage operations, always striving for detail in EXTREME

Research was extensive at the National Archives at College Park, Maryland (Archives II), with Nixon Project Watergate documents and presidential tapes. Countless days and hours were spent listening to and following tape guides in the Tape Room. I used finder's guides, key wording "**national security.**" Concerning were the number of "withholds" based on **national security.** Still, as of July 2014, non-released tape withholds involve thirty-seven hours, thirty-seven minutes, and three seconds. These withholds are based on review and recommendations of appropriate US governmental agencies. **National security** could involve foreign affairs as well as illegal Plumbers activity. Withholds also exist regarding Watergate grand jury proceedings. In 1975, President Nixon testified at a Watergate grand jury. About five pages are withholds based on **national security**. However, in the 1975 grand jury, Nixon and US government attorneys stipulated that no **national security** matters would be disclosed. Of all prior grand juries, only one page of withhold has ever been released. So there are an unknown number of citations which are still on **national security** withhold.

Know these withholds go back more than forty years; the American people will likely never know the entire truth about what their government did.

By USPS registered, receipted letter dated April 6, 2016, I requested Attorney General Loretta Lynch to do the following: "I am also attaching previously submitted FOIA requests to the FBI regarding Watergate that were denied disclosure. I request your cooperation in getting said matters released/disclosed."

There was zero reply to this letter request in regards to the Freedom of Information Act. This FBI FOIA request is cited in the Preface as pertains to pages fifty-eight and fifty-nine of the FBI Watergate Summary Report. There are other national security redactions on other pages of this report still not released.

Research also involved reading nearly every book dealing with Watergate by principals, jurists, newspaper journalists, and scholars. Research included efforts to obtain firsthand information of Watergate principals. This effort was extensive but did not yield much due to non-replies or non-responsive replies. There seemed to be an overall reluctance to provide any information whatsoever, even though said information was possessed.

The focus of this book was to get at the issue of what President Nixon himself called the grave **national security** matter. All during the immediate Watergate days and years, such was never disclosed or explained, even though the matter eventually lead to his departure from office. President Nixon's book *RN* did not explain "the grave **national security** matter." In reflection, President Nixon did not want the matter disclosed for fear that it would destroy the command and control of the US military. Such would clearly be a US Constitutional concern in his role as Commander-in-Chief. Watergate Counsel Samuel Dash was correct in observing that America almost lost its democracy.

I became aware in 1971 that some persons, not known then, were actively committing egregious crimes against me, a loyal Air Force officer, and in effect members of my family. I knew at the time the matter was a grave **national security** matter. Just how grave and who was responsible I did not know. As Watergate began to unfold in 1972 with head shots of Hunt and Liddy in the newspapers, disclosures of their break-in of the Democratic National Headquarters, and President Nixon's various actions and statements, I came to realize just how this all was indeed **a grave national security matter.** I believed then any reporting I did would be discounted and denied, and I discredited, dishonored and degraded. I did not want then to realize the hard truth that my promising Air Force career was finished at the eleven year point. I remained on active duty all as a major for another ten years until involuntarily, forced retired in 1981. Early on in my Air Force career, I was informed, "Don't mess with your career even if you are not at fault. If you embarrass the Air Force in any way, your Air Force career is OVER." I didn't want to admit it; I was enraged and felt betrayed, and this affected my attitude and duty performance. As shown, I did take actions to correct my situation, albeit unsuccessfully.

I have reported here my subsequent actions.

Absolutely no one knew what I knew about my exact Watergate involvement from its inception in 1971 to the present more than forty five years later. I believed following President Nixon's death in 1994 that the American people had and have an absolute right and need to know what happened. They have a right to know the truth about the grave **national security** matter as best I have been able to discover it.

And now, you, the citizen, have that information here, fifty-plus years later. During the Watergate era, no one, including the Nixon administration and Plumbers, Watergate special prosecutors, military officials, the press, or members of my immediate family had that knowledge. I am grateful that I did not get outed at the time or any time. If that had happened, I was prepared on any given day to immediately resign from the Air Force, requesting rapid separation from service. I am grateful to President Nixon (though his motivation was likely to avoid responsibility and accountability) and other unknown others for saving me from public Watergate identification. That spared me from me from spending the rest of my adult life wallowing in Watergate. Following my unsuccessful Air Force, career I was able to pursue other rewarding professional interests. My wife Pat and I had health problems as a result of Watergate exposure.

Throughout this book, I have presented "lessons learned" based on my own experiences and those of Watergate principals and scholars. Based upon what you have read here, I encourage you, the reader/citizen, to develop your own "lessons learned," be it today, tomorrow, or the next twenty to forty years.

People! Something needs to be learned from all this!

In saying this, I am aware that not many living in the Watergate era are still around. The new generations need to be concerned. It has been said that history has a tendency to repeat itself. We must learn and be vigilant for such abuses of power in the future. Again, now it is time that the American people know the truth. President Ford's previously quoted 1974 statement deserves notice:

"I believe that truth is the glue that holds government together, not only our government but civilization itself. That bond, though strained, is unbroken at home and abroad."

Lastly, I have highly valued my private professional, personal, and family life. It has been one of precious obscurity and blessed anonymity. My family and I treasure our personal privacy!! Thank you for reading my book.

The Lord is my Shepherd…
(Psalms 23)

Semper Fi

Appendix 1

"Security Could Imperil 'Plumbers' Prosecution"
Washington Star News, **November 20, 1973**
By Barry Kalb

A GENUINE NATIONAL SECURITY MATTER raised by the White House last summer is so sensitive it might bar future prosecutions involving the secret 'Plumbers' operations, former Atty Ten. Elliot L. Richardson believes.

Richardson told a reporter yesterday that information from special White House counsel J. Fred Buzhardt was so persuasive that he and former Watergate special prosecutor Archibald Cox have been prepared for the possibility that they might have to drop indictments in the case

One informed source, partially confirming Richardson's statement, said he was confident that Cox "would not have brought any indictments which he thought would fall." He indicated that Cox had taken the matter seriously.

In apparent corroboration of this, it was learned yesterday that federal indictments in connection with the Plumbers' 1971 burglary of Daniel Ellsberg's psychiatrist's office have been held up while the Watergate special prosecutor's office studies possible consequences to the allegedly sensitive matter.

The Plumbers were a special White House investigations unit so nicknamed because they were assigned to plug new "leaks."

Richardson said the security problem persists for Cox's successor, Leon A. Jaworski. "Jaworski, if he ever indicts, might have to [drop the indictments]—it's that genuine," he said.

While nobody contacted would reveal the nature of this matter, a lawyer for one potential defendant said Ellsberg was thought to have had access to information about it during his tenure on the National Security Council and later at the Rand Corporation. Extra line spacing

The White House knew at the time of the burglary that Ellsberg had given the secret *Pentagon Papers* about the Vietnam war to the press, and the White House also had information that Ellsberg had given the documents to the Soviet Embassy here, the lawyer said.

He said the investigation of Ellsberg, which President Nixon had admitted ordering personally, was aimed particularly at determining whether Ellsberg had given information on the sensitive matter in the press, the Soviets, or anybody else.

If his client is indicted, this lawyer said, "I would immediately subpoena certain documents," which he said would show why the Ellsberg operation was authorized and what its full extent was.

Rather than allow information about the allegedly sensitive matter to be introduced at trial, he predicted the White House would refuse on **national security** grounds to give up the documents, and Jaworski would be forced to drop the indictments.

President Nixon said at his Saturday night press conference that the chairman and vice-chairman of the special Senate Watergate committee—Sens Sam J. Ervin, Jr., (D-NC) and Howard H. Baker, Jr., (R-TN)—were aware of a highly sensitive **national security** matter in connection with the Plumbers and had agreed not to pursue it. It could not be determined whether this was the same matter about which Richardson had been informed.

A spokesman for Jaworski, reached yesterday for comment on Richardson's disclosure, replied that "Mr. Jaworski has received a briefing from the White House staff on some problems they see on the question of **national security**."

The spokesman said he assumed the allegedly sensitive matter was discussed, but he said Jaworski, like Cox, had not discussed details with anyone on his staff. Richardson said that he had told only one member of his Justice Department staff about the matter.

Cox reached at his home in Brooksville, ME, refused to discuss the situation. He said, "I just decided to make it a general rule that I won't say anything" about investigations formerly under his direction.

Richardson said a press report last Friday saying he and Cox had been pressured by Buzhardt not to indict certain former White House aides was inaccurate. The aides mentioned in the report were John D. Ehrlichman, Charles W. Colson, and Egil (Bud) Krogh, Jr.

"It's not fair to Mr. Buzhardt to say that he put pressure on me," Richardson said

"Buzhardt had brought to my attention a very significant **national security** aspect of the situation…a problem that could arise if asserted by a defendant. It was not a situation peculiar to any particular defendant. He did not mention any particular names."

A member of Cox's former staff agreed with Richardson, saying Buzhardt had not pressured Cox not to indict specific individuals. But if no names were mentioned, "it involved the Plumbers, all right." Richardson said.

He explained that anyone indicted in connection with an illegal operation, such as the Ellsberg burglary, could attempt to disclose the allegedly sensitive matter "to establish the overall legitimacy of what they did."

He said prosecutors at this point would have to consider the possibility that "the national interest at stake (in the operation) creates an overriding defense…to an otherwise illegal act."

"It would be a very tough call, especially in the present circumstances," Richardson said.

Krogh, former head of the Plumbers, former team members David Young and G. Gordon Liddy, and Ehrlichman, to whom Krogh reported, have already been indicted on state charges by a California grand jury. They are charged with the September 1971 burglary of the office of Dr. Lewis Fielding, then Ellsberg's psychiatrist.

Krogh, Liddy, and Ehrlichman apparently risk being indicted by a Jaworski grand jury on federal charges arising from the same incident. So do two of the original Watergate defendants, Bernard L. Barker and Eugenio R. Martinez, a friend of theirs, Felipe DeDiego, and Colson.

In September, attorneys for Colson, Barker, and Martinez said publicly that indictments were imminent and that they expected their clients to be indicted. But those indictments have been held up without explanation.

According to informed sources, assistant special prosecutor William H. Merrill, head of the Plumbers investigation, has been told about the allegedly sensitive matter—although he has not been given details—and has been told it poses a potential threat to any indictments from his task force.

He has therefore deferred the indictments while he studies how the issue might be raised, what his probable response would be, and what legal alternatives would be available to protect his indictments.

Questions about what constitutes a legitimate **national security** matter, and how far the government can justify otherwise illegal acts by claiming **national security**, have been hanging over the Watergate cases since the President first raised the issue last May.

In addition to his California indictment, Krogh has been indicted by Merrill's task force for allegedly lying to the Watergate grand jury last year concerning the travels of Liddy and former Plumber member E. Howard Hunt, Jr.

Krogh's attorney has argued that he lied because he was under strict instructions from Nixon to maintain secrecy about the Plumbers' activities. But US District Judge Gerhard A. Gesell rejected this defense last week.

This ruling seemed to leave Krogh with little or no firm defense to the charge and raised the possibility that he might therefore seek a deal with the prosecution and, in return for full cooperation in the Plumbers investigation, might be allowed to plead guilty to a less serious offense than lying to a grand jury.

Krogh, it is understood, might be able to corroborate testimony by former White House counsel John W. Dean III, who told the special Senate Watergate committee in June that Krogh had said his orders for the burglary came "right out of the Oval Office."

The President has hotly denied that he knew of the burglary in advance and has repeatedly labeled it "illegal."

A source close to the situation called ironic that the White House, by citing "**national security**" often in discussing Watergate, has created doubt about all such claims.

"Here turns out to be a situation that clearly did involve, and does involve, a matter of **national security**," this source said, "but the likelihood that it will be believed at this point has gone to hell."

*****

Appendix 2

"Jaworski to Push on 'Plumbers,'" November 21, 1973
Washington Post
By Mary Russell and Susanna McBee

SPECIAL PROSECUTOR LEON JAWORSKI SAID yesterday he plans to press for indictments in the Watergate case despite a **"national security"** problem brought to his attention by the White House.

He testified before the Senate Judiciary Committee that when presidential aides informed him of the problem last week, "my analysis was I could proceed, told them I expected to proceed."

Earlier, former Attorney General Elliot L. Richardson said White House Special Counsel J. Fred Buzhardt had told him last summer about "a very significant **national security** problem" in connection with the super-secret "Plumbers" operations.

The so-called White House Plumbers were set up in 1971 as a special investigative unit to plug news leaks of **national security** matters.

One Plumber project—the September 1971 burglary of the office of Daniel Ellsberg's psychiatrist—led last May to dismissal of the government's case against Ellsberg for leaking the *Pentagon Papers* to the press.

Richardson said the **national security** aspect of the Plumbers case, which he declined to specify, "could be" a serious impediment to Jaworski in bringing federal indictments. "It depends on how it is handled," the former attorney general said.

Richardson said he raised the problem with former Watergate Special Prosecutor Archibald Cox last September, "and he agreed it was a serious problem. We agreed it had to be thought through and anticipated."

Jaworski, however, did not seem overwhelmed by the problem in his testimony before the committee. He said Buzhardt and General Alexander M. Haig, Jr., White House Chief of Staff, "did call to my attention a matter related to **national security** and a problem which could arise from that."

The new prosecutor, whom President Nixon appointed November 1 after he had fired Cox, said Buzhardt and Haig promised to let him or a member of his staff listen to tapes and listen to any **national security** problem.

Jaworski added that he does not think "I would have to invade that area at all," and said he told the White House aides, "If the evidence justified bringing indictments, I would bring indictments."

"What assurances do you have that the veil of secrecy won't be drawn over the matter?" asked Sen. Edward M. Kennedy (D-MA).

"One, as much as I respect the issue of **national security**, I'm not going to be blinded by it," Jaworski replied, 'and, two, there was no resistance (from Buzhardt and Haig) when I said I thought some indictments could be brought, and I was going to pursue them."

Richardson, in a telephone interview, noted that he had raised the security problem in his testimony two weeks ago before the Senate Judiciary Committee.

He said a *Washington Post* article last Friday was "wrong" in saying that he and Cox were "lobbying efforts" to discourage possible indictments of former presidential aides John D. Ehrlichman, Charles W. Colson, and Egil (Bud) Krogh, Jr. because of **national security**.

Richardson said the article was "not fair" to Buzhardt in saying he had "lobbied heavily" on the issue. "He raised a problem that could arise if asserted by a defendant. He did not mention any particular names," Richardson said.

The security problem has been mentioned several times without being identified.

The lasted reference to it came last Saturday night from President Nixon in his news conference with the Associated Press Managing Editors at Disney World in Orlando, FL.

Mr. Nixon said he had told Assistant Attorney General Henry E. Petersen, who handled the Watergate probe until last May, "that the **national security** matters were not matters that should be investigated because there were some very highly sensitive, not only in Ellsberg, but another matter so sensitive that even Sen. Ervin and Sen. Baker (the chairman and vice-chairman respectively of the Senate Watergate Committee) decided they should not delve further into them."

Cox mentioned the problem on October 31 when he testified before the Senate Judiciary Committee. He indicated that indictments in the Ellsberg burglary case were held up by White House objections voiced to him through Richardson, concerning **national security**.

Petersen also discussed the matter when he testified before the Watergate committee last August.

He told of a phone conversation he had on April 18, 1973, with Mr. Nixon who he said told him that he (the President) knew about a report dealing with the Ellsberg break-in.

The President then said, Petersen testified, "That is a **national security** matter. You stay out of that. Your mandate is to investigate Watergate."

In a related matter, Jaworski told the Senate Judiciary Committee that the White House has been slow in giving him various documents he has requested on the Watergate case.

Author's Notes:

- Watergate Special Prosecutor Leon Jaworski stated he planned to pursue indictments in the Watergate case despite a **"national security"** problem bought to his attention by the White House.

- Jaworski stated he would not be blinded by the **national security** problem. These were possible indictments of former presidential aides John D. Ehrlichman, Charles Colson and Egil Krogh.

- Jaworski was briefed on the **national security** matter by White House attorney J. Fred Buzhardt and Chief of Staff General Alexander M. Haig, Jr. Buzhardt and Haig promised to let Jaworski listen to tapes and listen to any **national security** problem.

- Former Attorney General Elliot L. Richardson stated that Buzhardt told him in summer 1972 of "a very significant **national security** problem" in connection with Plumbers' operations. Richardson declined to specify the problem but thought it might be an impediment to Jaworski bringing federal indictments.

- The **national security** problem was addressed in Richardson's testimony before the Senate Judiciary Committee in early November 1973.

- Richardson apprised former Watergate Special Prosecutor Archibald Cox of the **national security** matter, and both agreed it was a serious problem that had to be thought through and anticipated. Cox mentioned the problem on October 31 when he testified before the Senate Judiciary Committee.

- Assistant Attorney General Henry E. Petersen also discussed the **national security** matter when he testified in August 1973 before the Senate Watergate Committee. He stated President Nixon told him to stay out of **national security** matters.

- The **national security** matter was the same one brought up at President Nixon's Associated Press news conference in Orlando, Florida: Ellsberg and another sensitive undisclosed matter.

Appendix 3

"Plumbers' Goal: Hid Spying on Soviets," November 29, 1973
Washington Star News
by Dan Thomasson

Excerpts:

The mysterious **"national security"** matter that President Nixon has said he hopes to keep secret involves a cover operation by the White House "Plumbers" to stop a threatened leak of highly sensitive information gathered about the Soviet Union.

And some who know about the matter believe disclosure of its details ultimately would endanger the life of a US intelligence source to the highest Russian official circles.

"I have no doubt that it is highly likely a life would be snuffed out," said one source aware of the operation. "It would, in the words of the CIA, put an individual in 'extreme prejudice.'"

Former Atty Gen. Elliot L. Richardson gave a hint of this in May during confirmation hearings before the Senate Judiciary Committee. Explaining why he had omitted certain passages from notes he had taken on a meeting with Egil Krogh, former White House aide and Plumbers chief, Richardson said.

"They (CIA) informed me that the words left out there are still subject to classification because their disclosure would prejudice an intelligence source." Richardson said further, "The omission…does refer to a genuine **national security** item."

Government officials aware of the various facets of the covert operation also agree that threat of disclosure that the United States possessed such sensitive information on the Soviet Union—and not the leak of the Pentagon papers or the US position on the strategic arms limitations talks—was the real reason for formation by the White House in June 1971 of the now defunct Plumbers, two of whose members later participated in the Watergate break-in.

Although most of those informed on the matter contend its disclosure would help the President's case in the Watergate affair, Nixon has steadfastly refused to do so.

These officials say it would legitimize the formation of the Plumbers which apparently came about because of a ban on the CIA's becoming involved in domestic intelligence activities and the refusal of the late FBI director, J. Edgar Hoover, to cooperate with the White House.

Nixon referred to the undisclosed **national security** problem ten days ago in an appearance before the Associated Press managing editors in Orlando, FL.

He said there is a matter "so sensitive" that the leaders of the special Senate Watergate committee had decided "they should not delve further into it."

"I don't mean by that that we're going to throw the cloak of **national security** over something because we're guilty of something." Nixon said, "I'm simply saying that where the **national security** would be disserved by having an investigation, the President has responsibility to protect it, and I'm going to do so."

Even such Nixon adversaries as ousted special Watergate prosecutor Archibald Cox and Senate Watergate Committee Chairman Sam J. Ervin, Jr., (D-NC) consider the matter an authentic **national security** problem.

Ervin refused to permit the committee to probe more deeply into the operation despite contentions by Senator Howard H. Baker, Jr., (R-TN), committee vice-chairman, that it was a vital "missing link" to the overall Watergate investigation.

Cox decided not to seek federal indictments against Krogh and his co-commander of the Plumbers, David Young, for the burglary of the office of Dr. Daniel Ellsberg's psychiatrist because to do so might expose the "**national security**" matter. Although Cox could see no direct link to the break-in the classified operation, he feared that defendants would use it as part of their defense.

The new special prosecutor, Leon Jaworski, however, apparently is moving ahead against Krogh, Young, and former presidential adviser John D. Ehrlichman in the Ellsberg matter. Sources close to the situation say Jaworski believes he must prosecute and then cross the **national security** bridge when he comes to it.

* * * *

The first public indication of the **national security** operation came last summer when Ehrlichman, in going over several known activities of the Plumbers, said there was another matter too sensitive to discuss.

A piece of that information previously had come to the special Senate Watergate committee's Republican investigators through an undisclosed source. When Baker pressed to know more, White House attorneys briefed Ervin, Baker, and their chief counsels, Samuel Dash and Fred E. Thompson.

Since then Baker and others, including acting White House counsel Leonard Garment, have urged Nixon to make it public.

While some officials believe Nixon has refused because of the ultimate threat to the intelligence source, other believe disclosure would bring about eventual revelation of other activities of the Plumbers along the lines of the Ellsberg break-in.

Another of those informed on the matter who has been highly critical of Nixon stated: "The only thing that makes me sympathize at all with the President's plight is the fact that, in this at least, he is sincerely motivated."

Baker said yesterday, before leaving for Puerto Rico, that if the **national security** matter were shown to be related to the Watergate investigation, "then I've got a problem."

Baker also said he told the committee that he believes the possible involvement of the CIA "and other agencies" into the break-in itself deserved more investigation.

He refused to elaborate on what evidence he had, but said there was a "little more" than what was contained in recent articles.

"The tip of the iceberg may be the only thing showing," Baker said of the Watergate investigation in general. "I'm not sure we can put it together" because of this major "missing piece."

* * * *

Appendix 4
"Nixon Cites <u>National Security</u>: 'Plumbers' Trials Pose Threat," December 7, 1973

<u>The Pittsburgh Press</u>
By Dan Thommasson

THE WHITE HOUSE PLUMBERS SUPERVISED during 1971 a massive still-undisclosed investigation of a leak within the Defense Department that President Nixon has told Senate Watergate leaders is of a matter of top **national security.**

The investigation, which focused on a middle-echelon military official whose duties included considerable foreign travel, employed the services of the Defense Intelligence Agency (DIA), the FBI, and possibly the Central Intelligence Agency (CIA). It was concluded in December 1971, when "the problem was isolated," according to those familiar with it.

But during the months the operation was in progress, the Plumbers became privy to much sensitive intelligence information.

Mr. Nixon and his present White House advisers now fear this may begin to come out in state and federal trials ensuing from the Plumbers' burglary of the office of a psychiatrist treating Dr. Daniel Ellsberg, who leaked the *Pentagon Papers*.

Those who know the situation say matters which Mr. Nixon contends are legitimate **national security** and must be protected include:

The identity of a military figure who was the target of the original investigation. Sources say he is still in service.

The fact that the country uses third-nation intelligence sources in gathering information on China and the Soviet Union.

Disclosure of these details might embarrass these nations, although the Russians and Chinese are aware of the practice.

That the United States intelligence sources, one of whom has been operating for nearly ten years, are close to the highest Russian circles.

One top federal source contends that generally the Plumbers were a "clearing house" with little actual operational status. Information poured into them from the various agencies, the source said. Except for the "aberration" of the Ellsberg break-in, they did nothing illegal.

But others contend G. Gordon Liddy and E. Howard Hunt, later arrested and convicted for burglarizing Democratic national headquarters in the Watergate office building here, were directly involved in other operations while serving under White House aides Egil Krogh and David Young.

Appendix 5

"The President and the Plumbers: A Look at Two Security Questions," December 8, 1973
New York Times
by Seymour M. Hersh

FOR MONTHS PRESIDENT NIXON HAS been citing **national security** as the reason for authorizing establishment of the secret White House investigations unit known as the Plumbers and as justification for restricting some aspects of the Watergate inquiry.

The President has never given any details of his **national security** concerns, noting they were "highly sensitive" matters.

Interviews over the last month by *The New York Times* with dozens of past and present administration officials, including men who were closely involved with the Plumbers, have suggested that at least two principal **national security** fears, neither of which has ever been substantiated, motivated the President. One was fear—nourished in part, some sources said, by Henry A. Kissinger, then the President's **national security** adviser—that Daniel Ellsberg, who said he turned over the *Pentagon Papers* to the press, might pass on to the Soviet Union secrets far more important than any information than any information contained in the Pentagon study of the Vietnam war.

Specifically, the sources said, the White House feared that Dr. Ellsberg, a former Rand Corporation and Defense Department official, may have been a Soviet intelligence informer who in the weeks after publication of the *Pentagon Papers* in June 1971 was capable of turning over details of the most closely held nuclear targeting secrets of the United States, which were contained in a highly classified document known as the Single Integrated Operations Plan, or S.I.O.P.

The second major concern was that a highly placed Soviet agent of the KGB, the Soviet intelligence agency, operating as an American counterspy, would be compromised by continued inquiry by the special prosecutor and the Senate Watergate committee into the Ellsberg case. The agent informed his FBI contacts that a set of the *Pentagon Papers* had been delivered to the Soviet Embassy in Washington shortly after a Federal court had ordered *The Times* to stop printing the series of articles on the papers. The series began June 13, 1971.

The administration thought the sources said that any extensive investigation by the Watergate prosecutors or the Senate Watergate committee would divulge defense secrets that Dr. Ellsberg possessed, expose the Soviet spy, and endanger communications and espionage secrets.

Officials interviewed by *The Times* disagreed sharply over the legitimacy of these fears and other **national security** secrets that the President has said he was trying to protect in 1971 by bypassing the usual police agencies in the federal government to set up the Plumbers and by insisting this spring—at the height of the Watergate controversy—that the Justice Department stop its inquiry into the Plumbers.

A number of well-informed persons, some of them with long careers in intelligence, openly questioned the President's motives in asserting **national security**. Based on the information available to them, they said they did not think that Mr. Nixon's fears were sufficient to justify setting up the Plumbers unit.

Moreover, they also raised the question of whether the President, in invoking **national security** last spring to restrict the Watergate's inquiry, was not in fact attempting to shield key aides from possible criminal disclosures.

* * * *

Appendix 6

"Nixon's Active Role on Plumbers: His Talks with Leaders
Recalled," December 10, 1973
The New York Times,
By Seymour Hersh

PRESIDENT NIXON PLAYED A FAR more active role in the secret operations of the White House Plumbers than either he or witnesses before the Senate Watergate committee have reported.

The President has publicly stated that he approved the bypassing of the Federal Bureau of Investigation to establish in 1971 the clandestine White House group designed to plug leaks of secret information. But he also insisted that he "did not authorize and had no knowledge of any illegal means used by the Plumbers."

Interviews in the last few weeks with federal investigators and with dozens of present and former government officials disclosed that the President developed a close working relationship with the leaders of the Plumbers through a series of meetings in the White House Oval Office in the summer of 1971.

In July 1971, authoritative sources said, when Mr. Nixon gave John D. Ehrlichman, his principal domestic adviser, overall responsibility for the activities of the Plumbers, he told him to urge the special investigators to read a chapter in his autobiography, *Six Crises*, dealing with Alger Hiss.

In the chapter, Mr. Nixon noted that as a Congressman investigating Mr. Hiss in 1950, he and committee aides "did not trust the Justice Department to prosecute the case with the vigor we thought it deserved."

Former White House officials said the President kept in personal touch with the Plumbers' operations in August and early September 1971, through a series of personal meetings with David R. Young, Jr., a former National Security Council aide who was a co-director of the group.

At his one meeting with the other co-director, Egil Krogh, Jr., these sources said, Mr. Nixon angrily declared that **national security** was more important than the "civil rights of some bureaucrats" and personally ordered Mr. Krogh to begin an extensive series of lie-detector tests of federal officials to determine the sources of some leaks. The tests began immediately.

The interviews by The Times produced no information conflicting with the President's statement that he had not known of plans for the Plumbers to break into the Los Angeles offices of the former psychiatrist of Daniel Ellsberg, the onetime Pentagon official who was accused in the *Pentagon Papers* case. The papers, which were obtained by the press, were a secret Defense Department study of United States involvement in the war in Vietnam.

Details of the **national security** rationale invoked by the President for setting up the Plumbers and demanding a limit on the investigation were reported by *The New York Times* today.

According to former White House officials, the President and his national security adviser, Henry A. Kissinger, now the Secretary of State, feared that a full inquiry into the Ellsberg case would eventually result in disclosure of United States nuclear secrets and compromise a Soviet KGB (intelligence) official operating as an American counterspy.

*****

One former high-level aide recalled that Mr. Young—whom he scathingly described as "Henry's Lord Chambermaid," demanded and received assurance that he would be equal to Mr. Krogh on the project. But, in fact, Mr. Krogh was always considered to be the nominal head of the operation.

******

Appendix 7

Baker on "Grave Matter," December 30, 1973
Watergate: Chronology of a Crisis, **page 472**

SENATOR HOWARD H. BAKER, JR. (R-TN), vice-chairman of the Senate Watergate investigating committee, said December 30 that he had strongly urged President Nixon to disclose a matter of "grave national importance" related to the Watergate case and perhaps touching on **national security**. "The odds are probably better that it would be helpful to the President than hurtful," Baker said, and the new information might "justify or at least explain some of the conduct that appears otherwise unexplainable."

Baker said he was referring to a matter Nixon described in his November 17 Orlando, FL, appearance before newspaper editors as "so sensitive that even Sen. Ervin (Sam J. Ervin, Jr., the committee chairman) and Sen. Baker have decided that they could not delve further" into it. News reports had speculated that it involved Nixon's concern that investigations into the activities of the White House Plumbers unit might reveal the name—and thus endanger the life—of a Soviet agent operating as an American spy (Nixon statement, page 438).

Baker made his remarks on ABC's *Issues and Answers*. Asked if he thought there were any more Watergate bombshells waiting to explode, he said, "There are animals crashing around in the forest. I can hear them, but I can't see them." Some of those undisclosed things did involve **national security**, Baker conceded, but he said that "there must be a balance at some point, a value judgment…on whether the requirements of **national security** are greater than the requirements of domestic tranquility."

* * * * *

Appendix 8

"Security Secret Is A Puzzle," January 15, 1974

Washington Post

By Laurence Stern

SIX MONTHS AGO, WHITE HOUSE attorneys J. Fred Buzhardt and Leonard Garment gave a private briefing to the cochairmen of the Senate Watergate Committee on a **national security** matter of "very urgent importance."

It was occasioned by a paragraph deleted from a 1971 memo from White House Plumbers Egil Krogh and David Young to presidential aide John H. Ehrlichman. The paragraph had become a subject of speculation at the public Watergate hearings.

In the course of the briefing, the White House attorneys unfolded for the first time to the Watergate committee chairman, Sam J. Ervin, Jr. (D-NC) and cochairman Howard J. Baker, Jr. (R-TN), the story of unauthorized leakage of National Security Council documents to the Pentagon by White House military liaison officers.

The affair of the leaked documents was one of Washington's most tantalizing secrets for months. Nonetheless, the episode figured in the request by White House attorneys that limits be drawn be drawn on grand jury inquiries into the operation of the Plumbers. And the Senate Watergate committee agreed to take no further testimony and press no further disclosures on the matter.

Yesterday, the story of "the **national security** issue" in the Watergate investigation took a further curious turn.

Baker, while confirming that the White House regarded the matter as "of very urgent importance" acknowledged that he did not know the specific basis of the White House concern or the nature of the documents which passed from the NSC to the Pentagon.

And a participant in the July secret meeting said Ervin's reaction at the time was that "it was more like the Keystone cops—comical rather than sinister—everyone in the room played it down and thought it was embarrassing."

Ervin was represented as being "surprised that the military people weren't arrested… Everyone agreed that it had nothing to do with Watergate and would explain nothing that the administration had done," the participant recalled.

Yet Baker acknowledged that the affair of the leaked documents, such as they were, was very much on his mind when he declared at Florida's Disney World in November that the American people may have "seen only the tip of the iceberg" in Watergate-related scandals. The Tennessee Republican followed President Nixon's appearance before the Associated Press managing editors convention.

President Nixon, at the AP editors session, alluded to inference in the White House Pentagon information snooping episode. He said that "**national security** matters were not matters that should be investigated, because there were some very highly sensitive matters involved, not only in Ellsberg but also another matter so sensitive that even Sen. Ervin and Sen. Baker have decided they should not delve into further into it."

Baker, in a telephone interview from his home in Huntsville, TN, said neither he nor Ervin were told last July or at any other time since then the precise nature of the White House concern for **national security**.

Asked whether there was a fear at the White House in 1971 that the material might fall into unfriendly foreign hands, Baker replied in carefully chosen words, "I would not urge you to think there was anything in the nature of foreign involvement…the nature of the concern has not been disclosure."

One attorney prominently associated with the criminal prosecution cases, who requested to remain anonymous, scoffing, questioned the priority of the document leaks as a **national security** breach of high consequence. "There were a good many things that ranked higher than that," he said.

In communicating Presidential concern over the alleged military snitching of documents, attorneys for the White House asked federal prosecutors to curtail investigation of the White House Plumbers in order not to divulge the **national security** secret.

In a recent appearance on the ABC program *Issues and Answers*, Baker anticipated the Pentagon information-grabbing case when asked if any more Watergate bombshells were in prospect.

Citing a "matter of grave national importance," Baker said, "There are animals crashing around in the forest. I can hear them, but I can't see them."

The White House, meanwhile, on Friday sought to clarify the basis of its concern over the entire episode in a statement issued by the press office. It said that while it will consider the matter inappropriate for public disclosure, it touched on "a matter peripheral to a **national security** issue…" That issue, said the White House, involved "deliberate leaks to the media of extremely sensitive information of interest to other nations."

It may be possible at a later time that "the facts can be made public without detriment to the national interest," the White House spokesman said.

One interpretation of the events was broadcast yesterday by CBS News, which theorized that the military documents snitching "appeared to be motivated by the aims of wrecking the Nixon-Kissinger plan for better relations with Communist nations."

Another conjecture, offered by a knowledgeable Senator source, was that the dissemination of the grave **national security** issue was an "effort by Sen. Baker to create a diversionary matter."

The entire story is, by agreement on all sides, yet to be told.

Author's Notes:

- Senators Ervin and Baker, Senate Watergate Committee, were briefed in July 1973 on **national security** matter of "very urgent importance" by White House attorneys J. Fred Buzhardt and Leonard Garment.

- President Nixon, at AP editor's convention in Orlando, Florida, earlier, stated that **national security** matters should not be investigated because highly sensitive matters were involved, not only on Ellsberg, but also another matter so sensitive that Senators Baker and Ervin decided not to pursue them.

- Baker stated in telephone conversation that neither Ervin nor he were briefed in July or later on precise nature of the White House concern for **national security**.

- It was speculated that the **national security** issue related to military snitching and leaking of sensitive documents related to diplomatic negotiations.

- The White House desired to limit grand jury inquiries into the operation of the Plumbers into this **national security** operation.

Appendix 9

"Chasing a Spy Ring: Its Secret is Safely Locked Away in Confusion," January 18, 1974

Washington Post

By Laurence Stern

Excerpts:

*****

"WAS THE ALLEGED MILITARY SPYING episode the much-advertised **national security** matter cited by the President and his lawyers in connection with the White House Plumbers investigation by federal Watergate prosecutors?

Yes, some sources told *The New York Times* and *The Washington Post*. No, said sources in both newspapers.

It was a critical difference. The White House had invoked the danger of a **national security** breach when it sought last summer to discourage criminal indictments of key aides associated with the Plumbers activities—specifically John D. Ehrlichman, Charles Colson, and Egil (Bud) Krogh. So the White House was informed, at any rate, by informed sources.

The White House said last Friday that its **national security** concern in the military spying episode was that it involved "deliberate leaks to the media" of sensitive information of interest to foreign powers.

*****

But there has been no explanation by the White House what **national security** interest might be endangered by prosecution of the White House special investigation unit operating under Ehrlichman's direction.

*****

Some White House officials registered the highest concern with one presidential aide contenting (*The New York Times*) that Mr. Nixon wanted it kept secret to protect the "whole military command structure."

Author's Notes:

- The article speculated the **national security** matter involved:

    1. Pentagon/JCS military spying on NSC/White House, also known as Admiral Moorer-Youman Radford activity

    2. Suspect wiretap of office of Secretary of Defense Melvin Laird

    3. Leak of minutes of Henry Kissinger White House meetings on strategy in the Indo-Pakistan war during December 1971

White House invoked danger of **national security** breach to discourage criminal indictments of Plumber activities involving:

- • John D. Ehrlichman

- • Charles Colson

- • Egil Krogh

- White House stated **national security** re: military spying involved deliberate leaks to the media of sensitive information of interest to foreign powers.

- Biggest asserted concern was the President Nixon wanted to protect **national security** matter to protect the "whole military command structure."

Appendix 10:
The Surrender of Lord Cornwallis

*Surrender of Lord Cornwallis painting at the U.S. Capitol Rotunda,
Washington, D.C, the symbolic center of America*

ON OCTOBER 19, 1781, LORD General Cornwallis surrendered
to General George Washington at the Battle of Yorktown. This final
victory concluded the Revolutionary War against Great Britain. The US
Constitution was signed on September 17, 1787.

The subject of this painting is the surrender of the British army at Yorktown, Virginia, in 1781, which ended the last major campaign of the Revolutionary War. The blue sky filled with dark clouds and the broken cannon suggest the battles that led to this event. In early September, entrenched with a force of 7,000 men, Cornwallis had hoped for rescue from the sea, but the British vessels were repelled by a French fleet. Within weeks General Washington had deployed a much larger army, and his artillery bombarded the British positions in early October. After American and French troops overran two British strongholds, Cornwallis surrendered on October 19.

In the center of the scene, American General Benjamin Lincoln appears mounted on a white horse. He extends his right hand toward the sword carried by the surrendering British officer, who heads the long line of troops that extends into the background. To the left, French officers appear standing and mounted beneath the white banner of the royal Bourbon family.

On the right are American officers beneath the Stars and Stripes; among them are the Marquis de Lafayette and Colonel Jonathan Trumbull, the brother of the painter. General George Washington, riding a brown horse, stayed in the background because Lord Cornwallis himself was not present for the surrender.

Surrender of Lord Cornwallis in the Capitol Rotunda is one of two paintings that Trumbull completed on this subject. He painted this version between 1819 and 1820, basing it upon a small painting (approximately twenty inches by thirty inches) that he had first envisioned in 1785, when he began to "meditate seriously the subjects of national history, of events of the Revolution." In 1787, he made preliminary drawings for the small painting. Although he struggled for a time with the arrangement of the figures, he had settled upon a composition by 1788.

To create portraits from life of the people depicted in this and other paintings, Trumbull traveled extensively. He obtained sittings with numerous individuals in Paris (including French officers at Thomas Jefferson's house) and in New York. In 1791, he was at Yorktown and sketched the site of the British surrender. He continued to work on the small painting during the following years but did not complete it; nevertheless, in January 1817 he showed it and other works in Washington, D.C., and was given a commission to create four monumental history paintings for the Capitol. *Surrender of Lord Cornwallis* was the second of these large paintings that he completed. He exhibited it in New York City, Boston, and Baltimore before delivering it to the Capitol in late 1820. He completed the small painting around 1828; it is now part of the collection of the Yale University Art Gallery.

Trumbull performed the first cleaning and restoration of his Rotunda paintings in 1828, applying wax to their backs to protect them from dampness and cleaning and re-varnishing their surfaces. Throughout the nineteenth and twentieth centuries the painting was cleaned, restored, varnished, and relined. In 1971, damage from a penny that was thrown hard enough to pierce the canvas was repaired. All of the Rotunda paintings were most recently cleaned in 2008.

John Trumbull was born in Lebanon, Connecticut, on June 6, 1756. His father, Jonathan Trumbull, was later Governor of Connecticut (1769–1784). John entered Harvard College in 1771 and graduated in 1773. He created numerous sketches of significant people and places, even during his service as an officer and General Washington's aide-de-camp during the Revolutionary War. Resigning his commission as colonel in 1777, he painted for two years and then went to England, where he studied under renowned history painter Benjamin West and at the Royal Academy of Arts.

In London, Paris, and New York City, he created scenes of the American Revolution and life portraits or sketches of many of the individuals who would appear in them. He also painted portraits of other notable persons and numerous religious scenes.

From 1794 to 1804, diplomatic postings in London interrupted his work, and his artistic skill suffered. However, he remained successful as a portrait painter, and exhibitions of his earlier canvases led to an 1817 commission for four large paintings to be placed in the Capitol Rotunda; these were installed in 1826, but he failed to secure a contract for additional Rotunda paintings. He returned to the religious subjects of his earlier career but fell on hard times. In 1831, he deeded many of his works to Yale College in exchange for a one-thousand-dollar annuity. Trumbull died in New York City on November 10, 1843, and was interred beneath the art gallery at Yale that he designed. In 1867, his paintings and his remains were moved to the new art gallery (now Street Hall).

While our family was stationed in Washington D.C we visited the US Capitol on at least two occasions and the Capitol Rotunda viewing the very large painting of the Surrender of Cornwallis at Yorktown. Ryan and I also visited the Rotunda at as part of a Washington DC trail medal for Scouting. The Capitol Rotunda is the symbolic center of the USA.

We also became aware that at the British surrender at Yorktown the British band played the tune "The World Turn'd Upside Down". This was the first song celebrating the new American Republic, a nation that can and does Turn the World Upside Down.

"The World Turn'd Upside Down"

General Cornwallis did not attend the surrender ceremony, saying that he was not feeling well. His substitute, General O'Hara, first tried to surrender to the Comte de Rochambeau who directed the British officer to General Washington who in turn directed him to Washington's subordinate General Lincoln. During the ceremony, a British band played the song **"The World Turn'd Upside Down."** *D James Thacher served with the Continental Army and published his account of the surrender some years later:*

AT ABOUT TWELVE O'CLOCK, THE combined army was arranged and drawn up in two lines extending more than a mile in length. The Americans were drawn up in a line on the right side of the road, and the French occupied the left. At the head of the former, the great American commander [George Washington], mounted on his noble courser, took his station, attended by his aides. At the head of the latter was posted the excellent Count Rochambeau and his suite. The French troops, in complete uniform, displayed a martial and noble appearance; their bands of music, of which the timbrel formed a part, are a delightful novelty, and produced while marching to the ground a most enchanting effect.

The Americans, though not all in uniform, nor their dress so neat, yet exhibited an erect, soldierly air, and every countenance beamed with satisfaction and joy. The concourse of spectators from the country was prodigious, in point of numbers was probably equal to the military, but universal silence and order prevailed.

It was about two o'clock when the captive army advanced through the line formed for their reception. Every eye was prepared to gaze on Lord Cornwallis, the object of peculiar interest and solicitude; but he disappointed our anxious expectations; pretending indisposition, he made General O'Hara his substitute as the leader of his army. This officer was followed by the conquered troops in a slow and solemn step, with shouldered arms, colors cased and drums beating a British march. Having arrived at the head of the line, General O'Hara, elegantly mounted, advanced to his excellency the Commander-in-Chief, taking off his hat, and apologized for the non-appearance of Earl Cornwallis. With his usual dignity and politeness, his excellency pointed to Major-General Lincoln for directions, by whom the British army was conducted into a spacious field, where it was intended they should ground their arms.

The royal troops, while marching through the line formed by the allied army, exhibited a decent and neat appearance, as respects arms and clothing, for their commander opened his store and directed every soldier to be furnished with a new suit complete, prior to the capitulation. But in their line of march, we remarked a disorderly and unsoldierly conduct. Their step was irregular and their ranks frequently broken.

But it was in the field, when they came to the last act of the drama, that the spirit and pride of the British soldier was put to the severest test: Here their mortification could not be concealed. Some of the platoon officers appeared to be exceedingly chagrined when giving the word "ground arms," and I am a witness that they performed this duty in a very unofficer-like manner; and that many of the soldiers manifested a sullen temper, throwing their arms on the pile with violence, as if determined to render them useless. This irregularity, however, was checked by the authority of General Lincoln. After having grounded their arms and divested themselves of their accoutrements, the captive troops were conducted back to Yorktown and guarded by our troops till they could be removed to the place of their destination.

Above text taken from Architect of US Capitol website.

"The Commander in Chief earnestly recommends that the troops not on duty should universally attend with that seriousness of Deportment and gratitude of Heart which the recognition of such reiterated and astonishing interpositions of Providence demand of us."
General George Washington, October 19, 1781, Yorktown

Appendix 11:
Watergate Lessons Learned

Nixon and Kissinger: Partners in Power
Robert Dallek
Harpers and Collins, 2007, page 622

"The scandal justifiably compelled an end to the president's political career. Nixon would never acknowledge wrongdoing. He attributed his resignation to errors that cost him his political support, but he refused to admit any legal misdeeds. The historical record, however, makes clear that he was guilty of obstruction of justice. History also refutes his assertion that resigning would ensure the office of the presidency. To the contrary, Nixon's departure from office has strengthened American institutions by demonstrating that even a president, however effective his policy-making skills, cannot escape the rule of law."

113th Landon Lecture at University of Kansas, Manhattan, Kansas
Howard H. Baker, Jr.
March 9, 1999

"...the institutional structures and framework of our government, I think it is unlikely our talented young fathers at the ending part of the eighteenth century could have understood how relevant the structures of government they gave us would be to the twentieth and twenty-first centuries. It is truly a remarkable system. There has probably never been a more sensitive and resonant system of government than that which we enjoy. It has withstood challenges to the independence, the internal strife of civil war, the industrial revolution, two world wars and the Cold War. For more than two centuries, the citizens of the United States have experienced sovereign authority, thus have instructed their government in remarkable and successful ways. Sometimes our decisions have produced conflicts, but all have led to a stronger and better country. Sometimes we are embarrassed as in Teapot Dome and Watergate, but we have learned from each of them. We have certainly learned that our best efforts at self-government are never perfect and almost always required significant change and mid-course correction."

I Gave Them a Sword: Behind the Scenes of the Nixon Interviews
David Frost
1978, page 319

"Yet of all the strengths he (Nixon) has talked about, the one he has ignored strikes me as the most critical. And that is the strength that comes from a nation's belief in the essential rightness of its own cause, in the integrity of its own vision, in the justice of its own ends, in the basic goodness of its own deeds. And that is the strength that was undermined, the faith that was shaken, by Vietnam abroad and by Watergate era at home."

Speech by President Gerald Ford at White House on August 8, 1974 after taking oath of office

"Our Constitution works: our great Republic is a government of laws and not of men. Here the people rule. But there is a higher Power, by whatever name we honor Him, who ordains not only righteousness but love, not only justice but mercy."

What the President Knew
Samuel Dash, Minority Counsel, Watergate Senate Select Committee
***PBS News Hour*, July 28, 2003**

"You know, this was a very serious tragic time in America; we almost lost a democracy and our constitutional government. And the good time was that our government worked as the Constitution wanted it to work. It was a strong Senate, a strong Congress that was carrying out its constitutional oversight function, that exposed the criminal activities of the president, but not only exposed them but informed the public who were the ultimate sovereigns. So here a president resigned on the exposure of this based on the separation of powers, without bloodshed. It wasn't a revolution, and a new president comes in without bloodshed. The government worked at this time."

"The Lessons that Watergate Holds for Lawyers,"
Judge Charles Breyer, US District Judge, San Francisco, CA
***Minnesota Lawyer*, Vol. 12, No. 15, April 14, 2008**

Breyer told the group that the real lesson of Watergate and its aftermath is seldom discussed and is taken for granted. The lesson is, the Constitution works, and the effectiveness of the legal process became apparent as the investigation and prosecution continued, he said. According to Breyer, some of the ways the system worked included:

- The First Amendment allowed stories in *The Washington Post* to break Watergate open and also led to stories about other abuses of power.

- The Senate hearings headed by Sen. Sam Ervin and the house impeachment proceedings showed the importance of the Congressional oversight responsibility.

- The independent judiciary was able to initiate an investigation, which a non-independent judiciary likely could not have done.

- The Saturday Night Massacre resulted in the largest spontaneous outpouring of outrage from the public that the White House had ever experienced. "It was the public exercising their right to petition the government for redress of grievances that made…an enormous difference," Breyer said.

Judge Charles Breyer, US District Court, San Francisco, on Watergate Lessons Learned
Stanford University Law School, November 11, 2008
Charles Breyer, District Court judge and former Watergate prosecutor, spoke to students at Stanford University Law School November 11, 2008, about lessons learned from Watergate, as well as connections between the issues of the time and the problems we face today.

Breyer, brother of Supreme Court Justice Stephen Breyer, was working as an assistant district attorney for California when he was asked by Archibald Cox to be involved in the Watergate prosecution.

"We were told repeatedly by the White House that this was a very dangerous investigation, and that we would somehow bring about the downfall of '**national security**' – something mysterious we've heard referred to often over the years," Breyer said.

He then told students what to take away from Watergate. "What was Watergate about?" Breyer asked. "People will say it was about the abuse of power. You can go through a whole list of government abuses and say that these were the lessons. I would say that these are not the lessons," he continued. "At that time, we were told that this investigation would bring about the end of the republic—that we could not afford to have the investigation. In fact, the opposite happened. We could not have afforded not to have this investigation."

Breyer listed freedom of the press, independent prosecution, and the system of checks and balances as important principles reaffirmed by the Watergate scandal.

"All [the branches of the government] worked together in an amazing way," he said. "Looking back, the writers of the Constitution were brilliant."

Right and the Power
Leon Jaworski
1976, page 278

"The tapes? The teachings of right and wrong were forgotten to the White House. Little evils were permitted to grow into great evils, small sins escalated into big sins. In the house and hours of tape-recorded conversations to which I listened, not once was there a reference to the Glory of God, not once a reference to seeking spiritual guidance through prayer. Our Lord was mentioned, yes, but on each pitiable occasion His name was taken in vain. If only there had been an occasional prayer for help, an occasional show of compassion? Why was there not just a simple statement such as, 'May we hold our honor sacred...' How different might have been the course of government if there had been an acknowledgement of God as the source of right instead of a denial of Him in a seemingly unending series of ruthless actions."

"The world is a dangerous place. Not because of the people who are evil but because of the people who don't do anything about it."
Albert Einstein

Abuse of Power
Stanley I. Kutler
1997, pages xxi to xxii
"Nixon never could publicly admit his involvement in anything illegal. Speaking of the abortive Houston Plan that would have authorized illegal break-ins for domestic counter-intelligence programs, Nixon said, 'Well, then to admit that were approved...illegal activities. That's the problem.' At another time he admitted, 'I ordered that they use any means necessary, including illegal means, to accomplished this goal (May 16, 1973). He then hastily added: 'The President of the United States can never admit that.' Most embarrassing of all probably was the break-in of the office of Ellsberg's psychiatrist, an action Nixon and his aides insisted was dictated by '**national security**' considerations, when, in fact, it was designed to discredit Ellsberg. Nixon knew the truth: 'I believe somehow I have to avoid having the President approve the break-in of a psychiatrist's office.'"

*****

"Nixon's inability to confront the truth about himself was institutional, as well as personal."

"Watergate Misremembered"
Professor Stanley Kutler
Slate, June 18, 2002
"Important lessons about Watergate remain to be learned. The institutions of government, established ones as well as some resurrected for the moment, such as the special prosecutor, did their work and did it well. Congress behaved intelligently, soberly, and in bipartisan

fashion, setting a pattern that sadly has not been followed in recent decades. The first thirty-seven days of hearings by the Senate Select Committee stand as an exemplary congressional investigation. Special Prosecutor Leon Jaworski, who led Texas Democrats for Nixon in 1972, should be remembered for his heroic achievement. The United States Supreme Court, in a unanimous opinion (Justice Rehnquist recusing himself), delivered its most historic opinion on executive privilege when it ruled that Nixon had to surrender the subpoenaed tapes."

"1972 Watergate Break-in Woke a Nation of Watchdogs"

Kenneth W. Olson
June 18, 2009
"As he left office, President Nixon admitted that some of his judgments were wrong, but claimed that whatever actions he took were in the nation's interest…and…defiantly defending status as the keeper of **national security**.

History will be the only judge… But sixty-five years ago, Learned Hand, one of this country's most important judges who never sat on the Supreme Court, reminded Americans that 'Liberty lies in the hearts of men and women; when it dies there, no constitution, no law, no courts can save it…'"

"Review of *SHADOW: Five Presidents and the Legacy of Watergate* by Bob Woodward"

John Ed Robertson
2002
"'*Shadow* is an authoritative, unsettling narrative of the modern, beleaguered presidency.' So states the dust cover of this book by Bob Woodward, who has arguably done as much as (or more than) anyone else to create the 'beleaguered' presidency he decries.

Woodward makes the point that there are two primary lessons to be learned from Watergate:

1. If there is questionable activity, release the facts, whatever they are, as early and completely as possible.

2. Do not allow outside inquiries, whether conducted by prosecutors, congressmen or reporters, to harden into a permanent state of suspicion and warfare."

"Nixon in Winter"
Monica Crowley

"Nixon Came To Understand His Tainted Legacy"
Jack Torry
Post-Gazette Washington Bureau, July 26, 1998
"And though Nixon expresses regrets about the Watergate scandal that drove him from office, Crowley's book shows that the former president never quite accepted his role. 'I had limited information the entire time,' Nixon says unconvincingly. 'Dean would come in and tell me one thing, Haldeman another, Ehrlichman another, and Haig something else.'
"And while railing away at the press, Nixon concluded, 'It was partly their creation, but mostly my own. It took me a long time to accept the fact that what happened was my fault.'"

Nixon in Winter
Monica Crowley
Page 294
Crowley: "Is that one of your biggest regrets related to Watergate?"
President Nixon: "There are so many regrets related to Watergate. First

of all was the way I handled the entire goddamned thing from the beginning. Instead I tried to keep it quiet... I should have gone straight to the American people and told them what the hell happened..."

For Information on

- How to order the book, paperback or virtual

- Jerry Rogers

- Where to post your comments and "lessons learned" from reading the book

- Where to sign up on Jerry's Facebook and Twitter accounts

www.nationalsecuritymatter.com

Made in the USA
Middletown, DE
11 January 2018